COMPETING CONSTITUTIONAL VISIONS

The Meech Lake Accord

Edited by

Katherine E. Swinton, B.A., LL.B., LL.M.
Professor, Faculty of Law, University of Toronto

and

Carol J. Rogerson, B.A., M.A., LL.B., LL.M.
Associate Professor, Faculty of Law, University of Toronto

CARSWELL
Toronto • Calgary • Vancouver
1988

Canadian Cataloguing in Publication Data

Main entry under title:

Competing constitutional visions

Papers originally presented at an inter-disciplinary
symposium held at the University of Toronto on
October 30, 1987.
Includes bibliographical references.
ISBN 0-459-32431-4 (bound)   ISBN 0-459-32421-7 (pbk.)

1. Canada - Constitutional law - Amendments -
Congresses.   2. Canada. Constitution Act, 1982 -
Congresses.   3. Canada. British North America Act -
Congresses.   4. Great Britain. British North
America Act - Congresses.   5. Federal-provincial
relations - Canada - Congresses.*   6. Federal
government - Canada - Congresses.   I. Swinton,
Katherine.   II. Rogerson, Carol, 1953-   .
III. Title.

C.2   JL65.1988 C65 1988   342.71'03   C88-094512-5

59,892

Contents

Preface vii
Contributors ix

Part I   **The Distinct Society: Concepts of Community and Principles of Interpretation**

The Concepts of "Distinct Society and Identity" in the
    Meech Lake Accord
—*Raymond Breton*   3

Aboriginal Rights and the Meech Lake Accord
—*J. Edward Chamberlain*   11

Perspective Féministe d'une certaine Société Distincte: Les
    Québécoises et L'Accord du Lac Meech
—*Lucie Lamarche*   21

The Distinct Society Clause in the Meech Lake Accord:
    Cound it Affect Equality Rights for Women?
—*Lynn Smith*   35

How Not to Drown in Meech Lake: Rules, Principles and
    Women's Equality Rights
—*Donna Greschner*   55

Linguistic Duality and the Distinct Society in Quebec:
    Declarations of Sociological Fact or Legal Limits on
    Constitutional Interpretation?
—*A. Wayne MacKay*   65

The Constitutional Priority of the Charter
—*Brian Slattery* 81

Part II   **National Institutions and the Spending Power**

Meech Lake and the Supreme Court
—*Peter H. Russell* 97

Meech Lake and the Future of Senate Reform
—*J. Peter Meekison* 113

Meech Lake and Federalism: Accord or Discord?
—*Thomas J. Courchene* 121

The Meech Lake Accord and the Bonds of Nationhood
—*A.W. Johnson* 145

Analysis of the New Spending Provision (Section 106A)
—*Peter Hogg* 155

Political Meaning and Social Reform
—*Keith Banting* 163

The Federal Spending Power and Meech Lake
—*Andrée Lajoie* 175

Meech Ado About Nothing? Federalism, Democracy and
the Spending Power
—*Andrew Petter* 187

Section 106A and Federal-Provincial Fiscal Relations
—*J. Stefan Dupré* 203

The Meech Lake Accord and the Federal Spending Power:
A Good Maximin Solution
—*Pierre Fortin* 213

The Economic Policy Implications of the Meech Lake
Accord
—*Robin Boadway, Jack M. Mintz and Douglas D. Purvis* 225

Part III   **Competing Visions of Constitutionalism**

Meech Lake and Constitutional Visions
—*Ivan Bernier* 239

The Limited Constitutional Vision of Meech Lake
—*Alan C. Cairns* 247

The 1987 Constitutional Accord and Ethnic
    Accommodation
—*John D. Whyte* 263

Political Vision and the 1987 Constitutional Accord
—*Jennifer Smith* 271

Competing Visions of Constitutionalism: Of Federalism
    and Rights
—*Katherine Swinton* 279

Meech Lake and Visions of Canada
—*Richard Simeon* 295

Appendix 1 307
Appendix 2 315

use pay 354 in lesson as well,

Preface

What is the significance of the Meech Lake Accord? The answer is far from clear, as was expected when a group of individuals from a variety of academic disciplines, including law, economics and political science; from different parts of the country; and with diverse backgrounds (some having represented interest groups or acted as governmental advisors) came together at a symposium held at the University of Toronto in the fall of 1987 to debate the question.

The papers in this volume reproduce much of the day's discussion. They contain diverse reactions to the impact of the distinct society clause, the spending power provisions, the changes to national institutions and the process by which the Accord was achieved. Some are positive; some are critical; while others express doubt about any long-term impact on Canadian life.

As editors, we chose to include all of the papers submitted to us. While there is thus some danger of repetition, there is the advantage that the volume reflects the richness of the debate about the Accord at the symposium and throughout the country. To save space, we have eliminated references to the Accord or the Constitution's provisions in the text of the papers and reproduced the relevant material in the Appendices at the end of the book.

While the volume bears our names as editors, it reflects the efforts of those who organized the symposium with us — David Beatty, Marsha Chandler, Steve Dupré, Robert Prichard, and Martha Shaffer — as well as the editorial assistance of Paula Hurwitz. Finally, we wish to acknowledge the contribution of President George Connell of the University of Toronto, for the symposium on Meech Lake was inspired by his concern that members of the university community engage in informed debate about the proposed constitutional amendment. His leadership guided us throughout the preparations for the symposium.

Contributors

KEITH BANTING is a member of the Department of Political Studies and of the School of Public Administration at Queen's University. A specialist in public policy and federalism, he is the author of *The Welfare State and Canadian Federalism* and co-editor of *And No One Cheered: Federalism, Democracy and the Constitution Act*.

IVAN BERNIER is a member of the Faculty of Law, Laval University and Executive Director of the Quebec Centre for International Relations. He was Dean of the Faculty from 1981-85 and served as Director of Research (Legal and Constitutional) for the Royal Commission on the Economic Union and Development Prospects for Canada (the MacDonald Commission).

ROBIN BOADWAY is a member of the Department of Economics at Queen's University. He is a specialist in public sector economics and his publications include *Public Sector Economics, Canadian Tax Policy*, and *Welfare Economics*. He is currently editor of the *Canadian Journal of Economics*.

RAYMOND BRETON is a member of the Department of Sociology at the University of Toronto. His research interests are the relations between ethnic and linguistic groups in Canada, the socio-political organization of ethnic communities and the politics and policies of ethnicity and language. He is the co-author of *Cultural Boundaries and the Cohesion of Canada* and *Why Disunity? An Analysis of Linguistic and Regional Cleavages in Canada*.

ALAN CAIRNS is a member of the Department of Political Science at the University of British Columbia. He is a long-time student of Canadian politics and has written widely on federalism and the Constitution. From 1983-85 he was Director of Research (Institutions) for the Royal Commission on the Economic Union and Development

Prospects for Canada (the MacDonald Commission). *Constitution, Government and Society in Canada*, edited by Douglas Williams, is a collection of his recent essays.

J. EDWARD CHAMBERLAIN is a professor of English and Comparative Literature and Principal of New College at the University of Toronto. He has served as an advisor to federal, provincial and aboriginal governments and has written extensively on aboriginal issues; his books include *The Harrowing of Eden: White Attitudes Toward North American Indians*.

THOMAS J. COURCHENE occupies the Stauffer-Dunning Chair at Queen's University and is the Director of the School of Policy Studies. He has written widely in the areas of monetary policy, fiscal federalism and Canadian socio-economic policy. His latest book is *Social Policy in the 1990's*. During 1987-88 he was Robarts Professor of Canadian Studies, York University.

J. STEFAN DUPRÉ teaches political science at the University of Toronto. He has served on over a dozen federal and provincial councils and commissions and has been writing about Canadian federalism for thirty years.

PIERRE FORTIN teaches at the Départment des sciences économiques of the Université du Québec à Montréal. He is a member of the Economic Council of Canada and the 1988-89 President of the Société Canadienne de science économique. He has written extensively on macroeconomic theory and policy in a Canadian context.

DONNA GRESCHNER is a member of the College of Law, University of Saskatchewan. A specialist in constitutional law and human rights, she has served as constitutional advisor for several national women's organizations.

PETER HOGG is a professor at the Osgoode Hall Law School, York University. He is the author of *Constititional Law of Canada*.

AL JOHNSON is a member of the Department of Political Science at the University of Toronto. Before entering academic life, he served as a senior advisor to the governments of Saskatchewan and Canada in the fields of federal-provincial and constitutional relations.

ANDRÉE LAJOIE is a professor at the Faculté du droit, Université de Montréal and a member of its Centre de recherche en droit public. She is the author of several books on constitutional law and has recently published on the federal spending power in the fields of health and higher education.

LUCIE LAMARCHE est professeure au Département des sciences juridiques de l'Université du Québec à Montréal. Elle est membre de l'executif national du Fonds d'Action et d'Éducation juridiques pour les femmes (LEAF/FAEJ).

A. WAYNE MACKAY is a professor of constitutional law at Dalhousie University. He has been involved as a litigator in several Charter cases, including one involving minority language rights.

J. PETER MEEKISON is Vice-President (Academic) and a professor of Political Science at the University of Alberta. As Deputy Minister of Alberta's Department of Federal and Intergovernmental Affairs he was involved in the constitutional negotiations leading to the Constitution Act, 1982. He continues to act as advisor to the Government of Alberta on constitutional matters.

JACK MINTZ is Director of the John Deutsch Institute for the Study of Economic Policy and a member of the Department of Economics, Queen's University. As a specialist in public finance, he has published several books and articles on taxation, public enterprise and fiscal federalism, one of which is *Commodity Tax Competition Between Member States of a Federation: Equilibrium and Efficiency.*

ANDREW PETTER is a member of the Faculty of Law at the University of Victoria. A specialist in constitutional law, he has written numerous articles on federalism and Charter issues.

DOUGLAS D. PURVIS is the Head of the Department of Economics at Queen's University. He is the author of numerous articles in professional journals, is co-author of a widely-used principles of economics textbook, and has written extensively in the public press on economic policy. Previous positions he has held include Director of the John Deutsch Institute for the Study of Economic Policy and Clifford Clark Visiting Economist at the Department of Finance, Ottawa.

PETER RUSSELL teaches in the Department of Political Science at the University of Toronto. He is a leading student of the judicial process in Canada and the author of the widely-used text, *Leading Constitutional Decisions.* His most recent book is *The Judiciary in Canada: The Third Branch of Government.*

RICHARD SIMEON is Director of the School of Public Administration, Queen's University. A leading student of Canadian politics, he is the author of *Federal-Provincial Diplomacy* and co-editor of *And No One Cheered: Federalism, Democracy and the Constitution Act*.

BRIAN SLATTERY is a member of faculty of Osgoode Hall Law School at York University. He has written widely in the fields of constitutional law, constitutional history, aboriginal rights, and criminal law and procedure.

JENNIFER SMITH teaches political science at Dalhousie University. She is a student of Canadian politics, and specializes in the Confederation period. Her published articles deal with questions of federalism and judicial review.

LYNN SMITH teaches law at the University of British Columbia. She has published on equality issues, including *Righting the Balance: Canada's New Equality Rights* (editor-in-chief and contributor) and is currently co-chair of the National Legal Committee of the Women's Legal Education and Action Fund (LEAF).

KATHERINE SWINTON is a professor of law at the University of Toronto. She teaches and writes in the constitutional law area.

JOHN WHYTE is Dean of the Faculty of Law, Queen's University. He teaches and writes in the area of constitutional law. He was also a constitutional advisor to the Blakeney government of Saskatchewan in the negotiations preceding the constitutional amendments of 1982.

Part I

The Distinct Society:
Concepts of Community and
Principles of Interpretation

The Concepts of "Distinct Society" and "Identity" in the Meech Lake Accord[*]

Raymond Breton

The definition of a society involves, in part, the processes whereby principles of inclusion and of exclusion are selected and established and those through which they become more or less generally accepted as the basis of membership. Such principles define who is an insider and who is an outsider. They can also define the conditions under which one can become a member and those under which one can be excluded. The Meech Lake Accord can be seen as a political exercise directly involved in this process which is not to say that it has succeeded in formulating principles that are either clear or that will generate consensus across the different segments of Canadian society.

Language constitutes one of the bases of social organization to which the notion of society in Canada has been applied. The expressions "French Canada" and "English Canada" are well established in the Canadian vocabulary, as are others used synonymously, such as "French-Canadian and "English-Canadian" society. One of the persistent issues in the politics of French-English relations has been the location of the "two Canadas": whom does each include? This question remains a source of intense controversy.

According to one view, French-Canadian society is located in Quebec, the rest of Canada being the homeland of English-speaking Canadians. This "segmentalist" conception of Canada is not new, but

[*] I wish to express my appreciation to Professors Albert Breton, Ronald Gillis and Robert Harney for their useful comments and suggestions on an earlier draft of this paper.

in recent decades it has been particularly strongly articulated by several nationalist groups in Quebec — the independentists in particular. A number of anglophones outside of Quebec share this view, rejecting the idea that French Canada exists in their part of the country. The fact that "Québécois" has replaced "French-Canadian" in the prevailing Quebec political vocabulary partly indicates the success of this idea.

The other view is "pan-Canadian". It conceives of both French- and English-speaking Canada as existing in all regions of the country. Of course, the presence of the two communities is not evenly distributed across the territory; nevertheless the pan-Canadian concept is seen as having an institutional existence in all parts of the country — an existence that should be maintained and strengthened. The difference between the two conceptions is not that one posits two and the other a single Canada. Indeed, both see Canada as segmented along linguistic lines.

One critical difference between these two views has to do with *where* the two Canadas are located: what *territorial* and, accordingly, what *socio-political space* and what *membership* are assigned to each of them. Underlying the "segmentalist" approach is the conception of community and society as space-bound — a territorial reality. When established as an "interpretive clause" in a constitutional document, such a view is likely to become determinant: the geographical space "assigned" to a community will progressively determine its social boundaries. The "pan-Canadian" conception, on the other hand, does not identify community and society with a particular geographical space. The boundaries are social, rather than spatial. The fluidity in this approach offers considerable flexibility for community development. It leaves the evolution of the linguistic communities to the operation of social, economic and political forces, rather than to the dictates of a constitutional document.

It is important to emphasize that the confrontation is between two *conceptions* of reality: of what Canada is and of what it should be. The controversy is between the definers of the socio-political reality. The proponents of each view read history differently, drawing different conclusions from given demographic trends. They see the necessity for different language policies and have different views of what is desirable or realistic in terms of institutional development. They have divergent prognoses for the future.

The Meech Lake Accord is significant because it takes sides in this controversy. Basically, it adopts the view of the segmentalists, recognizing the province of Quebec, not French Canada, as a distinct society. An important, but unsaid, implication of this proposition is that the rest of Canada is also a distinct society and that the governments of that society have the responsibility of preserving and promoting its distinct identity.

Second, while it defines Quebec as a society, it defines the rest of French Canada as a population (French-speaking Canadians are "also present elsewhere in Canada"). It similarly describes the segment of English Canada located in Quebec. Unless it is taken to mean a voluntary association or a social circle, a society implies a certain institutional structure designed for, and at least partly managed by, a given collectivity. A community cannot exist unless it has a minimal institutional system. By defining the "residual" French and English collectivities as populations whose presence outside the "homelands" "constitutes a fundamental characteristic of Canada", the Accord entirely avoids the matter of community and institutional development as a governmental responsibility. Professor Bastarache[1] has pointed out that while the Quebec government is recognized as having a role in preserving and *promoting* the distinct identity of Quebec, the Parliament of Canada and the provincial Legislature are only given the role of *preserving* the "fundamental characteristics of Canada". This, it should be noted, was a determined request made by a number of provincial premiers in the course of the negotiations.

The political discourse surrounding the Meech Lake Accord has been couched in terms of reconciliation and political harmony. It is, however, an ideological discourse that conceals an important exercise of power, in which one political faction has succeeded in imposing its view on a constitutional document. Many of those who have lost have been effectively silenced: by promoting their conception of Canada, they run the risk of being accused of being in favour of "confrontation politics" or of being anti-Quebec. (One senses from the debate on this issue that to challenge almost any aspect of the Accord exposes the critic to such an accusation.) In the event of a new wave of ultra-nationalism or separatism in Quebec, or a confrontation between anglophones and the Quebec government, or between a francophone minority and an English-speaking provincial government, then those who are proponents of a pan-Canadian French and English Canada will realize the extent to which they have lost.

In short, the definition of a society (or subsociety) that ultimately

---

1 *Le Devoir* [de Montréal] (2 July 1987).

prevails is the one that serves the political and related socio-cultural interests of the most powerful segments of a society. Political and economic power are gained and maintained by imposing particular ideological conceptions of the social order and orienting the institutional system to the service of the underlying interests.

The Meech Lake document uses another important concept — that of a distinct identity — but leaves it undefined. According to some newspaper reports, this was done deliberately at the request of the Quebec premier. It was also reported that attempts were made in l'Assemblée nationale to define the distinct identity in terms of language. Given the linguistic controversies of the past decades, it may be understandable that the authors of the document wanted to avoid the assignment of a linguistic basis to the identity of the "distinct society". But leaving it open-ended simply postpones and hands to others the issue of its definition.

Collective identities are not given once and for all. As the ongoing preoccupation with Canadian identity reveals, they may be very vague and ill-defined. Collective identities are socially constructed. They are systems of ideas about who "we" are and what we should be as a people and society. To a considerable extent, they are formulated by elites and then diffused among members of the society. The components of the collective identity that prevail at any point in time tend to be those that serve the interests of the most powerful segments of the society. For example, there is little doubt as to whose interest the definition of Quebec as a Catholic society served, and in whose interest it is to reject that identity. Similarly, leaving the identity undefined or ambiguous can also serve — especially when done deliberately — the power interests of particular groups or institutional authorities.

The use of two different concepts suggests that the authors of the Accord not only considered Quebec as a distinct society, but they also viewed this society as having institutions of a distinct character. Given the context in which the document was produced, the identity or character to which it refers can be termed ethnocultural (a notion that includes more than a distinctive language). Thus, while Canada as a whole has no official culture, only official languages, Quebec is encouraged to maintain and promote both an official language and a particular ethnoculture. On the one hand, Canadian society affirms through its government that it is multicultural but, on the other, intends to declare that one of its segments is a distinct society and encourages it to promote its ethnocultural distinctiveness.

In this context, what is the meaning of the word "Québécois" or of "Quebec society" whose distinct identity is to be promoted? Whom did the framers of the Accord have in mind? Did they mean to refer to those who are ethnically of French origin? Did they intend to include those who are francophone, but of non-French origins and those who are English-speaking? What does it mean to promote the distinctive identity of a society that is *de facto* multicultural and, in all likelihood, will become increasingly so? Is it a question of language, or does it also include religion, political ideology, ethnicity and race? The recent debate in Quebec as to whether or not immigration is a desirable or acceptable solution to the province's low fertility rate and eventual demographic decline indicates that this matter is not only of academic interest. Indeed, there seems to be considerable concern in some circles that immigration, particularly of people of non-European origins, will undermine the cultural character (that is, the distinct identity) of those who consider Quebec as their "homeland". (It should be noted in this connection that the first part of the text of the Accord expresses a concern with the demographic situation of Quebec and of the related importance of immigration. The implementation of the Accord's policy statements on this matter will make Quebec an increasingly multi-ethnic society, as is the rest of Canada.)

Furthermore, if Quebec society refers not to a culturally defined community but to a polity, the responsibility of the state is not to promote the distinct identity of a segment of the population, but to defend and promote the rights of all *citizens*. This is one of the senses in which the Accord is potentially in contradiction with the Canadian Charter of Rights and Freedoms[2] already incorporated in the Constitution. I say "potentially" because the notion of distinct identity is left undefined in the Accord. (It should be remembered that a provincial Legislature can decide to exclude some of its legislation from the dictates of the Charter — something that may become a real possibility when momentous matters such as "our identity as a people" are involved. The intensity of the political movements of the 60s and 70s should not be forgotten; nor should the re-emergence of such movements in the future be dismissed as "most unlikely".)

In its discourse, the Accord includes a distinction between "state" and "society", especially when it addresses the question of the

---

2 Being Pt. I of the Constitution Act, 1982 [enacted by the Canada Act 1982 (U.K.), c. 11, s. 1]. See relevant sections in Appendix 1 to this volume.

responsibilities of governments with regard to Quebec and Canadian society. For analytical purposes, it frequently makes sense to distinguish between the social, economic and political orders. This makes it possible to consider relationships between different institutional sectors in a society. But the distinction is analytical only. When state and society are dissociated (as several observers argue is the case in Poland, for example), the situation is considered an anomaly, a pathology to be dealt with. State institutions are an integral component of society. Accordingly, a distinct society implies distinct state institutions — the central theme of the independentist movement.

The Meech Lake Accord states that Quebec is a distinct society *within Canada*. But while it recognizes a special role for the Quebec government with regard to that society, it does not affirm the distinctive role that the central government would presumably have as well, since it is also the government of that distinct society. It could be argued that this is already clear in the Constitution; but so is the question of the "powers, rights or privileges" of the provincial governments.

The text of the Accord with regard to a distinct society and a distinct identity is a symbolic statement that seeks to recognize certain states of affairs or to assert the desirability of certain objectives. As a set of symbolic affirmations, the Accord is somewhat unbalanced. It selectively reaffirms certain realities, objectives, and governmental responsibilities, but ignores others. In addition, it can be noted that statements about Canada as a distinct society (that would be more than the juxtaposition of provinces) are absent. So are statements about the role and responsibilities of the central government in relation to the national level of societal organization. Of special interest is the absence of statements concerning the role that Quebec and the other provinces may have with regard to Canada as a whole.

The direction that the symbolic affirmations are given in the Accord should perhaps be placed in the context of the free trade negotiations with the United States, the other major policy initiative of the federal government. Indeed, it is possible to identify several levels of social, economic and political organization: local, regional, national, continental and international. Each level consists of networks of institutions and organizations within and between which complex patterns of social, economic and political transactions take place. Also, each level tends to involve different categories of individuals and groups. This is so, even if the interconnection among levels is extensive, as it tends to be in the contemporary world, despite the existence of formally defined political jurisdictions. It is suggested here that while the Meech Lake Accord emphasizes the provincial or regional level of political, socio-cultural, and economic organization, the free trade initiative promotes institutional development at the continental level. Wittingly or unwittingly, the national society appears neglected in this process too. Canada as a distinct level of social organization may be progressively eroded by emphasizing developments primarily in the other two directions. There seems to be an underlying assumption that the institutional system at that level will automatically take care of itself, while the other two levels need special attention and buttressing.

Another facet of constitutional documents as symbolic statements should be noted. They constitute a political resource that can be used by different groups in society, depending on the particular interests they are pursuing. Symbolic weapons are widely used in political battles, something that the politicians (who are among the experts in symbolic manipulation!) who have framed the Accord do not seem to have considered at great length. In addition, and most important, the statements of concern here are not only symbolic assets whose socio-emotional power can give them great significance in eventual political struggles, but also constitutional specifications, whose legal status can give them considerable import in legal and political battles. They are instructions to judges.

In analyzing the Accord it is important to raise questions as to who, in the more or less distant future, is likely to use the symbolism of distinct society and distinct identity, and what is the legal authority they will have been given in the pursuit of their cause. The definition of the collective identity and of changes in it is usually a conflictual process, mainly because different groups have diverging interests and life philosophies that they wish to incorporate into the character of the society and its institutions. Like any other political outcome, the collective identity that becomes established is a reflection of the distribution of power in the society and of the compromises reached among the competing interests. The Accord provides ammunition for certain groups, but deprives others who have competing interests.

What are likely to be the socio-political theories formulated around the concepts of distinct society and distinct identity? What political and socio-cultural objectives will they legitimate? It is not difficult to imagine the meanings that certain groups could give to these ambiguous symbolic statements in relation to issues such as immigration, language, culture, and the arrangements through which

Quebec is incorporated in the larger Canadian society. The very ambiguity of symbolic statements increases their political potential. For example, the notion of society itself is ambiguous and, accordingly, flexible. More specifically, the meaning articulated depends on the context in which it is used and on the particular interest groups using it. When used without a qualifier, it is generally understood to refer to a country — a possible meaning that is not likely to be lost by certain groups. As an exercise, the reader should speculate for a few minutes on how the symbolic statements would have been used in the 60s and 70s, had they been part of the British North America Act.[3]

Of course, the Accord itself will not trigger any social movement or set in motion particular socio-political processes. It is, rather, a symbolic resource with legal potential that may be used by groups in the future in ways that may not have been anticipated by the legislators. A substantial risk has been taken, by embedding in the constitution ambiguous notions that can be infused with meanings whose source and impact will depend heavily on the particular socio-political context, precisely because they are left undefined.

Finally, because the concepts of the Accord are ambiguous and because various groups have an interest in defining them differently, it gives a special *political* role to the courts. This feature is even more intriguing when we recall that several provincial governments had expressed concern that the Charter would diminish the role of Legislatures. The same provincial governments have agreed to give an enormous political role to the courts on a matter of central societal importance.

---

3 1867 (U.K.), c. 3 [now the Constitution Act, 1867].

Aboriginal Rights and
the Meech Lake Accord

J. Edward Chamberlin

When asked by Aunt Sally whether anybody had been hurt by the explosion on the Mississippi river boat, Huck Finn replied "No. Killed a nigger." "Well, it's lucky," said Aunt Sally, "because sometimes people do get hurt."

The Meech Lake Accord is the Aunt Sally of constitutional amendments. It is completely oblivious to the fact that the aboriginal people will be hurt by its provisions, though it has taken kindly concern about the welfare of everybody who in its view really counts. In constitutional terms, aboriginal people obviously don't count, though, like Huck Finn, the framers of this amendment mention them as an afterthought, in s. 16.

This is the fundamental flaw of the Meech Lake Accord. It perpetuates a habit of mind that produced provisions like that of the 1876 Indian Act which stated that "the term 'person' means an individual other than an Indian."[1] But this habit has never before been constitutionalized. (Australia, going much further, wrote into its 1900 Constitution that "in reckoning the numbers of the people of the Commonwealth, or of a State, or other part of the Commonwealth, aboriginal natives shall not be counted."[2] This was the legacy of a settler society that had appropriated a continent on the assumption that the land was *terra nullius* which in euphemistic Latin simply meant

---

1 Indian Act, 1876 (39 Vict., U.K.), c. 18, s. 12.
2 Commonwealth of Australia Constitution Act, 1900 (63 & 64 Vict., U.K.), c. 12, s. 127.

that there was no one there who counted). With the opening reference to the fundamental character of Canada in the "distinct society" provision of the Meech Lake Accord — a reference which though not exclusive is certainly prescriptive — the inclination to discount aboriginal people is for the first time in Canada given menacing constitutional encouragement.

The aboriginal people of Canada have routinely been the victims of someone else's language, and imprisoned in realities which are the product of that language. The language we use always tells something about who we are, and where we belong. If the language is someone else's, then our sense of identity and of nationality will in large measure be determined for us. Among other things, it may locate us on the margins as relentlessly as any economic or political logic.

Language looks in two directions at once. What is said indicates as much about the speaker as about the subject. This of course is as much a fundamental tenet of constitutional interpretation, as it is of literary criticism. I am therefore going to look at what the language of the amendment indicates not only about those whom it classifies as distinct but also those of us — which ultimately is all of us — who are responsible for this kind of language. I will be paying less attention to the specific subject of the amendment — French-speaking Canadians and the province of Quebec — than to its general implications, and especially to the way in which it maps out a geography of power, with boundaries that place some people at the centre looking out, and other people on the outside looking in.

There are three things that make the distinct society provision offensive. First, by being a definition *of* one group *by* another, within a general logic of *them* and *us*, it conditions the way in which we will make any other constitutional acknowledgement of fundamental differences between groups within Canada, and between governments which represent those groups. Second, the distinct society provision diminishes and distorts our sense of the fundamental character of Canada in some very specific ways, and narrows the range of models that we might contemplate in order to achieve a more accurate constitutional image of the country. Third, because it is so narrowly conceived, it fails to provide an informing vision of the country just at the point, both in the document and in the history of the country, when a vision is so crucial, and could be so useful in dealing with the realities that perplex us.

The first point is central. Any act of definition, being an act of language, draws attention to two parties: the defined and the definer.

When this definition is social or political, it creates a perception of difference between one group, which does the defining, and some other, which is defined in relation to the reference group. This kind of definition is an expression of power, and one of its features is that those who buy into the definition by accepting the dominant group's idea of them are typically caught up in a grim cycle of celebration and condescension.

This is not to say that difference or distinctiveness cannot be a positive element in a people's sense of themselves. It should be; and in some measure for all of us, individually or collectively, it must be. But it cannot be when the definition is provided by others. In a subtle but subversive way, this is what naming Quebec a distinct society does. It confirms the power of those who are implicitly *not* distinct — that is, of those who do not need to be designated as distinct because they are the reference group. Others are distinct *from them*. That is how this process always works. It involves an exercise of authority so natural that it seems inevitable. Just ask those who have over the centuries been represented by stereotypes or classified by a dominant society as different.

Some may say that this phrase about a distinct society is merely a constitutionally convenient way of speaking, a legal fiction of sorts. But Constitutions are much more than mere conveniences, and the fictions they express are intended to inform the political, social and economic realities that emerge within the country. An act of naming should never be taken lightly. The Indian people of Canada know this, having been mistakenly named in an act of European ignorance five hundred years ago, and having lived lives fundamentally determined by European values, including liberal values of sympathy and concern, ever since. Deciding the names by which they will be called, as the Dene have done, for example, has provided a significant new way in which Indian people have come to an awareness of their place in the country. Thus, the National Indian Brotherhood changed its name to the Assembly of First Nations, and now speaks of first peoples.

This kind of argument about the determining effect of names and categories in marginalizing individuals and groups is often dismissed as a distracting exaggeration. The definition of Quebec as a distinct society is not *intended* to do anything like this. But neither did Huck Finn intend harm to "niggers". Or at least no more harm than he — and they — were conditioned to accept. After all, one of his best friends was the "nigger" Jim. "The tongueless man gets his land took," says a Cornish proverb. Constitutions should give tongue to the dispossessed, instead of imposing words and names on them. For it is a sad but simple fact that the more liberal we are, the more likely we are to imprison others in our definitions of them, being committed to the delusion that those for whom we feel concern can share in our power if only they can learn the rules. And so we teach them. But the rules are precisely those that signify "them" (upon whom we bestow our sympathy) and "us." This is not an argument against liberalism, but a plea for a different constitutional amendment more scrupulous about its definitions and its language.

There was a cartoon that had wide currency when I was in Australia a couple of years ago. It showed a group of aborigines standing on the shore watching Governor Phillip land at Sydney Cove in 1788, and one saying to the others: "There goes the neighbourhood." We need to shift our perspectives to recognize this view of the country. We need to think of what it would be like to be labelled a distinct society by the Constitution. We need to come closer to the view expressed in a recent history of the West Indies that "Columbus did not discover a new world; he established contact between two worlds, both already old."[3] And the Meech Lake Accord does not help us do any of this. On the contrary, it is a very definite hindrance.

On the second point, the distinct society provision will diminish constitutional tolerance for effective expressions of aboriginal sovereignty, and distort constitutional acknowledgements of aboriginal rights. Naming is one way of imposing a definition upon other people. Another way is by territorial designations, in this case the identification of the province of Quebec as a distinct society. Putting people in their place is much more than a figure of speech. It is the basis of all codes of conduct; and it is the basis of colonial settlement. The process of making treaties with the Indians of Canada and surveying the country parcelled out the Dominion in ways that contradicted and contorted indigenous territorial affiliations. This constitutional amendment is a new parcelling. I am not addressing here the issue of whether it is one that benefits French-speaking Canadians. Rather, I am concerned that the parcelling itself, or at least the way in which it is undertaken, is fundamentally contrary to the long-term interests of aboriginal people trying to achieve a new set of relations with the dominant society.

Identifying the distinct society with a territorial region reinforces

---

3 J.H. Parry and P. Sherlock, *A Short History of the West Indies* (London: Macmillan, 1971) at 1.

the widely-held view that territorial designations provide the only feasible expression of distinctive authority, and certainly of the sovereignty that aboriginal people affirm as a central part of their heritage. This is a stubborn delusion, part of the mistaken notion that sovereignty is absolute and always territorially defined. In fact, it need be neither. The idea of contingent sovereignties is a comfortable part of most constitutional arrangements, including our own. And if we go back to the early forms of sovereign authority in Europe, tribal sovereignty unattached to a particular and defined place almost certainly preceded territorial sovereignty, and then ran concurrently with it for several centuries. Feudalism tended to shift the balance by linking personal rights and duties to ownership of land. The decline of the Roman Empire, and the rise of the reformed states in the north of Europe who would not accept the spiritual, much less the secular, authority of the See in Rome, meant that the idea of interdependent tribal sovereignties was replaced by the idea of independent territorial sovereignties. But the natural fact of groups whose territorial sovereignty was contingent or concurrent remained part of the picture, with a recognized sovereignty that ran parallel to, and differed in degree but not in kind from, that of other nation states.

The distinct society provision is therefore not only narrow in its conception of how one accommodates the anomalous character of the country, but it also entrenches a long-standing prejudice against developing models for aboriginal self-government that will take into account the large number of native people who are now without land. These models are notoriously elusive, but his provision makes them much more difficult to find, and even discourages us from looking. In terms of the collective interests which native people have always affirmed, it returns us to the era when individual rights were only enjoyed by property owners.

These collective interests have traditionally been represented in the language of sovereignty. This is not a new idea, but is one which goes back beyond Confederation, and is firmly grounded in the policy and practice of British and then Canadian governments in dealing with the aboriginal people of the country. I have used the term sovereignty because aboriginal people in all parts of the world have used it consistently for the past couple of decades. Granted, it is not their word; it is ours. But those who find it extravagant might do well simply to listen closely, for the ideal that it approximates has been around for a very long time, and is here to stay. Duncan Campbell Scott, who was Deputy Superintendent General of Indian Affairs from

1913 to 1932 and whose writings still provide one of the most reliable chronicles of Indian affairs policy in British North America, argued that from 1744, when William Johnson was appointed Indian agent by Governor George Clinton in the American colonies, to the present "there runs through the Indian administration a living and developing theory of government." What is the logic behind this theory? In Scott's words, "treaties and agreements defined the civil relation of the aborigines and the ruler. It was the British policy to acknowledge this Indian title to his vast and idle domain, and to treat for it with much gravity as if with a sovereign power."[4]

The anomalous character of these relations, and the sovereign character of aboriginal interests, intrigued British, American and then Canadian governments. From the time of Confederation in 1867, Canada has had a clear commitment to the notion that aboriginal interests are fundamentally political, and are most appropriately conceived in terms of national or sovereign rights. South of the border, things have occasionally taken a different turn. After nearly a century of signing treaties with Indian tribes, in 1871 the United States government passed an amendment to its Indian Appropriations Act to the effect that thereafter no Indian nation or tribe within the territory of the United States would be acknowledged or recognized as an independent and sovereign power with whom the Union might contract by treaty. This statutory initiative was in American historical and constitutional terms an aberration; and over the years the few such instances of American political impatience with the anomalous character of Indian tribal sovereignty have been routinely (albeit at times rather tardily) rejected by the courts. In contrast, Canada chose this particular year of 1871 to signal its commitment to the British tradition of recognizing aboriginal sovereignty, and its distance from American politics of the period, by beginning the process of treating with the Indians of the Northwest. This process, lasting over half a century, resulted in the eleven so-called numbered treaties, and in the main features of Canadian Indian policy and administrative practice. In proceeding with treaty-making in such obvious contrast to contemporary American policy and practice, Canada recognized precisely what American legislators at that time were rejecting — the sovereign status of Indian nations.

To the extent that the distinct society provision encourages the

---

4 D.C. Scott, "Indian Affairs, 1763-1841" in *Canada and Its Provinces*, A. Shortt and G. Doughty, eds. (Toronto: Publisher's Association of Canada, 1913-1914), vol. 4 at 689 to 697.

development of constitutional arrangements which move away from explicit recognition of inherently sovereign aboriginal rights that are governmental in character, the development of imaginative and flexible relationships among federal, provincial and aboriginal governments will be impaired. Ironically, for all its occasional vacillation, the United States has from its beginning had a constitutional logic in place that accommodates aboriginal sovereignty. Its courts have confirmed this logic; and its politicians have (sometimes grudgingly) accommodated these awkward facts of constitutional life which, like the facts of geography in North America, are part of the challenge of creating a federal system of contingent sovereignties bound together by a sense of common purpose. And with all of this, the Union has not collapsed. This should provide some comfort to those who worry about the collapse of the Canadian Confederation under the weight of so much supposedly foreign freight. There are obviously significant differences between the ways in which Canada and the United States conceive inherent and delegated rights, both provincial and aboriginal. But over the past two centuries, room has been found in the American scheme for a combination of ideology and practicality that accommodates aboriginal sovereignty. Canada has good reason to think that a constitutional accommodation is possible here too. And partisan ideology should be no impediment. Over a fifty-year period, in a couple of radically different political situations, the United States has acknowledged the governmental authority of aboriginal people: in the "New Deal" reforms of the 1930s, for example, which confirmed the authority of Indian tribal governments, and at the opposite end of the political spectrum in the recent assertion by President Reagan that the United States government recognizes the sovereignty of Indian governments and acknowledges that its dealings with them are on a government-to-government basis.

This brings me to my third point. The Meech Lake Accord and the distinct society provision, which claims to articulate a fundamental characteristic of Canada, incorporate no vision of the country that expresses the aspirations of aboriginal people. In fact, the Accord and its provisions heighten their anxiety. There is a disturbing implication, reinforced by the territorial designation of Quebec as a distinct society, that we are moving back towards the alternatives of separation or assimilation, alternatives that have plagued native affairs for the past two or three hundred years in Canada. In the early days of European settlement, assimilation of the aboriginal people was proposed as a solution to the "Indian problem" both by idealists and by those who wanted land. Separation, on the other hand, was proposed by other idealists and by those who wanted even more land, and no trouble. Confined in their thinking to this strictly limited set of alternatives — separation or assimilation — even the best-intentioned eighteenth and nineteenth century legislators and administrators prepared the way for the alternatives that bedevil the twentieth century — the rural Indian slum and the urban Indian slum. The alternatives of separation or assimilation present false choices: both inappropriate and unnecessary, and ultimately pernicious. It should not be a matter of choosing between drowning or being marooned on an island, but a matter of choosing which of several ways to take advantage of living by the shore, with access both to the land and to the sea.

We need to give some articulate energy to finding a way beyond these alternatives, and to finding a language that will celebrate a vision of the country which includes aboriginal rights. This vision is both comparable and consistent with the great visions of national unity and progress which have driven Canada, and which inspired the constitutional amendments found in the Meech Lake Accord. This is a national opportunity, not a set of local problems. My concern is that in meeting one national opportunity, the first ministers may be foreclosing another.

Curiously, Canada has not recognized this opportunity. We have a long tradition of participation in international affairs; and all around the world, something significant is happening with aboriginal people. From widely different regions, at various and very different stages of political involvement, aboriginal people are expressing their determination to have their rights recognized. This is not some highly orchestrated world-wide conspiracy. But it is a startlingly widespread development. Probably the most accurate analogy is to be found in the late eighteenth century, when revolutions against Old World authority seemed to spring up in a number of places, as political action combined with philosophical thought about the rights and duties of individuals in relation to the power of the state. The questions now have more to do with the relation between various forms of collective authority, but they are no less challenging, and no less urgent. National constitutions are still the place for these questions to be addressed. In this latest round of constitutional deliberations, Canada is acting like some *ancien régime*, doing a New World imitation of an Old World minuet.

At the very least, the federal and provincial first ministers must commit their governments to the proposition that bringing aboriginal people into the constitution now has the same priority that for the past three years was given to bringing Quebec into the Constitution. In my view, the distinct society provision is an impediment to doing this: it fails to reconcile the theory of the country, and the sense of the place of the Constitution in national affairs which it embodies, with a theory that is central to the full and active participation of aboriginal people.

If we do not try, we will continue like Huck Finn and Aunt Sally. Nice enough people, to be sure, but with a profoundly flawed view of our country, and of the million or so of our fellow Canadians who have an inheritance of aboriginal rights. And we will, like Huck, continue to see Indian territory as something out there, rather than right here.

Perspective féministe d'une certaine société distincte : Les Québécoises et l'Accord du Lac Meech

Lucie Lamarche

Nous avons été invitée à soumettre quelques réflexions, d'une part sur la participation d'une culture féministe québécoise au concept de société distincte et d'autre part sur le sort réservé aux droits à l'égalité dans le cadre de l'Accord du Lac Meech. Notre point de vue dépend à la fois de notre expérience de chercheure et d'avocate praticienne aux prises quotidiennement avec la réalité de l'égalité au Québec. Après avoir distingué la culture juridique féministe de la culture québécoise nous tenterons d'illustrer le contentieux de l'égalité sexuelle au Québec pour mieux affirmer que les Québécoises ont tout intérêt à se préoccuper des effets de l'Accord sur leur droit à l'égalité.

MAIS QUELLE EST DONC CETTE SOCIÉTÉ DISTINCTE?

Il importe d'abord de vérifier comment nous avons été à ce jour instruites sur le contenu réel de la notion de société distincte. À l'occasion, par exemple, des audiences du Comité conjoint du Sénat et de la Chambre des communes, il a été soumis[1] que la définition suggérée par Claude Ryan dans le *Livre Beige* de 1981 devait être retenue:

> . . . les lois, les systèmes judiciaires, les institutions municipales et provinciales, les associations volontaires, les médias, les arts, les lettres, le système d'ensei-

---

1 Voir audiences du Comité conjoint de la Chambre des communes et du Sénat du 26 août 1987, Fédération des femmes du Québec (p. 13:44).

gnement, le réseau des services sociaux et sanitaires, les institutions religieuses, les institutions d'épargne populaire.

Quant au gouvernement québécois, il a généralement soutenu dans le cadre des discussions entourant la ratification par le Québec de l'Accord que le concept de société distincte avait tout au moins une dimension linguistique et culturelle. Le ministre Gil Rémillard a cependant exprimé de plus grandes ambitions, référant tantôt à la place que pourrait occuper dorénavant le Québec sur le plan des télécommunications, des relations bancaires internationales ou des affaires extérieures. Le professeur André Tremblay, quant à lui, a soutenu que le principal acquis "consistait en la reconnaissance du Québec comme société française à l'intérieur du Canada".[2] Le Québec avait déjà, avant la lettre de l'Accord du Lac Meech, soumis aux tribunaux un contenu du concept de société distincte. Ainsi, dans l'affaire du "droit de veto",[3] le procureur général du Québec soumettait à la Cour suprême que la société distincte allait bien au-delà des questions linguistiques et culturelles. Le concept visait tous les aspects de la société québécoise : les valeurs sociales, les lois, la religion, l'éducation, les ressources naturelles, la souveraineté de son assemblée législative. Il est vrai que la Cour suprême avait alors rejeté le principe de la dualité linguistique suggéré par le Québec. Par ailleurs, dans sa décision relative aux droits linguistiques garantis aux minorités québécoises en vertu de l'article 23 de la Charte canadienne des droits et libertés[4] la Cour n'avait pas non plus disposé des arguments relatifs à la société distincte.

Comme Québécoise, nous partageons l'espoir que l'article 2 de la Loi constitutionnelle de 1867[5] serve dorénavant de façon significative de guide d'interprétation aux tribunaux dans la reconnaissance du fait québécois distinct.[6] Ceci ne nous empêche pas de questionner d'une

---

2 16 septembre 1987. Causerie de l'Association du Jeune Barreau de Montréal.

3 *P.G. Québec c. P.G. Canada* (1982), 140 D.L.R. (3d) 385 à 1a p. 401.

4 Pt. I de la Loi constitutionnelle de 1982 [décrétée par la Canada Act 1982 (U.K.), c. 11, s. 1], dans la décision de *P.G. Québec c. Quebec Association of Protestant School Boards*, [1984] 2 R.C.S. 66 (C.S.C.).

5 (U.K.), c. 3.

6 Peu d'experts en droit constitutionnel voient dans le libellé des alinéas 2.1(1) (b) et 2.1(3) de l'Accord, la possibilité que soit fondamentalement affecté le partage des compétences de l'État fédéral canadien. Cependant, il apparaît évident que l'argument de la société distincte permettra à la Cour suprême de trancher en faveur du Québec dans quelque zone grise relative au partage des compétences (auquel cas l'ensemble des provinces pourraient bénéficier de la décision). La règle d'interprétation que constitue pour le pouvoir législatif et exécutif du Québec la reconnaissance et la promotion de la société distincte s'appliquera tant à la Constitution qu'à la Charte canadienne des droits et libertés et notamment à l'art. 1 de la Charte.

part le contenu réel du concept de société distincte, eu égard aux droits des Québécoises, et d'autre part, l'effet de cette reconnaissance constitutionnelle sur le droit des Canadiennes à l'égalité, compte tenu qu'à l'évidence, aucun groupe d'intérêts au Québec n'a tenu compte de ce droit avant la ratification de l'Accord par le Québec.

LES QUÉBÉCOISES ET LA SOCIÉTÉ DISTINCTE

A tout le moins, le caractère distinct de la société québécoise, d'un point de vue sociologique, autorise la référence aux droits collectifs des francophones, lesquels sont souvent assimilés aux droits de la "majorité", concept qui, s'il peut constituer un non-sens juridiquement, n'en est pas moins un fait politique. Le caractère distinct du Québec, tel qu'invoqué par le(la) citoyen(ne) réfère essentiellement au fait français et à ses répercussions sur le plan institutionnel et surtout scolaire. Or, le fait français est légitimement la préoccupation des francophones, majoritaires au Québec, dans leur rapport institutionnel avec les "minorités" anglophones et allophones du Québec. Mais voilà qu'il a été soumis que le caractère distinct de la société québécoise comprendrait, dans sa dimension culturelle, l'égalité des sexes comme valeur fondamentale et assurée.[7]

Qu'en est-il donc de cette égalité et plus précisément du droit des Québécoises à l'égalité? A cet égard, le Québec est effectivement différent sinon distinct. Le régime de droit civil, les acquis aux termes de l'expression législative de l'égalité formelle et la présence de la Charte des droits et libertés de la personne du Québec[8] ont entretenu l'illusion d'une "meilleure égalité" pour les Québécoises. Cependant l'adoption de mesures d'égalité formelle peut aussi entraîner des effets discriminatoires. A titre d'exemple, l'entrée en vigueur du nouveau Code civil du Québec a consacré l'obligation solidaire des conjoints aux charges du mariage et aboli le mandat domestique (445-446 C.C.Q.). Or, en 1981, le lobby des Québécoises les plus démunies,

---

(Voir audiences du Comité conjoint: Monsieur R. Décary, 4:66 et le professeur Gérald Beaudoin, 2:65).

Nous souscrivons à l'argument voulant que le fait que le pouvoir exécutif du Québec doit aussi assurer la promotion de la société distincte reflète essentiellement la mesure de l'engagement du Québec à l'égard de son caractère distinct et non une attribution supplémentaire de pouvoirs.

7 26 août 1987 — audiences du Comité conjoint de la Chambre des communes et du Sénat sur l'Entente constitutionnelle de 1987; présentations de la Fédération des femmes du Québec et du Conseil du statut de la femme du Québec.

8 L.R.Q., c. C-12.

lesquelles prétendaient que cette mesure n'avait pour seul but que d'appauvrir les femmes d'une crédit qu'elles n'ont pas au profit des créanciers, a été complètement négligé. Citons aussi le cas des travailleuses domestiques (lesquelles sont majoritairement des femmes immigrantes), exclues de l'application de la Loi sur les normes du travail[9] lorsque leur travail consiste essentiellement dans le gardiennage d'enfants, et celui des conjointes âgées et divorcées, lesquelles sont exclues de la définition de conjointe survivante prévue à la Loi sur le régime de rentes du Québec.[10]

Par ailleurs, l'adoption de mesures économiques compensatoires à l'occasion de la rupture du mariage n'a pas atteint ses objectifs. Ainsi, l'article 559 du nouveau Code civil du Québec, en vigueur depuis le 1er décembre 1982, prévoit qu'au moment où il prononce le divorce, le tribunal peut ordonner à l'un des époux de verser à l'autre, en compensation de l'apport en biens ou en services de ce dernier à l'enrichissement du patrimoine de son conjoint une part compensatoire. Cinq années de décisions judiciaires révèlent une banalisation dramatique de cette mesure, au point de créer un effet discriminatoire pour les femmes. D'ailleurs, le gouvernement envisagerait des amendements à l'article 559 C.C.Q. pour y inclure expressément que certaines contributions autres que financières, mais encore inconnues, doivent être prises en compte dans l'attribution de la part compensatoire. Les Québécoises avaient pourtant à l'époque manifesté une vive opposition au libellé de l'article 559.

Nous sommes aussi préoccupée du rapport entre le droit à l'égalité et les pratiques gouvernementales et institutionnelles qui entraînent des effets discriminatoires dont les femmes sont victimes. A titre d'exemple, citons l'opération "bou-bou macoutes" : plus de 60% des ménages bénéficiaires d'aide sociale au Québec sont dirigés par des femmes chefs de familles monoparentales. Bien que le langage de la Loi sur l'aide sociale[11] traite également les hommes et les femmes, ces dernières ont été récemment les principales victimes de l'opération d'enquêtes administratives consistant à procéder à des coupures dans les ménages où quelque indice permettait de croire qu'un homme pouvait prendre en charge les besoins de la famille, peu importe le choix de vie de la bénéficiaire. Pour contester ces pratiques et leurs effets discriminatoires auprès des Québécoises les plus pauvres, les

---

9 Loi sur les normes du travail, L.R.Q., c. N-1.1, art. 1 (6e).

10 Loi sur le régime de rentes du Québec, L.R.Q., c. R-9, art. 132 et ss.

11 Loi sur l'aide sociale, L.R.Q., c. A-16.

garanties fondamentales et le droit à l'égalité contenus à la Charte canadienne des droits et libertés ont été invoqués.[12]

Il est probable que la période 1975-1981 a facilité au Québec l'émergence dans le droit d'une expression formelle de l'égalité au profit des femmes participant activement au fait politique français et majoritaire. Le discours politique égalitaire du gouvernement du Parti québécois a favorisé cette émergence. Il est aussi exact d'affirmer que les lois du Québec ont, depuis 1975, une longueur d'avance, aux termes de l'expression de l'égalité formelle des sexes, sur les lois des autres provinces.[13] Mais si l'État québécois s'est préoccupé de dire l'égalité, il ne s'est guère plus que les autres gouvernements impliqué dans l'"opérationnalisation" de l'égalité et ce, dans les sphères d'activités qui touchent les femmes par leurs effets discriminatoires : telles le travail, la sexualité ou la famille.[14] C'est pourtant dans ces domaines socio-économiques que les femmes sont le plus touchées non seulement en vertu des effets de la discrimination sexuelle mais surtout en vertu d'une combinaison de facteurs discriminatoires alliant à leur sexe, l'âge, l'origine ethnique, la pauvreté ou le statut matrimonial.

Le revenu annuel moyen des Québécoises chefs de familles monoparentales est de $12,571. Le taux de participation des Québécoises à la main-d'oeuvre est de 8% inférieur à la moyenne canadienne, soit de 45%.[15] Le gouvernement québécois s'apprête à couper les budgets des services externes de main-d'oeuvre, lesquels sont gérés par des femmes et constituent le réseau le plus efficace d'insertion des femmes à l'emploi dans des secteurs qui ne constituent pas des ghettos d'emplois féminins.

Compte tenu de ces exemples, comment peut-on prétendre que ces Québécoises, victimes de discrimination non seulement en fonction de leur sexe mais aussi de leur origine ethnique, leur âge, leur situation familiale et leur état civil, tirent un "meilleur avantage" d'une "culture de l'égalité" qui ferait partie du concept de société distincte?

Nous en concluons que si une telle culture existe, elle est

---

12 *Laforest c. Paradis*, [1987] R.J.Q. 364 (C.S. Qué.).

13 Voir par exemple les dispositions du Code civil du Québec relatives au régime matrimonial primaire (art. 441 et ss) et à l'exercice de l'autorité parentale (art. 645 et ss). Cependant, le régime matrimonial de la communauté de biens (abrogé, mais qui touche encore 30% des Québécoises âgées de plus de 50 ans) prévoit encore que le mari est le seul administrateur de la communauté.

14 Car l'"opérationnalisation" de l'égalité ne s'exprime pas seulement par l'énoncé de la norme législative mais aussi par les pratiques administratives de l'État ou l'activité judiciaire.

15 Mercier, *Les Femmes ça compte*, Québec, Conseil du statut de la femme, Gouvernement du Québec, 1984.

essentiellement blanche et d'allégeance néo-libérale. Elle résulte de la participation de ces femmes à la poussée nationaliste des années 75 par la majorité francophone au Québec. Ceci légitimerait l'affirmation selon laquelle une certaine culture féministe fait partie du concept de société distincte.

Les Québécoises ont, tout autant que les autres Canadiennes, à se préoccuper de l'influence de l'article 2 de la Loi constitutionnelle de 1867 et de l'article 16 de la Loi constitutionnelle de 1987 sur les droits à l'égalité énoncés aux articles 28 et 15 de la Charte canadienne des droits et libertés. Les femmes, victimes de discrimination sur des bases multiples, ont besoin de l'ensemble des garanties d'égalité contenues à la Charte, et les Québécoises doivent partager les préoccupations des autres Canadiennes. Ainsi, il n'est pas inconcevable qu'à court d'arguments politiques ou économiques valables, le gouvernement québécois tente de légitimer certaines politiques d'éducation (par exemple, la formation offerte aux femmes par des commissions scolaires éloignées des centres urbains à l'égard des métiers non traditionnels est déjà insuffisante ou inexistante), d'immigration ou de santé par son obligation de promouvoir le caractère distinct du Québec, et ce, au détriment du droit des femmes à l'égalité.

Par ailleurs, on sait que l'utilisation actuelle de l'article 15 de la Charte canadienne des droits et libertés est faite surtout par des hommes ou des personnes morales issus des groupes majoritaires de la population. On sait aussi que ces demandeurs fondent surtout leur recours sur des motifs non mentionnés à l'article 15 et que sont surtout invoquées les garanties procédurales plutôt que les garanties d'égalité substantive.[16] Tant que les articles 15 et 28 de la Charte ne seront pas clairement confirmés dans leur qualité de droits substantifs, il n'est pas inconcevable que l'omission d'énumérer à l'article 16 de l'Accord les articles 28 et 15 de la Charte puisse signifier que ce droit à l'égalité, que toutes et tous aimeraient croire fermement acquis, soit ébranlé en vertu des règles interprétatives que sont la société québécoise distincte et la dualité linguistique du Canada.

Il n'est pas à ce point évident que l'introduction de nouveaux principes d'interprétation n'aurait qu'un effet marginal sur le droit à l'égalité, à l'égard duquel l'histoire jurisprudentielle n'est pas encore écrite.

---

16 Voir à ce sujet le mémoire de LEAF (Legal Education and Action Fund for Women)/FAEJ (Fonds d'action et d'éducation juridiques pour les femmes), intervenant devant la Cour suprême dans l'affaire *Law Society of British Columbia v. Andrews* (22 septembre 1987).

L'ARGUMENT POLITIQUE DE LA PRÉSENCE DE LA CHARTE DES DROITS ET LIBERTÉS DE LA PERSONNE DU QUÉBEC

On sait que le Québec a choisi de soustraire les législations québécoises à l'application de la Charte canadienne des droits et libertés en adoptant la Loi concernant la loi constitutionnelle de 1982.[17] Le Québec avait alors utilisé le mécanisme dérogatoire de l'article 33 de la Charte. La Cour d'appel du Québec a rappellé à l'ordre le gouvernement québécois en lui reprochant, à l'occasion de sa décision dans l'affaire *Alliance des professeurs de Montréal c. P. G. Québec*,[18] d'évincer de la protection de la Charte toutes les lois québécoises sans démontrer le rapport entre la loi à l'abri et le droit dont on voulait la protéger. C'est à titre de justification *a posteriori* que le gouvernement québécois a prétendu que la protection offerte par la Charte des droits et libertés de la personne du Québec était plus généreuse que celle offerte par la Charte canadienne. Mais qu'en est-il vraiment?

D'abord, l'article 9.1 de la Charte prévoit que le gouvernement peut fixer la portée et aménager l'exercice des droits et libertés fondamentaux prévus aux articles 1 à 9. Ensuite, le droit à l'égalité devant la loi (art. 10), tout comme les droits et libertés fondamentaux sont soumis au mécanisme de l'art. 52 de la Charte[19] qui prévoit que:

> Aucune disposition d'une loi, même postérieure à la Charte, ne peut déroger aux articles 1 à 38, sauf dans la mesure prévue par ces articles, *à moins que cette loi n'énonce expressément que cette disposition s'applique malgré la Charte.*

Enfin, le droit à l'instruction publique (art. 40), le droit à l'enseignement moral et religieux (art. 41), le droit de choisir l'enseignement privé (art. 42), le droit à l'information (art. 44), le droit à des mesures sociales et d'assistance financière (art. 45) et le droit à des conditions de travail justes et raisonnables (art. 46), sont des droits qui ne font l'objet d'aucune protection.

Bien sûr, la Charte lie la Couronne (art. 54), mais l'État peut expressément lui déroger ou bénéficier d'exemptions dans la mesure prévue à chaque article pour chaque droit.[20] Donc, la Charte ne garantit

---

17 L.Q. 1982, c. 21.

18 [1985] C.A. 376 — présentement en appel devant la Cour suprême.

19 La régle de prépondérance édictée à l'art. 52 de la Charte n'a son plein effet que depuis le 1er janvier 1986 (Loi modifiant la Charte des droits et libertés de la personne, L.Q. 1982, c. 61, art. 34.)

20 Sur la protection de la Charte contre l'action étatique, voir A. Morel, *"La Charte québécoise: un document législatif unique dans l'histoire législative canadienne"* (1987), 21 R.J.T. 1 à la p. 20.

pas de droits à l'encontre de l'État lui-même. Le gouvernement québécois a refusé de se lier pour l'avenir à l'égard de conditions de forme plus exigeantes en regard des modifications qui pourront être apportées à la Charte.[21] Enfin, les tribunaux n'ont pas encore réglé la question de savoir si l'article 52 permet de déclarer invalide une législation ou simplement d'appliquer la règle de prépondérance à la Charte.[22] Pour reprendre les propos de Pierre Mackay, voilà un outil qui représente bien peu la mesure d'autonomie et de maturité d'un peuple.[23]

Dans un autre ordre d'idées, il n'est pas à négliger que la Commission des droits de la personne du Québec (C.D.P.Q.) est une institution célèbre par son inefficacité, tant au niveau de ses pouvoirs que de son fonctionnement. Faute de directives, d'enquêtes complétées dans des délais utiles et de poursuites devant les tribunaux de droit commun,[24] l'énoncé très progressiste des concepts d'égalité[25] contenus à la Charte québécoise quant aux normes anti-discriminatoires, demeurent lettre morte. A titre d'exemples :

— L'article 19 de la Charte québécoise consacre le principe "A travail équivalent-salaire égal". Cette mesure est souvent utilisée pour distinguer le Québec des autres régimes législatifs qui ne reconnaissent le principe du salaire égal que pour un travail "égal".[26] Cependant, une seule décision judiciaire a à ce jour fourni une illustration de ce principe,[27] faute par le C.D.P.Q. d'entreprendre les poursuites appropriées suite aux plaintes déposées auprès d'elle par les syndicats;

---

21 Sur la constitutionnalisation progressive de la Charte, voir J.Y. Morin, "*La constitutionnalisation progressive de la Charte des droits et libertés de la personne*" (1987), 21 R.J.T. 25 — contra: P. Mackay, "*La Charte canadienne des droits et libertés ou le déclin de l'empire britannique*" dans R.D. Bureau et P. Mackay, ed, "*Le droit dans tous ses états*, (Montréal, Wilson & Lafleur, 1987), 13 à la p. 30.

22 Morin, precité, note 21 à la p. 38 et ss.

23 Mackay, precité, note 21, à la p. 31.

24 En vertu des articles 82 et 83.2 de la Charte québécoise, la Commission ne peut que recommander diverses formes de réparation à la discrimination prouvée. Advenant le non respect de cette recommandation, elle peut prendre fait et cause devant les tribunaux de droit commun, en reprenant à zéro une nouvelle enquête judiciaire.

25 Encore ici, notons que l'interdiction de discriminer en raison de la grossesse (L.Q. 1980, c. 11, art. 34) et de l'orientation sexuelle (L.Q. 1982, c. 61, art. 3) sont des précisions législatives qui ont été apportées à la Charte durant les "années-lumière" de l'expression de l'égalité formelle au Québec, bien qu'elles constituent une réponse à de cuisants échecs judiciaires.

26 Voir L. Lamarche, "L'égalité des femmes en matière d'emploi: rien n'est acquis" dans R.D. Bureau et P. Mackay, ed., *Le droit dans tous ses états*, Montréal, Wilson & Lafleur, 1987, 163.

27 *Senay c. Les Aliments Ault*, [1984] C.S.P. 1056.

— L'article 10.1 de la Charte énonce que le harcèlement sexuel constitue une forme de discrimination basée sur le sexe. Mais encore là, l'inertie de la C.D.P.Q. et ses exigences franchement discriminatoires quant à l'administration du fardeau de preuve[28] des plaignantes font que les Québécoises ont tout intérêt à s'en remettre aux tribunaux de droit commun qui ont été à ce jour plus progressistes que la C.D.P.Q. en la matière;[29]

— Ce n'est que depuis juin 1985 que sont en vigueur les articles 86.1 et suivantes de la Charte prévoyant que les programmes d'accès à l'égalité ne constituent pas de la discrimination. Seuls les programmes imposés par les tribunaux de droit commun et les programmes recommandés par la C.D.P.Q. suite à une plainte[30] doivent être établis conformément au règlement[31] et supervisés par la C.D.P.Q. Pourtant la C.D.P.Q. paralyse les initiatives volontaires en les soumettant à un formalisme administratif excessif. Par ailleurs, le gouvernement québécois n'est pas soumis à l'implantation de tels programmes;[32]

— Enfin, le gouvernement québécois n'a pas à ce jour jugé nécessaire d'implanter des mécanismes équivalant à l'obligation contractuelle des fournisseurs du gouvernement fédéral, non plus qu'il ne met en oeuvre des mesures s'apparentant à la Loi sur l'équité en matière d'emploi[33] qui contraint les employeurs soumis à la législation fédérale à épurer l'ensemble de leurs pratiques d'emploi discriminatoires.

L'argument économique prônant l'intérêt des Québécoises d'avoir recours à la C.D.P.Q. par voie de plainte, à cause de la gratuité du recours, est presque sans fondement. L'inefficacité juridique et administrative de l'organisme constitue un élément fort dissuasif. Dans la mesure où les pratiques administratives qui découlent de l'utilisation

---

28 Voir le mémoire du Groupe d'aide et d'information sur le harcèlement sexuel au travail de la région de Montréal Inc. déposé devant la Commission parlementaire des Institutions portant sur l'examen des orientations, des activités et de la gestion de la C.D.P.Q.

29 Voir *Foisy c. Bell Canada*, [1984] C.S. 1164 et *Diane May Halkett c. Ascogifex Inc. et S. Stephenson* (1 octobre 1986), Montréal 500-04-008308-41 (jugement de M. le Juge L. De Blois).

30 *Charte des droits et libertés de la personne*, L.R.Q. 1977, c. C-12 telle qu'amendée par L.Q. 1982, c. 61, art. 21, introduisant l'article 86.3.

31 *Règlement sur les programmes d'accès à l'égalité*, en vigueur le 1er septembre 1986, 118 G.O. II, 1959.

32 *Charte des droits et libertés de la personne*, L.R.Q. 1977, c. C-12, telle qu'amendée par L.Q. 1982, c. 61, art. 21, introduisant l'art. 86.7.

33 Loi sur l'équité en matière d'emploi, S.C. 1986, c. 31, en vigueur depuis le 9 septembre 1986.

du recours à la Charte comportent en elle-mêmes des effets discriminatoires, la Charte canadienne revêt une grande importance pour les
Québécoises. A cet égard, une recherche privée est actuellement en
cours au Québec. Par ailleurs, une commission parlementaire relative
à l'étude du fonctionnement de la C.D.P.Q. et au bilan de la première
décennie de la Charte québécoise a été convoquée et les audiences
sont très attendues des groupes de femmes du Québec.[34]

En conclusion, lorsqu'il s'agit de contrôler l'effet discriminatoire
d'un loi québécoise ou des effets d'une pratique de l'administration
étatique au Québec, il n'y a aucune raison de prétendre sérieusement
que la Charte québécoise constitue une garantie suffisante à l'égard
du droit des femmes à l'égalité et que la Charte québécoise ajoute
à la confiance des femmes dans le concept de société distincte.

LA SOCIÉTÉ DISTINCTE COMME RÈGLE D'INTERPRÉTATION

Il est généralement admis que la Charte canadienne des droits
et libertés consacre des droits individuels, sous réserve des articles 25
(droit des peuples autochtones) et 29 (droits confessionnels). Cependant, la reconnaissance du Québec comme société distincte comporte
une dimension purement collective, laquelle, plus particulièrement à
l'égard des droits linguistiques, ne va pas de soi. Par exemple, alors
que le juge Deschênes affirmait que les droits linguistiques sont d'abord
exercés par des individus, et donc individuels,[35] certains auteurs
affirment que ces droits sont collectifs parce qu'attribués à une
collectivité.[36] Le juge en chef de la Cour suprême dans la décision
Société des Acadiens[37] reconnaît que les droits linguistiques revêtent un
caractère social. Cette affirmation fait partie des indices positifs
permettant de croire qu'il existerait des droits collectifs dans la Charte.

Bien que nous ne tenterons pas ici de démontrer que les femmes
constituent politiquement une classe de citoyennes défavorisées,[38] il

---

34 Voir note 28.
35 *Quebec Association of Protestant School Boards c. P.G. Québec*, [1982] C.S. 673.
36 P. Carignan, "De la notion de droit collectif et de son application en droit scolaire au Québec" (1984), 18 R.J.T. 1.
37 *Société des Acadiens du Nouveau-Brunswick Inc. c. Association of Parents for Fairness in Education, Grand Falls District 50 Branch*, [1986] 1 R.C.S. 549 à la p. 566.
38 Voir W.W. Williams, "The Equality Crisis: Some reflections on Courts, Culture and Feminism" (1982), 7 Women's Rights Law Reporter 175 et J. Saint-Arnaud, "L'argument de la différence et le contrôle des rôles sociaux" (1985), 1 Revue Juridique la Femme et le Droit 69.

existe des raisons jurisprudentielles de croire que les femmes peuvent aussi invoquer des droit collectifs. Ainsi, la Cour suprême dans les décisions *Action Travail des Femmes c. Canadien National*[39] et *Robichaud c. Sa Majesté la Reine*[40] affirme fermement que les plaignantes étaient victimes de discrimination seulement en raison de leur sexe, laquelle forme de discrimination est spécifique aux femmes comme groupe.

Par ailleurs, l'article 16 de l'Accord du Lac Meech énonce que l'article 2 de la Loi constitutionnelle de 1867 ne doit pas être interprété comme portant atteinte aux droits conférés par les articles 25 et 27 de la Charte. On peut s'interroger, sous réserve de la portée réelle et inconnue de l'article 28 de la Charte, quant à la priorité donnée au multiculturalisme sur la culture des femmes au Canada, qui selon nous existe et est distincte de la culture de la majorité francophone au Québec.

En effet, la portée de l'article 28 de la Charte n'est pas encore claire. Les références les plus pertinentes en matière d'égalité sexuelle, soit les décisions *Boudreau v. Family Benefits Appeal Board*[41] et *Shewchuck v. Ricard*,[42] sont contradictoires. La première affirme que l'article 28 de la Charte ajoute aux garanties d'égalité contenues à l'article 15 de la Charte et rend les garanties d'égalité sexuelle supérieures aux autres garanties. La deuxième affirme que l'article 28 n'ajoute rien à l'article 15 de la Charte. La portée réelle de l'article 28 de la Charte à l'occasion de l'analyse par les tribunaux des limites raisonnables pouvant justifier une dérogation aux droits et libertés garantis par la Charte dans le cadre de l'article 1 n'est pas non plus évidente.[43]

Enfin, l'article 28 lui-même n'a pas encore été confirmé quant à sa portée substantive ou son autonomie propre. Et pourtant le gouvernement affirme que la protection interprétative offerte au multiculturalisme et aux peuples autochtones à l'article 16 de l'Accord se justifie d'une part par le caractère collectif de ces droits et d'autre part s'oppose aux garanties substantives offertes par l'article 28 de la Charte en matière d'égalité sexuelle.[44] Nous croyons plus simplement que l'effet de l'article 2 de la Loi constitutionnelle de 1867 et de l'article

39 [1987] 1 R.C.S. 1114 (C.S.C.).

40 (1987), 40 D.L.R. (4th) 577 (S.C.C.).

41 *Boudreau c. Family Benefits Appeal Board (N.S.)* (1984), 66 N.S.R. (2d) 271 (N.S. C.A.).

42 *Shewchuck c. Ricard*, [1986] 4 W.W.R. 289 (B.C. C.A.).

43 Voir à ce sujet M. Eberts, "Sex-based discrimination and the Charter" dans M. Eberts et A. Bayefsky, eds. *Equality Rights and the Canadian Charter of Rights and Freedoms* (Toronto: Carswell, 1985) 183.

44 Comment alors interpréter la présence de l'art. 35 de la Loi constitutionnelle de 1982 et de l'art. 91(24) de la Loi constitutionnelle de 1867 à l'art. 16 de l'Accord du Lac Meech?

16 de l'Accord sur les garanties d'égalité contenues aux articles 28 et 15 de la Charte n'ont tout simplement pas suscité l'intérêt de la part des premiers ministres.

Un amendement garantissant au droit à l'égalité le même poids interprétatif qu'aux garanties visées à l'article 16 de l'Accord serait tout au plus superflu, mais n'est pas superflu à l'évidence. Il faut éviter *absolument* qu'à l'occasion de l'examen d'une règle de droit portant atteinte aux droits et libertés garantis par la Charte, les limites raisonnables d'une société libre et démocratique, telles qu'interprétées à la lumière de l'article 2(a) de la Loi constitutionnelle de 1867, puissent permettre que la reconnaissance du Québec comme société distincte se fasse au détriment des énoncés d'égalité contenus à la Charte.[45]

POURQUOI LES GOUVERNEMENTS PRATIQUENT-ILS LA POLITIQUE DU REFUS?

Il nous apparaît que quatre réponses sont théoriquement possibles :

1— Malgré qu'il soit à ce jour sensibilisé aux préoccupations des Canadiennes, le gouvernement préfère laisser aux soins des tribunaux le mandat de définir le contenu et la portée des droits à l'égalité. Implicitement, il néglige qu'au Québec cela puisse signifier que s'opposent le droit des femmes à l'égalité et les droits collectifs d'une société distincte. Il est à noter que cette opposition n'est pas exclusive au Québec si l'on tient compte des principes de dualité linguistique et du respect du multiculturalisme et des droits des peuples autochtones.

2— Compte tenu de la sérénité avec laquelle le gouvernement affirme que l'article 28 de la Charte a une portée substantive et autonome et considérant les limites apportées à l'article 2 de la Loi constitutionnelle de 1867 par l'article 16 de l'Accord, le concept de société distincte serait vidé de sa valeur interprétative.

3— L'article 16 de l'Accord est un compromis purement politique, juridiquement superflu.

4— Dans une société libre et démocratique, le gouvernement n'estime pas politiquement nécessaire ou rentable d'ouvrir la "Boîte de Pandore" que constitue l'Accord du Lac Meech dans le seul but de garantir aux femmes, *sans l'ombre d'un doute*, leur droit à l'égalité.

Les deux premières hypothèses prêtent au gouvernement des

---

45 Cela sans envisager l'hypothèse où l'art. 2 de la Loi constitutionnelle de 1867 ajouterait aux pouvoirs législatifs et exécutifs du gouvernement québécois.

intentions qui ne sont certes pas les siennes et élaborent des situations que nous ne saurions accepter comme Québécoise. Les troisième et quatrième réponses sont sans doute assez proches de la réalité. Il est à remarquer que si l'article 16 est lui-même superflu, il est difficile de croire que seuls quelques hommes autour d'une table de négociations constitutionnelles aient le privilège du superfétatoire. Reste donc la quatrième possibilité. Et essentiellement à cause de notre scepticisme par rapport à l'affirmation qui veut que l'égalité soit une composante implicite du concept de société distincte, nous misons, comme femme, juriste et Québécoise, sur l'ouverture de la boîte de Pandore! Dans les faits, il s'agit à peine de soulever le couvercle, puisque tous les gouvernements affirment que le droit à l'égalité est un acquis et qu'il n'a jamais été question de le mettre en péril. Faut-il entendre par là que, dans le cadre de la négociation de l'Accord, il n'a jamais été question d'égalité?

The Distinct Society Clause in the Meech Lake Accord: Could it Affect Equality Rights for Women?

Lynn Smith

According to the first ministers responsible for drafting the Meech Lake Accord, it is not intended to, nor does it, affect the constitutionally guaranteed rights to equality[1] in the Canadian Charter of Rights and Freedoms.[2] However, some constitutional experts, national women's groups and the Canadian Advisory Council on the Status of Women, have argued to the contrary.[3] Similar arguments have been made with respect to the effects of the Meech Lake Accord on the equality rights of disabled people, members of cultural or social communities which are neither English nor French, and aboriginal people.[4] I will limit

---

1 Premier MacKenna of New Brunswick, elected since the Accord was framed, has given some indication that he would oppose its implementation without clarification regarding its effect on the position of women and minorities under the Charter: *The [Toronto] Globe and Mail* (October 22, 1987) at A1 and A5.

2 Being Pt. I of the Constitution Act, 1982 [enacted by the Canada Act, 1982 (U.K.), c. 11, s. 1].

3 Some of the women's organizations in Quebec have said that they find no cause for concern in the terms of the Accord. The divergent views will be discussed in the text and notes below.

4 There are differences between the arguments from case to case, arising from differences in the Charter protection for various equality rights (compare Charter ss. 15, 25, 27, 28 and 29) and from differences in the sorts of equality problems which can arise for different groups. However, the common feature is a concern that the effect of the Meech Lake Accord may be to weaken protection for equality rights both inside and outside Quebec.

this discussion to the possible effect of the distinct society clause,[5] which the Accord would add as a new s. 2 to the Constitution Act, 1867,[6] on women's equality. However, many of the arguments described would also apply in the context of the debate about the effect of the Accord on equality rights for other groups designated by the wording of s. 15 of the Charter.

The discussion will begin in Part I with an examination of issues which I will characterize as "burden and standard of proof", to be followed in Part II by a description of the debate incorporating a review of the arguments on both sides. Part III will then offer some conclusions about the arguments.

As a preliminary matter, it will be helpful to set out the questions which logically could be asked about the distinct society clause and s. 2 in general:

(1) Might the proposed new s. 2 of the Constitution Act, 1867 affect the protection of the equality rights of women and minorities under the Charter? If the protection of equality rights might be affected, in what ways?
(2) If there might be effects, are such effects necessary and desirable in order to achieve some purpose connected with the recognition of linguistic duality in Canada or of Quebec as a distinct society?
(3) If so, should those purposes have primacy over the protection of equality rights for women or minorities?
(4) If those purposes should not have primacy over the protection of equality rights, how should the Accord be amended in order to prevent equality rights from being affected?

Although these are the four questions which logic would seem to dictate, the debate so far has focused almost entirely upon the first. This is because those responsible for the Meech Lake Accord have refused to concede that it may have any real effect on equality rights. To use a predictably watery metaphor, the supporters of the Accord have remained daintily on the shoreline defined by the first question, and have successfully refrained from getting their feet wet in a discussion of the second, third and fourth questions. Nevertheless, I will argue that, given the statements of the first ministers that the Accord was not intended to affect Charter equality rights, unless there

---

5 I refer to the proposed new s. 2 of the Constitution Act, 1867 as a whole, although it is only in para. 2(1)(b) that the term "distinct society" is used.
6 (U.K.), c. 3.

is an overwhelmingly clear case that the Accord cannot affect those rights, the question "Why not amend it to eliminate any doubt?" must be answered. The supporters of the Accord have given unsatisfactory answers to that question to date, which suggests that either they truly believe that equality rights are *necessarily* unaffected, and there is no benefit in opening up the Accord for the addition of clarification, or that (very quietly, in their own minds) they have addressed the second and third questions, and reached conclusions which would give distinct society and linguistic duality considerations priority over the protection of Charter equality rights.[7]

PART I: ISSUES OF BURDEN AND STANDARD OF PROOF

This part of the discussion will attempt to describe how the debate about the effect of the Meech Lake Accord would be conducted in an atmosphere in which logic and reason are of primary importance, and in which women's interests are not systematically discounted.

First, in this hypothetical world, there would be a process of consultation before and after the amendments were drafted, in which the views of those potentially affected would be taken into account,[8] rather than the presentation of *faits accomplis*. As Alan Cairns has pointed out, in the view of many Canadians, the process of constitution-making no longer belongs solely to the eleven first ministers. Whether realistically or not, women and minorities had placed a great deal of hope in the entrenchment of constitutional equality rights as a protection against the kind of discrimination which they have so recently experienced in the Canadian legal system. Whether or not there is a sense of "ownership" of those rights by the groups which invested considerable effort in obtaining their entrenchment,[9] there is certainly a sense that representatives of those groups belong at the

---

7 The latter explanation gains support from the apparent political priority that has been given to Quebec's support for the Accord, at the expense of other interests. For example, Senator Lowell Murray has said that the governments involved cannot respond to concerns raised by women and other groups since to do so would risk "unravelling the whole accord" and jeopardize the primary achievement of reconciliation of Quebec with Canada: Ross Howard, *The [Toronto] Globe and Mail* (26 August 1987) A3; Joel Ruimy, *The Toronto Star* (26 August 1987) A1.

8 The process might, for example, have approached the level of consultation often conducted with respect to proposed tax amendments.

9 As Alan Cairns suggests: see "The Limited Constitutional Vision of Meech Lake" in this volume, p. 247.

table when modifications to those rights are being considered.[10]

Second, a primary question would be whether the burden should be placed on the "modern Fathers of Confederation" to justify, to some standard of proof, the wisdom of proceeding to amend the Constitution in the way they have proposed. Alternatively, should the burden be on the women and minorities who are concerned about the effects of the Accord to justify the wisdom of not proceeding? In the hypothetical context I have proposed, the fact that the first ministers proposed the amendment and were responsible for its wording and the timing of its presentation, tends to support the placing of the burden of justification on them insofar as it may affect Charter rights. As to standard of proof, should it be established that there have or have not been "egregious errors" in the drafting of the document?[11] Or should it demand showing some plausible ways in which equality rights might be affected? In the hypothetical world of reason and gender equality, given the nature of a Constitution and the length of time for which it is expected to last,[12] tendencies toward perfectionism and away from the "quick and dirty" approach would be encouraged in the framing of amendments. Thus, if the burden of proof were on those proposing the Accord, they would be obliged to establish either that the Accord could not possibly affect equality rights for women under the Charter or that, if it did, this weakening of constitutional rights was necessary to achieve a more important purpose. If the burden were on the critics of the Accord, they would be obliged to show some plausible way in which equality rights could be affected. The burden would then shift to the supporters of the Accord to justify the change to the status of those rights.

I need not belabour the point that the reality has been otherwise. The burden has been placed on the critics, not the drafters, of the

---

10 Further, to state the obvious, the demographic characteristics of a collection of first ministers are not such that the interests of women and minorities will necessarily come to mind.

11 On August 4, 1987, Senator Lowell Murray, speaking on behalf of the federal government, told the Special Joint Committee of the Senate and the House of Commons (Joint Chairpersons Senator Arthur Tremblay and Chris Speyer M.P.) that alterations to the Meech Lake Accord would be made only where there was evidence of an egregious error, and where such alterations were unanimously approved by the provinces and the federal government: *The Toronto Star* (4 August 1987) A1.

12 Although it may be true that the shelf-life of constitutions is now assumed to be much shorter than it was in the previous one hundred years, I am not sure whether that is an assumption to be encouraged.

hastily-drafted agreement, to establish an egregious error.[13] Because of the shoreline strategy described above, the supporters of the Accord had offered no specific justifications for altering the status quo of protection of equality rights. At the same time, from the shoreline, they are able to take shots at those who are in the water.[14] What are the situations contemplated by the first ministers in which the primacy of the distinct society clause over Charter equality rights could be of such importance that amendments to remove this prospect would be viewed as seriously jeopardizing the Accord?[15] Indeed, it may be that the first ministers have not formulated any long-term policy in this area. This is irrelevant, of course, if the wording of the Accord leaves open the possibility of its affecting the meaning given to the equality rights in future judicial determinations. For the reasons which follow, I think it does.

PART II: DESCRIPTION OF THE DEBATE

In this section I will review the main arguments and counter-arguments in the debate which has been conducted between critics and supporters of s. 2. Although my main sources for arguments have been the *Report of the Special Joint Committee of the Senate and the House of Commons on the 1987 Constitutional Accord*[16] and the briefs submitted to that committee by national women's organizations,[17] I have also

---

13 As well, in the case of Quebec and the federal government at least, to do so under very early deadlines. Many of the submissions to the Special Joint Committee mentioned the problems with the timing of the presentation of the Accord and the committee hearings — even those from groups such as the Fédération des femmes du Québec which were supportive of the Accord.

14 For example, the accusations levelled against the national women's groups that they were "anti-Quebec". See Carol Goar, "How PM Infuriated Women's Groups," *The Toronto Star* (27 August 1987) A2, in which she describes the Prime Minister's statement of August 19, 1987 based on an assessment by Montreal columnist Lysianne Gagnon. The Prime Minister stated that he shared Ms. Gagnon's opinion that the women's groups' opposition to Meech Lake masked a real opposition to Quebec's desire for distinct status. As Goar points out, in fact the women's groups had consistently supported the recognition of Quebec's distinct status.

15 See Senator Lowell Murray's comments quoted above, note 7.

16 (Ottawa, Queen's Printer, 1987). The report will hereinafter be referred to as the JCR.

17 Including the briefs of the Women's Legal Education and Action Fund (LEAF), National Association of Women and the Law (NAWAL), and the National Action Committee on the Status of Women (NAC), all of which expressed concerns about the possible effect of the distinct society clause on protection for women's equality rights in Quebec and the rest of Canada. The federal Canadian Advisory Council on the Status of Women (CACSW) also submitted a brief strongly stating similar concerns. The amendments sought by the groups varied somewhat, although all agreed that s. 28 of the Charter should be mentioned in s.

drawn upon other sources in setting forth these arguments,[18] and have in some cases extrapolated from arguments actually made to ones which seem to follow from them.[19]

There are three main ways in which it has been argued that the proposed new s. 2 might affect women's Charter equality rights: (1) through providing a constitutionally-stated justification for limiting equality rights; (2) through stating a fundamental compromise of Confederation enabling the passage of legislation immune from Charter review; and (3) with regard to the overall context of the foundation of the Meech Lake Accord, through making a statement which creates the negative implication that in general women's equality rights have lower priority than other rights and interests in the Canadian polity. Each of these arguments will be dealt with in turn.

(1) Through Providing a Constitutionally-Stated Justification for Limiting Equality Rights

Arguments by the critics

I note at the outset that none of the women's groups nor the Canadian Advisory Council on the Status of Women expressed reservations about the merits of recognizing linguistic duality or the distinctiveness of Quebec society; on the contrary, the briefs tend to begin with statements endorsing the constitutional recognition of those principles and applauding the inclusion of Quebec in the Constitution.[20] Nor do I intend to dispute the merits of such recognition and inclusion.

---

16 of the Accord if it remained in its present form. As well, all of these groups criticized the process which led to the Accord, and the lack of consultation. I have also referred to the briefs of two Quebec women's groups, the Fédération des femmes du Québec (FFQ) and Femmes regroupées pour l'accessibilité au pouvoir politique et économique (FRAPPE). The Quebec Government Conseil du statut de la femme also presented a brief. The conclusion of the FFQ and the Conseil du statut de la femme was that the distinct society clause poses no threat to women's equality rights in Quebec, although the FFQ stated that it did not oppose an amendment to s. 16, adding a reference to s. 28 of the Charter, to make the matter clear. The third group (FRAPPE) supported the position taken by NAWAL.

18 Including personal communications and news reports.

19 Thus, this review includes some arguments because they have in fact been made by one side or the other, and other arguments because they seem logically to bear on the determination of the issue; it does not purport to be a complete and exhaustive historical record.

20 Compare the Prime Minister's accusation that women's groups contesting the present wording of the Charter harbour opposition to Quebec's recognition as a distinct society, note 14. Nor have I come across statements by any critic of the distinct society clause which begin with the premise that those matters should not be recognized or that it is immaterial whether or not Quebec endorses the constitutional amendments which took place in 1982.

Beginning from those premises, however, the critics argue that the wording of the proposed amendments in the Accord could weaken the protection of equality rights for women.

The argument in global terms is this: while presumably courts have always been free to take into account facts about the linguistic duality of Canada and the distinctiveness of Quebec society in assessing the reasonableness and justifiability of limits on equality rights under s. 1 of the Charter, the proposed amendments could be taken by the courts as directions to give those considerations priority over Charter equality rights, or at least equal weight to Charter equality rights, when a conflict arises. The arguments in support of this conclusion follow.

Section 2(1) says that the Constitution "shall be interpreted" in a manner consistent with the recognition of the facts set out in subss. (a) and (b). Sections 2(2) and (3) suggest the possibility that there is a grant of legislative power in s. 2 and the wording of s. 2(4) does not eliminate that possibility.[21] But whether or not there is a grant of legislative power in s. 2, a new interpretive direction will be added to the Constitution: this much is conceded by the supporters of the Accord.[22] Thus, with respect to the recognition of Quebec as a distinct society in s. 2(1)(b), there are conceivably circumstances in which a Quebec government[23] could seek to defend legislation on the basis that it furthers that goal despite an adverse effect on gender equality.

21 For this argument see the opinion letter from Mary Eberts and John B. Laskin of Tory, Tory, DesLauriers & Binnington dated August 25, 1987, to the Ad Hoc Committee of Canadian Women on the Constitution, and submitted to the Special Joint Committee. See also the LEAF brief at p. 9, where the argument is made that s. 2 does not contain a provision "capping" the extension of legislative authority, as in s. 31 of the Charter; rather, s. 2(4) only provides that nothing "derogates" from the powers of the governments.

22 See the brief dated August 4, 1987 presented by Gérald Beaudoin to the Special Joint Committee, in which it is said at 18:

Pour plusieurs juristes dont je suis, la déclaration de la société distincte ne modifie pas le partage des pouvoirs, non plus que la Charte canadienne des droits et libertés. C'est une règle d'interprétation expresse, importante certes, mais une règle qui ne change pas *matériellement* le partage des pouvoirs et la Charte des droits. Cependant, elle peut, comme toute règle, en certains cas, notamment sous l'article 1 de la Charte, ou dans une zone grise du partage des pouvoirs, faire pencher la balance d'un côté ou de l'autre.

See also the JCR above, note 16, at 32:

. . . [the linguistic duality and distinct society clauses] do not in themselves override existing substantive rights. They become two additional constitutional values that, when balanced with other values already represented in the Constitution, will be used to arrive at a fair and proper interpretation in the decision of a particular case.

23 Section 2(2) refers to the Parliament and provincial Legislatures; s. 2(3) refers only to the Legislature and Government of Quebec. Thus, the only government which could directly

An example might be matrimonial property legislation which excludes business assets from the definition of matrimonial property and thereby has the effect of disadvantaging women (since men are usually the partners in the marriage with business assets in their names). Under ss. 15 and 28 of the Charter, such a provision could be attacked as an infringement of equality, on the basis that it is a facially neutral rule which has an inordinate impact on women.[24] A government defending such legislation might well argue that the legislation does not offend s. 15 of the Charter, being reasonable and fair in the circumstances taking into account the fact that it relates to the internal arrangements of families, that families are fundamental institutions of the society both for linguistic and cultural purposes, and that the legislation forms part of the unique and distinct Quebec civil law system.[25] Thus, s. 2 of the Constitution Act, 1867 could be invoked in the argument about whether there was a violation. Alternatively, s. 2 could be invoked at a second stage of the inquiry, under s. 1 of the Charter, in assessing whether, despite its limitation on s. 15 equality rights, the exclusion of business assets is reasonable and demonstrably justified in a free and democratic society. For either of these uses of s. 2, it seems to be irrelevant whether or not one assumes that there is a new grant of legislative power, so long as one assumes that "distinct society" is not read in a very narrow and artificial sense.

With respect to the recognition of linguistic duality in Canada, there are conceivably circumstances in which legislation pursuant to the goals reflected in subs. (a), either inside or outside Quebec,[26] could

---

rely on s. 2(3) is Quebec. (However, insofar as the recognition of a distinct society in s. 2(1)(b) is a new interpretive direction in the Constitution, any government could make reference to it in the context of a constitutional argument. This effect of the distinct society clause is discussed below.) It is also possible as a result of the preamble to the Meech Lake Accord, recognizing "the principle of the equality of all the provinces", that a provincial government would argue that its society is "equally distinct" and that legislation in furtherance of goals related to community interests within the province should be reviewed in the same way as legislation in furtherance of Quebec's distinct society is.

24 The Supreme Court of Canada decisions under other parts of the Charter (particularly the guarantee of freedom of religion) strongly suggest that not only the purpose but also the unintended effects of legislation will be reviewable under s. 15: see R. v. Big M Drug Mart Ltd. (1985), 18 D.L.R. (4th) 321; R. v. Edwards Books & Art Ltd., [1986] 2 S.C.R. 713.

25 This could be the form of argument if the test for violations of equality is similar to the one enunciated by the British Columbia Court of Appeal in Re Andrews and Law Society of B.C. (1986), 27 D.L.R. (4th) 600 at 605 ff. (The appeal has been heard by the Supreme Court of Canada but not yet decided.)

26 Any provincial government or the federal government could make direct reference to s. 2(2), and any government (presumably including the territorial governments) could use the interpretive direction in s. 2(1)(a).

conflict with claims to sex equality by women. Suppose that an affirmative action program is in place for women and racial minorities with respect to employment in a government's public service. In order to promote the linguistic duality purpose recognized in s. 2(1)(a), the government then decides that it will remove resources and administrative support from the first affirmative action program in order to support a new program for members of the linguistic minority in the province. This governmental decision could be challenged under s. 15(1) by women and racial minorities. The government's defence would likely be mounted under s. 15(2), which may save affirmative action programs from being struck down under s. 15(1). It is not yet known what principles the courts will develop to decide such cases, where a government has chosen between two meritorious options, both of which could be defended under s. 15(2). However, the use of the proposed new s. 2 (s. 2(2) in conjunction with s. 2(1)(a), or just the interpretive direction in s. 2(1)(a) on its own) could lead to a tilting of the balance against women and minorities.[27]

In resolving a dispute about legislation where s. 2 was argued, the court would examine the wording of the Accord as a whole and the historical setting in which it occurred. Section 16 of the Accord expressly states that s. 2 does not affect ss. 25 or 27 of the Charter, nor s. 35 of the Constitution Act, 1982 or s. 91(24) of the Constitution Act, 1867.[28] The failure to state in s. 16 that s. 2 does not affect ss. 28 and 15 of the Charter gives rise to the inference that those sections *are* to be affected.[29] Similarly, the proposed new s. 95B of the Constitution Act, 1867, relating to agreements on immigration and aliens, specifically states that the Charter applies in respect of any such agreement that has the force of law and in respect of anything done pursuant to such agreements by the federal or provincial

---

27 This example is drawn from one given in the Eberts/Laskin opinion, above, note 21. It may be seen, in the fact that I cite this example, that I do not agree with the statement in the JCR above, note 16, at 64, para. 45, that it "does not raise a Charter issue at all".

28 See Appendices to this volume for the relevant sections.

29 This argument is put forcefully by Beverley Baines in the *Financial Post* (September 7, 1987) at p. 10, in response to the contrary argument put forward by William Lederman, *Financial Post* (August 31, 1987) at p. 10. It was addressed by many briefs and submissions to the Special Joint Committee, including those of all of the women's groups, above, note 17, except the Quebec government's Conseil du statut de la femme. The JCR above, note 16, comments at 61:

> It must be acknowledged at the outset that various distinguished constitutional experts appearing before the Joint Committee had great difficulty in providing a legal rationalization as to why certain sections are included in section 16 and why others are left out.

Legislatures or governments. This could give rise to the inference that the Charter is not to apply with respect to other parts of the Accord.

The consequence of s. 2 affecting Charter equality rights (as suggested by s. 16) or of the Charter not applying to s. 2 (as suggested by s. 95B) may be to set a priority among those values which are liable to be considered in determining the constitutionality of legislation under s. 15 of the Charter, with linguistic duality or distinct society considerations being given primary importance.[30] Thus, the distinct society clause could effectively lead to different levels of scrutiny for review of different alleged violations depending upon whether the equality claim related to linguistic, multicultural, aboriginal, or other considerations.[31] Once established, differential levels of scrutiny could well be applied outside the context of claims actually involving competing distinct society or linguistic duality values.

Even if the effect of s. 2 is not to set priorities, at a minimum it adds an interpretive principle of equivalent weight to the statement of Charter gender equality, and this alone affects the future interpretation of such rights.[32] In the context of s. 1 of the Charter, the

---

30 Although the Supreme Court of Canada has yet to give reasons in which the Charter equality rights are discussed, it seems safe to say that in determining the constitutionality of legislation alleged to infringe or deny s. 15 equality rights, the courts will take account of matters such as the purpose of the legislation, whether it furthers a pressing and substantial governmental purpose, the severity of its effect on individuals or groups, the proportionality between the purpose and the effect, and so on, wherever the assessment takes place, whether under s. 15 (determining whether there has been a *prima facie* violation of equality rights) or under s. 1 (determining whether the legislation, despite the violation, should be upheld as being a reasonable limitation, prescribed by law, and demonstrably justified in a free and democratic society). The linguistic duality or distinct society purposes could be argued at either stage.

31 As the LEAF brief above, note 17, points out at 11, this could go further:

In effect, saying that aboriginal and multicultural provisions will not be affected by section 2 implies that courts are free to find that, and allow, equality rights to be affected by section 2. A hierarchy of rights is thus created. This ranking, this preference for aboriginal and multicultural rights, may likely weight these preferred rights over sex equality rights in cases of conflict, may restrict the progressive use of analogies between adjudications on these issues and sex equality issues, and may affect the comparative attitude of gravity toward sex equality cases across the board.

32 This point is conceded in the JCR above, note 16, at 68, para. 62. In fact, there is a suggestion that if it were not the case that the distinct society clause adds something to the weight of such considerations under s. 1, it would be meaningless. The Joint Committee says:

Under the terms proposed by the 1987 Constitutional Accord neither gender equality rights nor the "linguistic duality/distinct society" rule of interpretation will be given automatic paramountcy in all situations. Neither overrides the other. Neither is automatically subordinate to the other. The courts are entrusted with the task of

question the courts ask themselves could become, "Is this limit on equality rights prescribed by law, reasonable and justifiable in a free and democratic society *fundamental characteristics of which are linguistic duality and the distinctiveness of Quebec society?*" It must also be remembered that the Supreme Court of Canada is the final court of appeal for equality claims from all provinces and that a formulation of equality rights developed in the context of cases coming from one province can influence the understanding of equality rights in all cases.

Arguments by the Supporters of the Meech Lake Accord

I will try to set out the arguments on this side of the debate in parallel to the arguments of the critics, although this is not always possible. In summary, the supporters of the Accord argue that s. 2 is purely interpretive, and does not grant a new head of power. As an interpretive section, it only confirms what has always been the case, that the courts may take into account under s. 1 of the Charter factors such as linguistic duality and the distinctiveness of Quebec society. In discussing the meaning of Quebec's "distinct society", the Special Joint Committee said:

> What is the "distinct society" that Quebec is to preserve and promote? Undoubtedly, it includes the language and culture of French-speaking Canadians and that of the English-speaking minority, but such a statement does not do justice to the variety and richness of the many other cultures and peoples within Quebec's borders, including aboriginal peoples. The expression "distinct identity", in its ordinary meaning, is broad enough to include anything and everything that makes Quebec recognizably different, both in its many constituent parts and in the relationship they bear to one another.[33]

However, it is argued, to take such factors into account does not necessarily indicate that they will be given priority. Therefore, constitutional equality rights of women are not affected. The Fédération des femmes du Québec put it this way:[34]

> L'accord du lac Meech ne constitue donc pas d'après notre analyse, une ménace ni expresse ni même potentielle aux droits à l'égalité des femmes du Québec. Nous ne voulons pas dire par là que des atteintes à nos droits ne sont pas possibles

---

maintaining a proper balance. The outcome will depend on the particular circumstances of the case. If the proposed interpretive rule on occasion is invoked to justify an alleged infringement of gender equality rights, the courts will be called upon to decide whether the infringement is "demonstrably justified" or not.

33 JCR above, note 16, at 32-33.
34 FFQ brief, above, note 17, at 3.

en terre québécoise; nous disons plutôt que l'histoire des droits des femmes démontre que nous n'avons pas besoin de "sociétés distinctes" pour que nos droits soient compromis et que le concept de société distincte est un concept neutre sous ce rapport.

Thus, this side of the argument begins with the contention that the wording of the opening phrase of s. 2 establishes that it is purely interpretive:[35] it does not create a new head of power authorizing legislation by any level of government.

Second, it is only remotely possible that there would be cases in which the "distinct society" and linguistic duality values reflected in s. 2 actually conflict with the principle of gender equality, given the Quebec government's record in respect of women's rights over the last decade.[36] In fact, gender equality should be seen as an integral part of the distinct society which is to be recognized, preserved and promoted.[37]

Section 16, which specifies that particular provisions respecting aboriginal and multicultural rights will not be affected by s. 2, is explained by political reasons. Therefore, the section has no significance (even as stating priorities) because it was otherwise unnecessary.[38] Alternative explanations for s. 16 contend that ss. 25 and 27 of the Charter, mentioned in s. 16, are interpretive sections, while ss. 28 and 15 are not,[39] or that ss. 25 and 27 refer to "group" or "collective" rights dealing with cultural considerations, rights which are only vaguely defined in the Charter and in need of extra protection, rather than clearly stated individual rights, as found in s. 15.[40] Further, the application of the Charter clause in the proposed s. 95B of the Constitution Act, 1867 does not compel the interpretation that the Charter fails to apply to the rest of the Accord since that is inconsistent

---

35 See JCR, above, note 16 at 32.

36 See, for example, the quotation from Yves Fortier at JCR 60, above, note 16.

37 The FFQ brief above, note 17, states at 3:

> Nous ne croyons pas qu'on puisse se servir davantage du concept de société distincte que de la caractéristique fondamentale du Canada — francophones concentrées au Québec et anglophones dans le reste du Canada — pour faire reculer les droits des femmes. Au Québec, le respect des droits des femmes fait de plus en plus partie de la culture politique. Les progrès marqués faits au chapitre de la condition féminine ne sont pas étrangers à ce caractère de société distincte.

38 This is one of the arguments which I mention because it was actually made — see JCR above, note 16 at 62-63, para. 37.

39 See Senator Lowell Murray, quoted in the JCR, *ibid.*, at 61.

40 This argument is referred to although not, seemingly, adopted at JCR, *ibid.*, at 62.

with the statement in s. 16 that two sections of the Charter are unaffected.[41]

Section 2 confirms established constitutional values to be balanced against others in the Constitution but does not create new values or establish that such a balancing process should take place, the latter having been established when s. 1 was enacted as part of the Charter.[42] There is nothing in the Meech Lake Accord which expressly establishes a priority for the values recognized in s. 2, or renders legislation in furtherance of s. 2 goals immune from Charter review.[43] Courts will most likely balance competing interest by preferring the combined effects of ss. 15 and 28 of the Charter, which are substantive rights as opposed to principles of interpretation, over s. 2, but if they do not, that is a consequence of s. 1 of the Charter conferring such powers on courts. It is not a consequence of the Meech Lake Accord.[44]

Finally, the first ministers responsible for the Meech Lake Accord have said that it was not intended to and does not affect Charter equality rights. Many constitutional experts agree.[45] Therefore the supporters of the Accord argue that it is safe to conclude that, as a matter of law, the Accord will not have such effects.

Replies by the Critics

These replies involve five main points.

First, the concern that s. 2 affects s. 15 of the Charter does not

---

41 For a discussion of this issue, see the opinion letter from Professor Robin Elliot attached to the LEAF brief above, note 17, at 3-5.

42 I must confess that I cannot understand the argument which the Special Joint Committee seems to make, that because the assessment will likely take place under s. 1, the critics are wrong in their argument about the possible effect of a new interpretive direction. (See JCR, above, note 16 at 66-68.) The conclusion does not seem to follow from the premise.

43 The JCR, *ibid.* at 57 said:

> Is there anything in the "linguistic duality/distinct society" clause to suggest that this normal principle would not apply? On its face, there is nothing in the 1987 Accord to suggest that the values of linguistic duality or Quebec's distinct society are to override the Charter or that legislation or governmental acts in furtherance of these values are to be immune to Charter review.

44 JCR, *ibid.*, at 65. See also Lederman, above, note 29.

45 See JCR, *ibid.*, at 55-68; citing Yves Fortier, Gérald-A. Beaudoin, William Lederman and Senator Lowell Murray. However, there are also constitutional experts who disagree. A partial list would include Senator Eugene Forsey, Brian Slattery, Mary Eberts, John Laskin, Robin Elliot and Gerald Gall. Even Peter Hogg, whom the JCR cites as opining that effects on equality rights are "unlikely", indicates thereby that he must consider such effects to be possible.

depend upon it amounting to a new head of power. It can affect s. 15 through its operation as a principle of interpretation.[46] In any event, there is a possibility, although small, that s. 2 does grant some measure of legislative authority. This interpretation would explain the use of the term "promote" in s. 2(3).

Second, with respect to the argument about Quebec's record in the area of sexual equality rights, the record of Quebec or any other province is not the issue. Presumably, few would argue that Quebec's record has been any worse than that of other provinces. But without knowing what criteria of evaluation are being used — the existence of formal guarantees of equality? protection against physical assault? equality in family life? availability of daycare? entry into the professions? equal pay for work of equal value? — it is impossible to accept that Quebec's record has been clearly better. Lucie Lamarche points out that there may be broad guarantees on paper but the absence of mechanisms for their enforcement can make them hollow.[47]

Third, the concerns arising from s. 16 of the Accord remain despite the arguments of the Meech supporters since s. 28 could well be seen as an interpretive section, yet it is excluded from s. 16 while ss. 25 and 27 of the Charter are included;[48] s. 35 of the Constitution Act, 1982 and s. 91(24) of the Constitution Act, 1867 are as substantive as s. 15 of the Charter, yet they are included in s. 16 while it is excluded.[49] Furthermore, the distinction between group and individual rights is specious, since s. 15 of the Charter recognizes both kinds of rights[50] and women's rights to equality under ss. 28 and 15 of the Charter have some important collective features.[51] As well, the strong cultural

---

46 As discussed above, this much was conceded by the Special Joint Committee. If the linguistic duality/distinct society considerations come into play at the s. 1 stage of analysis, they may affect the outcome of equality claims. If they come into play at the stage of defining the right to equality, then they will help to shape that definition. Either way, the considerations could have an effect.

47 See L. Lamarche, "Perspective féministe d'une certaine société distincte: Les Québécoises et l'Accord du Lac Meech" in this volume at p. 21.

48 While s. 28 may have both substantive and interpretive effects, at least when it is used in conjunction with s. 15 of the Charter it must either have an interpretive effect or be redundant, as is pointed out in the CACSW brief above, note 17, at 7. See also the NAC brief, *ibid.*, at 6.

49 The JCR, above, note 16, recognizes this: see 62, para. 33.

50 The reference to "disadvantaged groups" in s. 15(2) provides evidence of this.

51 This has been recognized recently in the Supreme Court of Canada in *Cdn. National Railway v. Action Travail des Femmes* (1987), 40 D.L.R. (4th) 193. The CACSW brief, above, note 17, at 9 discusses this argument, referring to the Ontario Court of Appeal definition of "collective or group" rights as opposed to "individual" rights in *Reference re an Act to Amend the Education Act* (1986), 53 O.R. (2d) 513 at 566 (affirmed (1987), 40 D.L.R. (4th) 18 (S.C.C)).

component of gender inequality in all societies must be recognized.[52] As for the argument that "political reasons" explain s. 16 and that therefore it is meaningless, this fails to deal with the principle that courts will attempt to give effect to constitutional wording wherever possible.[53]

Fourth, with respect to the argument that the proposed s. 95B of the Constitution Act, 1867 could not give rise to the inference that the Charter *only* applies to that part of the Accord, because of the internal inconsistency between that inference and the statement in s. 16 that ss. 25 and 27 are not to be affected, it is possible to draw the contrary inference that the only applications of the Charter outside s. 95B are those specifically provided for in s. 16.

Finally, with respect to the argument from the intention of the first ministers, it has been clearly stated in the Supreme Court of Canada[54] that statements from the drafters of a constitutional document as to their understanding of its meaning will be given very little if any weight. The meaning of s. 2 and the Meech Lake Accord as a whole will be determined by the courts after a lengthy interpretive process, the outcome of which is not notably predictable. There are many examples of constitutional interpretation which the framers and constitutional experts would have found surprising.[55] Courts, societies, and prevailing views about the desirability of gender equality all change over time, and the sensible approach to a constitution is to clarify as much as possible wherever there is ambiguity. While the record of the presently-constituted Supreme Court of Canada may

---

52 The CACSW brief, above, note 17, at 10 also refers briefly to the notion of a "women's culture" which has gained some prominence in feminist literature.

53 See, for example, the discussion in the British Columbia Court of Appeal decision in *Re Andrews and Law Society of B.C.*, above, note 23, at D.L.R. 603-611, about the necessity to give effect to the word "discrimination" in s. 15(1) of the Charter.

54 *Reference re Section 94(2) of the Motor Vehicle Act*, [1985] 2 S.C.R. 486 at 508.

55 The *Reference re Section 94(2) Motor Vehicle Act* case, *ibid.*, is a good example of an interpretation of the Charter which differed from that which had been predicted by the majority of the experts. Other examples of interpretation which differed from the intention of at least some of the framers may be found in the trilogy of cases on freedom of association: *Reference re Public Service Employee Relations Act, Labour Relations Act and Police Officers Collective Bargaining Act* (1987), 51 Alta. L.R. (2d) 97 (S.C.C.); *Public Service Alliance of Canada v. Canada* (1987), 87 C.L.L.C. 14,022 (S.C.C.); *Saskatchewan v. Retail, Wholesale & Department Store Union* (1987), 87 C.L.L.C. 14,023 (S.C.C.). *Edwards v. A.-G. Canada*, [1930] A.C. 124, [1929] 3 W.W.R. 479, sets a standard for constitutional interpretation in Canada which treats the Constitution as a living document that should be read in the light of current realities, regardless of what the framers may have had in mind at the time of drafting. The very recent decision in *R. v. Morgentaler* (1988), 82 N.R. 1 (S.C.C.), would clearly find a place on many lists of unexpected decisions.

found some optimism with respect to the protection of women's equality rights, such optimism has not been possible until very recently, and times and courts can change.[56]

(2) Through Section 2 Forming Part of a Fundamental Compromise of Confederation, Insulating Legislation Thereunder from Charter Review

Arguments by the Critics

The effect of the recent decision of the Supreme Court of Canada in the *Separate High Schools Funding Reference*[57] may be to insulate legislation in furtherance of linguistic or distinct society goals from Charter review or to add further weight to claims that such goals are more important than those underlying the equality guarantees. In the *Separate Schools Reference*, Ontario legislation granting full funding to Roman Catholic denominational schools was upheld despite a challenge based upon its violation of religious freedom and equality rights. The Court found it unnecessary to resort to the Charter guarantee of denominational schools in s. 29, given the express grant of legislative power in s. 93 of the Constitution Act, 1867, which represents a fundamental part of the Confederation compromise.[58] It is quite likely that the linguistic duality and distinct society principles recognized in the proposed new s. 2 of the Constitution Act, 1867 would be seen as forming a fundamental part of the Confederation compromise, similar to s. 93 of the same Act, and it is therefore possible that legislation in furtherance of those goals would be sheltered from Charter review.[59]

Arguments by the Supporters of the Accord

The supporters of the Accord argue that because s. 2 does not grant constitutional power, the analogy with s. 93 of the Constitution

---

56 As recent events surrounding the near confirmation of Justice Bork in the Supreme Court of the United States illustrate.

57 (1987), 40 D.L.R. (4th) 18 (S.C.C.) (*sub nom. Reference re An Act to Amend the Education Act (Ontario)*).

58 For more detailed discussion of the Supreme Court ruling and its implications see Brian Slattery, "The Constitutional Priority of the Charter" in this volume at p. 81.

59 This possibility would exist if s. 2 were seen as empowering legislation, but not if it were merely interpretive. The argument is developed more fully in the LEAF brief, above, note 17, and in the Eberts/Laskin opinion letter, above, note 21.

Act, 1867 fails.[60] Furthermore, even if s. 2 did grant such power, they argue that the correct interpretation of the *Separate School Reference* is a narrow one, restricted to situations such as those under s. 93, where the legislative power must necessarily be exercised in a manner which discriminates contrary to s. 15 of the Charter. In contrast, legislation pursuant to distinct society or linguistic duality objectives would not necessarily have to violate the equality rights of women.[61] The broad interpretation of the *Separate School Reference* is viewed as leading to the absurd proposition that the Charter does not apply to any exercise by Parliament or a provincial Legislature of its powers under ss. 91 or 92 of the Constitution Act, 1867. Such an interpretation would essentially render the Charter useless.[62]

Possible Reply by Critics

Even if the *Separate Schools Reference* were read as limited to situations where legislation under a head of power in the Constitution must necessarily violate Charter rights in order to carry out the purposes for which the head of power was granted, its notion of a provision which is a fundamental part of the constitutional compromise could prove important. Section 2 is to be placed in the fundamental constitutional document, the Constitution Act, 1867, and it reflects a crucial part of the reconciliation between Quebec and the rest of Canada. This could be seen as a direction to give it primacy in the resolution of conflicts.

(3) Through Creating a Negative Implication as to the Importance of Gender Equality in the Constitutional Scheme of Things

Arguments by the Critics

The Meech Lake Accord makes a symbolic statement which has negative implications with respect to the importance of gender equality as a value in Canadian society. In support of this point, it is argued that symbolism can be important in the context of constitutional formation, as the example of the Meech Lake Accord itself illustrates. While Quebec was legally subject to the provisions of the Constitution

---

60 See the JCR, above, note 16, at 58.

61 JCR, *ibid.*, at 59-60.

62 *Ibid.*

Act, 1982 including the Charter, from April 17, 1985 onward, its exclusion from the final stages of formation of that constitutional amendment led to a strong and quite understandable push to bring Quebec into the constitutional family at the symbolic level.[63]

The symbolic statement made by the failure to mention women's equality rights in the Meech Lake Accord, while other similar rights are mentioned, is that women's rights, along with equality rights for other minorities, have secondary status, and that the goal of achieving equality for those groups is secondary to other goals. The negative impact of the symbolic statement is heightened by the fact that this is the second occasion in a short period of time that women's equality rights have been placed in a secondary position, either through inadvertence or intention.[64] When values are important enough, steps are taken to protect them even if those steps are quite likely redundant. An example may be found in s. 29 of the Charter, protecting the continued existence of denominational schools. Although redundant because of s. 93 of the Constitution Act, 1867, it was included out of caution.[65]

The consequences of such a symbolic statement could include not only a direct effect on specific issues of constitutional interpretation, but also an indirect influence in other contexts in which courts must take account of public policy and community values, through a lessening of the regard paid to gender equality as a value. As Catharine MacKinnon has put it:[66]

> Perhaps the deepest cause for concern is the effect of the Accord on the social process of constitution-building: the relationship between the Charter's political culture and its actual delivery of promised rights. In addition to being law, the Accord works politically to set priorities and agendas, affect resource allocations and provide an edge in close cases. Such a document is a political act. It enters into the atmosphere that surrounds the seriousness of commitment to equality rights on the day-to-day level that is the level on which a constitutional right either becomes meaningful or dies as a piece of paper. On this level, a constitution affects outcomes from family court to rape trials to Human Rights adjudications; it shapes women's fortunes in board rooms and

---

63 Ivan Bernier and Alan Cairns, among others, have referred to the importance of symbolism in their discussions: see I. Bernier, "Meech Lake and Constitutional Visions" at p. 239, and A. Cairns, above, note 9.

64 The previous occasion being the temporary demotion of s. 28 to make it subject to s. 33 in the "November Accord" version of the Charter.

65 This point was suggested to me by my colleague Robin Elliot, who was also generous with his thoughts and time in connection with discussions as to other aspects of this paper.

66 In an opinion dated September 6, 1987, appended to the brief of LEAF, above, note 17.

at the bargaining table, in the home and on the street, in places where the Charter itself would seldom formally venture. A political act like the Accord supports or detracts from a climate of concern in a way that affects the results of particular cases, shifts the ground beneath legal arguments, determines what becomes persuasive. It gives life to law. On this level, constitutional process begins as politics but ends as law. The status of sex equality itself as a fundamental commitment of society is thus as much constituted by such documents as it is reflected in them.

Arguments by the Meech Lake Supporters

I have not found any arguments directly addressing this issue, but I imagine that they would consist of a reiteration of the starting position that the Accord is not intended to and does not affect Charter equality rights, and there is no symbolic statement being made. Alternatively, it might be argued that, even if there is a symbolic statement, that is an amorphous concept which has no place in constitutional decision-making.

PART III: CONCLUSIONS

The Joint Committee Report clearly confirms that Charter equality rights will be affected, in the sense that a new interpretive rule will be added to the process of balancing interests under s. 1 of the Charter or, alternatively, under s. 15, if the balancing takes place there. In addition, the second two arguments, relating to the fundamental compromise of Confederation and the symbolic importance of exclusion, raise plausible concerns. Although the risk of outcomes in women's equality litigation being different because of the Accord is probably quite low, it is not negligible. As Donna Greschner has pointed out, s. 28 of the Charter is written in very strong language.[67] Nevertheless, the courts' reading of that language is highly uncertain.

Thus, there is reasonable cause for concern that the proposed new s. 2 will directly or indirectly tend to restrict the scope of Charter equality rights, both inside and outside Quebec. Given the continued reiteration by the "modern Fathers of Confederation" that the Accord will not affect the rights of women, native people, and minorities, and given the difficulties of predicting in advance how Constitutions will be interpreted, the question "Why not amend to clarify this

---

67 See D. Greschner, "How Not to Drown in Meech Lake: Rules, Principles and Women's Equality Rights" in this volume at p. 55.

matter?" is a powerful one. The answer that it is not desirable to open up and therefore imperil the Accord only increases the concern of the critics, who begin to suspect even more strongly that the impairment of Charter equality rights is intended and is seen as necessary and desirable. Otherwise, why the difficulty in making the desired change?

In fact, I think the best explanation for the current situation is that the supporters of the Meech Lake Accord have cannily chosen the dry-land strategy. Were a discussion of the possible effects of s. 2 on equality rights to open up, the situations in which the supporters think those rights ought to be affected would inevitably be revealed. There would then follow a discussion about the comparative importance of rights in which the real political issues would emerge from the muddy waters.

How Not to Drown in Meech Lake: Rules, Principles and Women's Equality Rights

Donna Greschner

Constitutional politics, as conducted by both politicians and judges, historically have submerged the concerns and experiences of women. Recall, for instance, the political battles of 1980-81, in which women's groups swam doggedly against a current of apathy and hostility in the political forum for an express proclamation of sex equality in the Canadian Charter of Rights and Freedoms.[1] Although the campaign did result in s. 28 of the Charter, the very need for the protracted fight is still too fresh in the memories of national women's organizations for them not to be suspicious of the Meech Lake Accord, a deal struck in private by eleven men. The close scrutiny that women's groups have given the Accord is thus not unexpected. We may be saddened but we are not surprised by our findings. The conclusion of many women's groups is that the linguistic duality/distinct society clause of the Accord (the proposed new s. 2(1) of the Constitution Act, 1867,[2] contained in s. 1 of the Accord), could be interpreted by the courts to detract from the Charter's declaration of equal rights of women and men, particularly when read in

---

1 Being Pt. I of the Constitution Act, 1982 [enacted by the Canada Act 1982 (U.K.), c. 11, s. 1].

2 (U.K.), c. 3. See the Appendix to this volume for relevant sections of the Constitution Acts and the Accord.

conjunction with s. 16 of the Accord.[3]

The Special Joint Committee, in dismissing the concerns of women,[4] stated that s. 28 of the Charter and the new s. 2(1) of the 1867 Act were of equal weight; their interrelationship would be determined by a balancing exercise undertaken by the courts in each case.[5] For women afraid of drowning in Meech Lake, being told to trust the courts is not much of a lifeline. Consider that in the five years since its entrenchment, s. 28 has been overwhelmingly ignored by the courts and, when it has attracted judicial attention, has received interpretations narrower than the expectations of its proponents.[6] If the battle for entrenchment was "the taking of 28",[7] persuading the judiciary to take s. 28 seriously will be its "retaking". This paper will try to do that. I will argue that the Committee's view of the weight of s. 28 and its relationship with the Accord is not the only view, and indeed is not the best one. An analysis of the constitutional text reveals that s. 28 is the superior provision, with the capacity to prevent s. 2(1) of the 1867 Act and s. 16 of the Accord from adversely affecting women's equality rights. The development of this argument requires an exploration of a peculiarly Canadian type of constitutional provision — what I call the "instruction provision".

One initial point must be clarified, however. The availability of an argument that s. 28 takes precedence over the linguistic duality/distinct society clause does not mean that the analysis conducted by women's groups was erroneous. Their conclusion was based on a prediction of what the courts would do, given what has been done in the past. My argument does not deny that conclusion; rather, it

---

3 For a review of the arguments made by women's groups, see L. Smith, "The Distinct Society Clause in The Meech Lake Accord: Could it Affect Equality Rights for Women?" in this volume at p. 35.

4 Women's groups were dismissed without even being heard; they spoke to the Special Joint Committee but their voices were not heard. See B. Baines, "ACCORDing to the Committee . . ." (1988, Queen's Quarterly).

5 Canada, *The Report of the Special Joint Committee of the Senate and the House of Commons on the 1987 Constitutional Accord* (Ottawa: Queen's Printer, 1987) at 68:
   Under the terms proposed by the *1987 Constitutional Accord* neither gender equality rights nor the "linguistic duality/distinct society" rule of interpretation will be given automatic paramountcy in all situations. Neither overrides the other. Neither is automatically subordinate to the other. The courts are entrusted with the task of maintaining a proper balance. The outcome will depend on the particular circumstances of the case.

6 See, for example, the harshly negative opinion by a judge in a non-judicial capacity: K. Fogarty, *Equality Rights and Their Limitations Under the Charter* (Toronto: Carswell, 1987) at pp. 120-124, 304-307.

7 The history of the entrenchment struggle is told in P. Kome, *The Taking of Twenty-Eight* (Toronto: Women's Press, 1983).

posits an alternative approach for the courts to adopt in the future. Nor is my argument a reason to ignore or halt the political struggle for an express affirmation in the Accord that it does not negatively affect the equality rights of women. Since the approach advanced here must be accepted by the courts, efforts to strengthen the argument are to be welcomed. Given the history of judicial reaction to claims of sex equality, we can rightfully demand that the constitutional text announce with as much certainty as possible the priority and importance of women's equality rights. An explicit statement in the Accord that sex equality is not affected may not avoid injurious interpretations altogether but it ought to reduce the risk.

Both s. 28 of the Charter and s. 2(1) of the 1867 Act are instances of the unique Canadian contribution to constitutional texts — the instruction provision. I use the term "instruction provision" to refer to those constitutional provisions which do not create institutions of government or enunciate specific rights and freedoms, but rather give instructions about the meaning of other provisions and how they are to fit together. Not only do instruction provisions differ from other provisions; they also differ among themselves. Although any taxonomy of instruction provisions will necessarily be tentative and rough, the following types of provisions appear to cluster under this rubric. First, interpretation sections can be identified, such as the linguistic duality/distinct society clause or s. 27 of the Charter which uses the language of interpretation. Second, non-abrogation and non-derogation sections are found, such as ss. 21 and 22 of the Charter, which specify the limits of substantive provisions. (Note the hybrid sections, such as s. 25 of the Charter which has both the language of interpretation and non-abrogation.) Third, there are miscellaneous sections, such as s. 28 which does not announce a new right but declares the strength of others.

I acknowledge that the label of instruction provision to delineate a subset of constitutional provisions would be thought inapt by some jurists, such as those of Kelsenian persuasion. They would argue that every legal provision, from a mundane statutory driving offence to an important constitutional right, is a normative instruction to a judge about what ought to be done with respect to a fact situation before the court. Be that as it may, the term instruction provision does seem to capture a characteristic that sets some of our constitutional provisions apart from others. One unique feature of our Charter is the extent to which it contains instruction provisions — a situation unparalleled in the Constitutions of other liberal or post-liberal democracies. For example, the only analogous section in the American Bill of Rights is the Ninth Amendment, similar in form to s. 26 of the Charter.[8]

Other than the discussion of s. 29 in the *Separate High Schools Funding Reference*,[9] instruction clauses have not received more than passing reference by the Supreme Court of Canada nor been the subject of sustained academic scholarship. And now, before there has even been much thinking about instruction provisions in the Charter, the Accord has introduced two new complexities. First, the interpretive requirements of the proposed s. 2(1) of the 1867 Act will apply to the entire Constitution of Canada, not just the Charter. Second, s. 16 of the Accord, that strange, solely free-standing part of the Accord, proceeds to give instructions about another instruction clause, s. 2(1) of the 1867 Act. Section 16 addresses a variety of different relationships: as between two interpretation clauses (ss. 27 and 25 of the Charter and s. 2(1) of the 1867 Act); as between a non-Charter recognition of rights and an interpretation clause (s. 35 of the Constitution Act, 1982 and s. 2(1)); and as between an interpretation clause and a head of legislative power (s. 91(24) of the Constitution Act, 1867 and s. 2(1)). Before we had analyzed the simple, we were given the difficult.

A theory of the Canadian Constitution needs to account for the existence, function and implications of instruction provisions. Although an instruction provision, like any other constitutional statement, is directed at all political actors, my concern will be with what instruction provisions say to the courts. What is the impact of these provisions on interpretation generally? How do they differ in form, rationale, and function from each other — for they are not homogeneous — and from other sections? How do they influence not just how we go about the interpretive task, but the very nature of interpretation? In other words, does their existence change our conception of the concept of interpretation? I cannot answer these questions within the confines of this paper, but I can raise some initial issues about instruction provisions that will help clarify the enterprise, and suggest one

---

8 Both the Ninth Amendment to the American Constitution and s. 26 of the Charter state that the inclusion of certain rights and freedoms in the constitutional text shall not be construed as denying the existence of other rights and freedoms. The word "construed" also appears in the Eleventh and Seventeenth Amendments, dealing with the jurisdiction of the federal courts and the election of Senators.

9 *Reference Re An Act to Amend the Education Act (Ontario)* (1987), 40 D.L.R. (4th) 18 (S.C.C.).

conceptual structure[10] that makes sense of the provisions. Happily, that suggested structure should ease some of the fears of women's groups that women will drown in Meech Lake.

The interpretive enterprise, at least as propounded by Dworkin, seeks to achieve coherence of a community's legal data in the case at hand.[11] The various components of the community's legal morality — as revealed for instance by statutes and precedents — are woven together insofar a possible with a good result in a particular case being one with a close fit to what has been done in the past. Constitutional adjudication is no different in that the goal of coherence requires a melding of the provisions in the text, as understood in light of their historical and philosophical contexts. The repeatedly endorsed purposive method of Charter interpretation clearly meets these criteria of an interpretive enterprise.

Instruction provisions have some small role to play in the exercise of constitutional interpretation. To say that they are irrelevant because they do not enunciate rights and freedoms of individuals or duties of government is antithetical to the concept of interpretation, and also goes against our constitutional grain. Words are added to constitutions by politicians because they think the words will make a difference. Moreover, courts do pay attention to the words; within the purposive method of adjudicating Charter cases, the linguistic context is firmly placed as one of three important contexts within which to define and find purposes of Charter provisions. Arguments from the text have already been decisive in Charter cases, as illustrated by the first Charter decision, *Skapinker*.[12] Of course, to admit that instruction provisions are relevant says nothing about how they will be relevant. And, as will be discussed, merely because they are part of the constitutional methodology does not necessarily entail that they will change the results in particular cases.

When instruction clauses are placed in the context of the adjudicatory enterprise, it may be tempting to classify all instruction clauses as principles in the Dworkinian sense, inclining a judge toward

---

10 I recognize that using established jurisprudential concepts in aid of women's equality rights is an enterprise fraught with potential danger. Women have long realized that the master's tools cannot easily be used to dismantle the master's house. However, they may provide the best arguments for protecting women's equality rights if the Meech Lake Accord is ratified, and we avoid their use at our peril.

11 R. Dworkin, *Taking Rights Seriously* (Cambridge: Harvard University Press, 1977); R. Dworkin, *Law's Empire* (Cambridge: Belknap/Harvard University Press, 1986).

12 *Law Society of Upper Canada v. Skapinker*, [1984] 1 S.C.R. 357.

one interpretation over another. But to do so would be a mistake because the language of instruction clauses indicates that not all are principles — some are rules. The difference between principles and rules rests upon the force that they have in adjudication. A rule determines the result in a particular case; a principle only influences the result.[13] The non-abrogation and derogation species of instruction clauses seem to be rules. They assert that nothing in other sections can be used to take away that which they protect, such as the protection given by s. 22 to legal rights with respect to any language other than French or English. In the Hartian scheme, such rules are secondary rules of adjudication: secondary because they do not relate to the behaviour of a citizen, and adjudicatory because they are directed toward what a judge does in a case.[14]

Those instruction provisions which are of the interpretive variety, however, seem clearly to be examples of Dworkinian principles. Section 27 of the Charter, for example, does not direct behaviour nor dictate a result in a particular case, but enunciates a factor that a judge must take into consideration in deciding a case. The judge does have an obligation to bear in mind the preservation and enhancement of our multicultural heritage. In that sense she cannot ignore the possible influence of s. 27, but that does not mean s. 27 dictates a result. All Dworkinian principles are obligatory, in that judges must take them into account; they are simply not decisive of result.

If interpretation clauses contain principles, what sort of principles are they? Here we run into complexity. Principles are thought of as ethical statements. But, as John Whyte has pointed out,[15] the proposed s. 2(1) of the 1867 Act contains sociological descriptions. So too does s. 27 of the Charter. By telling the judges to preserve our multicultural heritage, s. 27 is implicitly stating that multicultural heritage is a sociological fact. It also has a normative component, the enhancement of our multicultural heritage. The linguistic duality/distinct society clause is an even stronger sociological statement than s. 27; the latter part, for example, says Quebec *is* a distinct society. The normative aspect appears in s. 2(3) of the proposed amendment to the 1867 Act in the obligation placed on Quebec to promote that distinct society.

---

13 Dworkin himself, it has been argued by some commentators, has abandoned the distinction between rules and principles. Be that as it may, other legal theorists have not. See N. MacCormick, *Legal Reasoning and Legal Theory* (Oxford: Clarendon Press, 1978).

14 H.L.A. Hart, *The Concept of Law* (Oxford: Clarendon Press, 1961).

15 J. Whyte, *Submission to the Special Joint Committee of the Senate and the House of Commons on the 1987 Constitutional Accord* (20 August 1987).

How are the normative and sociological components to fit together? What happens when a sociological/normative principle meets one that is purely normative?

Such a purely normative principle is contained in s. 28. Equality between men and women is not a sociological fact. According to Alison Jaggar's minimalist description of feminism, all varieties of feminism are committed to ending the subordination of women.[16] If that is the goal, the premise must be that there is subordination now. And even those who would not call themselves feminists would have an onerous task in denying the current and persistent inequality of women with respect to all of the things that currently count in society, such as money, power and prestige. So s. 28 contains a purely normative principle: equality of women and men is something to be attained; it is not a state that exists and needs to be preserved. To preserve the present situation would be to perpetuate inequality.

Does this difference in form between sociological description and purely normative principle have any bearing on interpretation? As noted above, the point of at least a Dworkinian interpretation is to weave all of the legal principles together into a coherent whole. Law as Integrity respects a community's highest values, and interpretation gives effect to those values in particular cases.[17] But it seems implicit that the principles Dworkin uses are ethical or normative principles, not sociological descriptions. Does this mean that sociological descriptions are entitled to lesser weight, that they can be trumped by purely normative principles? If that were so, the concerns of women's groups about the effect of the Accord would be eased.

But the answer is not so straightforward. Interpretation takes place within a community and gives effect to community aspirations. The Dworkinian enterprise is a historically-based one; the interpreter looks at the history of the community and tries to continue the stories of the community.[18] A description by the community of what the community "is" ought then to be entitled to serious consideration. It may even set the foundation for the interpretive exercise, forming the base on which the competing and complementary normative principles are then interwoven into a coherent whole. In Marxist terminology, the sociological descriptions are the base, and the

---

16 A. Jaggar, *Feminist Politics and Human Nature* (Totowa: Rowman and Allanheld, 1983), at 5.

17 *Law's Empire*, above, note 11.

18 *Ibid.*

normative principles are the superstructure. From this perspective, sociological descriptions are the more important aspect of the interpretive exercise — at least more important than the superstructural principles. In this view, what I have called purely normative principles would need to correspond to the sociological base. Hence, any conflict between s. 28 of the Charter and s. 2(1) of the 1867 Act would be resolved in favour of the latter.

This is not a happy conclusion for a feminist, but there is a solution. One aspect of s. 28 has not yet been discussed: s. 28 is not just a principle, it is a rule. It states that rights and freedoms *are guaranteed* equally to female and male persons. This is an assertion of a legal result, not just an announcement of a principle which merely lends weight to a particular interpretation. Women's groups thought that the words were the strongest of any of the instruction clauses in the Charter; after all, one point of s. 28 was to trump s. 27, in that a discriminatory law could not be justified as being necessary to preserve or enhance a group's cultural heritage. According to the Dworkinian-based dichotomy of rules and principles, if s. 28 is a rule, then any conflict between it and a principle, such as the new s. 2(1) of the 1867 Act, would be resolved in favour of the rule.

Interpretation provisions will still have some effect under this approach. Principles enter adjudication by their influence on the interpretation of the substantive provisions. It would still be possible, for example, for a court to interpret mobility rights in such a way that a law justified by the linguistic duality/distinct society clause would be held not to violate the s. 6 rights. Nevertheless, mobility rights could not be defined as entailing fewer rights for women than for men, because to do so would offend the *rule* in s. 28 that Charter rights are guaranteed equally to women and men. Interpretation provisions may have the potential to restrict the meaning of rights, but because of s. 28, the restriction must affect women and men equally.

The other way an interpretation provision may affect Charter adjudication is through s. 1. A discriminatory law may be held to violate a substantive provision, such as sex equality in s. 15, but there is the possibility that the violation could be permitted by s. 1 of the Charter.[19] The new s. 2(1) of the 1867 Act may provide a government with one justification for the violation. Again, if we see s. 28 as being a rule, not just a principle, it ought to trump the principle stated in s. 2(1).

Some jurists would argue that the distinction between rules and

---

19 I say "could" because the interrelationship between s. 1 and s. 15 is still very contentious.

principles cannot be maintained because all so-called rules are in effect principles. Even if this is so (and the intricacies of the arguments are beyond the parameters of this paper), the same conclusion would result. All principles have the dimension of weight, in that some principles have more force and are weightier, than others. Accordingly, the same arguments that can be made to show that s. 28 is a rule can also be deployed to prove that if it is a principle, it is stronger than the linguistic duality/distinct society clause. To hold otherwise, for instance, would render meaningless the word "guarantees" in s. 28. In other words, whether s. 28 is regarded as a rule or as a principle, the Special Joint Committee is wrong to assert that it is of equal weight to the proposed s. 2(1) of the 1867 Act.

The conclusion, then, is that if attention is paid to the differences between types of instruction provisions, one can conclude that s. 28 is a far stronger instruction than the proposed s. 2(1) of the 1867 Act. This is so even though s. 28 is not mentioned in s. 16 of the Accord, because s. 28 by its nature is stronger than s. 2(1). To have added sex equality to s. 16 would have been most desirable since any doubt would then have been removed, but as I have tried to show, conceptual arguments are available that give s. 28 sufficient force to trump interpretation provisions.

This is a far happier conclusion for a feminist. But women's equality rights may still be submerged in Meech Lake. These conclusions turn on how a court will view the language of s. 28 and the interpretation clauses. The task for feminists is to convince the courts that the words and form of s. 28, as read in their historical and philosophical contexts, mandate its supremacy over an interpretation provision, be it s. 27 of the Charter or s. 2(1) of the 1867 Act. The argument in this paper is one attempt at that task. With theories of interpretation such as that of Dworkin being invariably complex, I can only hope not to be misleading in the course of my brief foray into the unmapped waters of constitutional interpretation in the post-Meech Lake era. Further analysis is needed of the role of instruction provisions in constitutional interpretation generally, not just with respect to s. 28. I hope these comments will serve as a catalyst and as a lighthouse for that analysis — specifically as a life-line to rescue women from the bottom of Meech Lake.

Linguistic Duality and the Distinct Society in Quebec: Declarations of Sociological Fact or Legal Limits on Constitutional Interpretation?

A. Wayne MacKay

The Canadian Constitution is an increasingly complicated jigsaw puzzle. For more than a century the crucial document was the Constitution Act, 1867,[1] which, apart from setting up the basic governmental structures in Canada, also distributed powers between the federal and provincial levels. As a matter of constitutional interpretation, the major challenge was to fit federal and provincial pieces into the puzzle without distorting its shape or causing undue overlap. Then, as a result of the Constitution Act, 1982, which patriated the Constitution, Canada acquired the Canadian Charter of Rights and Freedoms.[2] Individual and collective rights had to be fitted into a game, which in the past involved an attempt to harmonize federal and provincial claims to power. The fit is sometimes difficult and the result a different kind of puzzle.

Barely had the constitutional interpreters adapted to the changes in the game precipitated by the Charter of Rights, when further changes emerged from Meech Lake, in the form of the 1987 Constitutional Accord. Once again, new pieces were proposed for the jigsaw puzzle

---

1 (U.K.), c. 3. See the Appendices to this volume for relevant sections of the Constitution Acts and the Accord.

2 Being Pt. I of the Constitution Act, 1982 [enacted by the Canada Act 1982 (U.K.), c. 11, s. 1].

and the precise shape of some of these pieces, such as linguistic duality and the distinct society, is far from clear. Furthermore, it is not yet apparent how Meech Lake will change the fit of both the distribution of powers pieces and the Charter of Rights pieces in the puzzle.

This paper is concerned with certain aspects of this larger question of constitutional fit. I shall attempt to give some shape to the concepts of linguistic duality and the distinct society in Quebec.

While the Charter is primarily concerned with individual rights and national standards, linguistic duality and the distinct society involve collective rights to a particular kind of culture and a recognition of regional differences. To further complicate matters, the various signatories to the Accord have quite different views about the intended shape and purpose of the linguistic duality and distinct society clauses. The political actors have agreed upon the words and set the process in motion, but the judges have the difficult task of giving the words meaning.

LINGUISTIC DUALITY/DISTINCT SOCIETY

The two interpretive clauses proposed as s. 2 of the Constitution Act, 1867 generated the most controversy and consumed the most time at both the first ministers' meetings which gave birth to the Accord and the Special Joint Committee hearings which followed.[3] While the proposed interpretive clause is often referred to as the "distinct society" provision, it really has two branches. Section 2(1)(a) recognizes linguistic duality in Canada, with the French fact centred in Quebec and the English fact concentrated in the rest of Canada. In s. 2(1)(b), Quebec is recognized as a distinct society. As a declaration of sociological fact, there is little dispute that linguistic duality and a distinctive Quebec society have been important aspects of Canadian identity. What has been hotly disputed is the effect of giving constitutional recognition to these sociological facts.[4]

---

3 In *The Report of the Special Joint Committee of the Senate and House of Commons on the 1987 Constitutional Accord* (Ottawa: Queen's Printer, 1987) at 55, A. Tremblay and C. Speyer acknowledged that the interaction between these interpretive phrases and the Charter generated the most controversy in their hearings. Dr. Norman Spector, Secretary to the Cabinet for Federal-Provincial Relations, indicated that this interaction was one of the most time-consuming for the First Ministers: *Minutes of Proceedings and Evidence of the Special Joint Committee of the Senate and House of Commons on the 1987 Constitutional Accord*, Issue 16:24.

4 There is not even unanimous agreement on the sociological facts. Former Prime Minister Pierre Trudeau, in his evidence before the Joint Committee, attacked the whole concept of the distinct society in Quebec as a threat to the federal state in Canada. He saw constitutional

Section 2(2) of the Constitution Act, 1867 will affirm the roles of Parliament and the provincial Legislatures of *preserving* linguistic duality, but the role of the Quebec Legislature and government is to *preserve* and *promote* the distinct society. Preserving smacks of maintaining a status quo, while promoting evokes a more positive image of advancing beyond it. Even though s. 2(4) guarantees that there is no derogation from the existing distribution of powers under the Constitution Act, 1867, it may be possible to expand the legislative powers of Quebec without derogating from the federal level. The use of the term "affirmed" in ss. 2(1) and (3) emphasizes existing powers rather than new ones, but old powers can be interpreted in an expansive way. Quebec officials from Premier Bourassa down have assumed that the distinct society clause can be used to expand Quebec's control over its own culture.[5]

Senator Lowell Murray and other federal officials tried to reassure the Joint Committee that the distinct society clause would have little impact on either the distribution of powers under the Constitution Act, 1867 or the Charter of Rights. At most, it would come into play in a few grey areas at the fringes of the Constitution.[6] It is difficult to reconcile the views of the Quebec and federal officials on the real impact of the distinct society clause. There are even inconsistencies within the federal position. On the one hand, Senator Lowell Murray reassures the Joint Committee that there will be no change in the distribution of powers and little impact on the Charter of Rights.[7] On the other hand, he warns those who wish to exempt the Charter of Rights from the distinct society clause that such a change would

---

recognition of a distinct Quebec society, not as an act of reconciliation, but as an acceptance of separation. This view was not shared by either the members of the Joint Committee or the majority of witnesses who appeared before it. (See Canada, *Minutes of Proceedings and Evidence of the Special Joint Committee of the Senate and House of Commons on the 1987 Constitutional Accord*, Issue 14:136 (Ottawa: Queen's Printer, 1987). These proceedings are hereafter referred to as Joint Committee Hearings.)

5 Above, note 4 (referring to Mr. Rémillard) and Joint Committee Hearings, Issue 16:27-28 (Mr. Donald Johnston quoting Mr. Bourassa's statements to the National Assembly of Quebec).

6 This is the essence of the federal position, as summarized in Chapter 5 of Tremblay and Speyer, above, note 3. We should keep in mind the observation of John Whyte and the breadth of the grey area in constitutional interpretation:

> Of course, you only get to construe terms of a Constitution when they are ambiguous. On the other hand, they are always ambiguous. So you get to construe, according to this social norm, in almost every case.

Joint Committee Hearings, above, note 4, Issue 10:61 (testimony of J. Whyte).

7 Joint Committee Hearings, *ibid.*, Issue 2:9 *et seq.* (L. Murray).

never be accepted by Quebec.[8] Presumably Quebec officials take this position because they believe that the effect of the clause is to limit the application of the Charter to Quebec and that this is important for Quebec's cultural survival as a distinct society within Canada.[9]

The federal position with respect to linguistic duality is somewhat clearer. There is an agreement only to preserve the rights of linguistic minorities in Canada — not to promote them. Senator Murray indicates that this is as far as the premiers were willing to go at this time, but that the constitutional recognition of the duality of the country is something that should not be minimized.[10] Because of the simultaneous recognition of English majorities outside Quebec and a French majority within Quebec, others question whether the linguistic duality clause really preserves the position of linguistic minorities in Canada. Senator Eugene Forsey argues that the effect of both branches of the interpretive clause will be to reduce the rights of the English minority in Quebec.[11] John Whyte was skeptical that the Accord would enhance the rights of francophones outside Quebec.[12]

JUGGLING INTERPRETATION DOCTRINES

Many problems will arise because linguistic duality and the distinct society are general interpretation doctrines. Even those constitutional experts who argued that the new interpretive phrases would not significantly alter the existing constitutional puzzle, admitted that they would have more impact as an interpretation doctrine than as part of a constitutional preamble.[13]

There is a clear distinction between substantive and interpretive

---

8 Joint Committee Hearings, *ibid.*, Issue 16:5 *et seq.* (L. Murray).

9 The importance of limiting the Charter's application to Quebec as part of a strategy of cultural survival is well articulated by H. Brun, "'The Canadian Charter of Rights and Freedoms as an Instrument of Social Development" in C. Beckton and W. MacKay, eds., *The Courts and the Charter* (Toronto: University of Toronto Press, 1985) at 1-36.

10 Joint Committee Hearings, above, note 4, Issue 2:36, 37 (L. Murray).

11 Joint Committee Hearings, *ibid.* Issue 2:97 *et seq.* (E. Forsey), and Written Submission to the N.D.P. (Alberta) Hearings on the 1987 Constitutional Accord. As examples of the potential reduction of the powers of the English minority he refers to unilingual French signs and limitations on the protestant separate schools in Quebec.

12 Joint Committee Hearings, *ibid.*, Issue 10:58-82. Groups such as Acadians in the Atlantic Provinces fear that they will be forgotten now that Quebec has been constitutionally recognized as the distinct French society in Canada. They fear the creation of "two solitudes" among francophones in Canada. In their view their recognition as a constitutional minority outside Quebec is less significant than the implicit rejection of Acadians as a distinct society.

13 Joint Committee Hearings, *ibid.*, Issue 2A:33 (G. Beaudoin).

constitutional provisions. In the original Constitution Act, 1867 there were no full blown interpretive clauses, but some guidance was given to the courts in the form of preambles. The phrase "a Constitution similar in Principle to that of the United Kingdom", in the preamble to the Constitution Act, 1867, was used by both Canadian courts and the Privy Council although rarely did it change the substantive result of constitutional interpretation.[14] The major interpretation doctrines used by the courts in resolving distribution of powers disputes were developed by the judiciary itself.[15]

With the arrival of the Charter of Rights in 1982, new interpretation problems arose. The only references to guaranteed rights in the Constitution Act, 1867 were to collective rights. Certain rights of the English linguistic minority in Quebec and French linguistic minorities elsewhere were protected by s. 133 as part of the Confederation deal. Similarly the rights of the protestant and Roman Catholic denominational groups were guaranteed by virtue of s. 93 of the Constitution Act, 1867. Madame Justice Wilson in the *Separate High Schools Funding Reference*[16] found that the guarantees contained in s. 93 were also part of the basic Confederation bargain and thus could not be altered by the Charter of Rights. She did not rely on s. 29 of the Charter of Rights, which could be regarded as an interpretive clause, in favour of maintaining denominational rights.[17]

Because the *Separate High Schools Funding Reference* addresses how one part of the Canadian Constitution affects another part, it is central to the assessment of the impact that the Meech Lake amendments will have on the Charter of Rights. Based upon the broad language of Wilson J., speaking for the majority of the Court, many groups appearing before the Joint Committee expressed fear that governments would be immune from Charter review, so long as they were acting

---

14 Attempts to use this phrase as importing an implied Bill of Rights into the Constitution Act, 1867 met with little success.
15 P. Hogg, *Constitutional Law of Canada*, 2nd ed. (Toronto: Carswell, 1985) at 313-344 describes the many judicial doctrines devised in respect of distribution of powers under the Constitution Act, 1867.
16 *Reference Re An Act to Amend the Education Act (Ontario)* (1987), 40 D.L.R. (4th) 18 (S.C.C.).
17 *Ibid.* The key passage in Wilson J.'s judgment is at 60:

> . . . the special treatment guaranteed by the constitution to denominational, separate or dissentient schools, even if it sits uncomfortably with the concept of equality embodied in the Charter because not available to other schools, is nevertheless not impaired by the Charter. It was never intended, in my opinion, that the Charter could be used to invalidate other provisions of the Constitution, particularly a provision such as s. 93 which represented a fundamental part of the Confederation compromise.

within their plenary constitutional authority under the Constitution Act, 1867.[18] Thus, linguistic duality and the distinct society as part of the Constitution Act, 1867 would prevail over Charter guarantees such as equality, in the same way that the denominational rights guaranteed in s. 93 of the Constitution Act, 1867 prevailed over Charter guarantees of freedom of religion and equality in the *Funding Reference*.

Such fears are not justified for several reasons. First, the rights to denominational schools are substantively guaranteed in the Constitution Act, 1867 and reinforced by s. 29 of the Charter of Rights as either an interpretive provision or a reaffirmation of substantive rights. Linguistic duality and the distinct society are only interpretive provisions designed to assist the courts in interpreting the rest of the Constitution. There is a qualitative difference between substantive constitutional provisions, such as the various guarantees of rights in the Charter of Rights, and interpretive provisions such as the proposed s. 2 of the Constitution Act, 1867. The *Separate Schools Funding Reference* involves a conflict between substantive rights in different parts of the constitution and thus is not directly analogous to the potential conflicts between s. 2 of the Constitution Act, 1867 and substantive Charter guarantees.

Secondly, I agree with the narrower interpretation of the *Funding Reference* adopted by the Joint Committee, relying on the views expressed by William Lederman:

> In the separate school system of Ontario, yes, the denominational characteristics, the religious characteristics, have special protection. But this does not mean there can be sex discrimination in the hiring of teachers. Section 28 would apply. Section 15 would apply.[19]

While it might be argued that linguistic duality and a recognition of the distinct society in Quebec are part of the new Confederation compromise, surely all that Wilson J. would suggest is that the Charter not be interpreted in such a way as to totally destroy these principles. If every time a government acts within its plenary powers under s. 91 or 92, it is immune from Charter challenge, then most of the Supreme Court decisions on the Charter of Rights are wrongly decided. Such a broad interpretation would put an end to most Charter challenges

---

18 This was one of the foremost concerns of women's groups appearing before the Joint Committee such as the National Association of Women and the Law, the Women's Legal Education and Action Fund, the Canadian Advisory Council on the Status of Women and the Ad Hoc Committee of Canadian Women on the Constitution.

19 Tremblay and Speyer, above, note 3, at 59.

and was not what Wilson J. intended. The case will be limited and thus not have the dramatic impact that some fear.[20] That does not mean that linguistic duality and a distinct society will have no impact on the Charter of Rights. The nature of this impact will be explored in the next sections of this paper. In any event, linguistic duality and the distinct society are not immune from Charter challenges.

Apart from s. 29 of the Charter of Rights, there are other provisions (ss. 25-28, 30 and 31) which may be regarded as interpretive provisions. There is some debate about whether non-derogation clauses are interpretive or substantive provisions, but they are relevant to the process of interpretation, as they must be considered in relation to other parts of the Constitution.[21]

Sections 25 and 27 are exempted from the proposed s. 2 of the Constitution Act, 1867, but other than that it is left to the courts to juggle these various interpretation doctrines. There is no indication other than the hierarchy implicit in s. 16 of the Accord, as to which interpretation doctrine should prevail when there is conflict. There is no guidance in the Accord about how linguistic duality and the distinct society should be treated when they conflict with the equality guarantee in s. 28 of the Charter. If the latter is regarded as a substantive rather than interpretive clause, the result may be clearer. The net effect of the ambiguity surrounding these interpretation provisions and their interaction is to transfer very significant value choices about the nature of the Canadian state to the judges. There will be conflict between the various interpretation doctrines, even those that are supposedly exempted by s. 16 of the Accord, and in resolving these conflicts judges will be making policy decisions about the nature of Canada.[22]

---

20 This narrower interpretation of the *Separate Schools Funding Reference* was adopted by the Fédération des Femmes du Québec in their submission to the Joint Committee. Joint Committee Hearings, above, note 4, Issue 13:42-57.

21 This debate surfaced in the Joint Committee Hearings in respect to s. 28 of the Charter of Rights, the guarantee of equality to male and female persons. The question was whether it was a provision like those relating to multiculturalism and the rights of Canada's aboriginal people and therefore appropriate for inclusion in s. 16 of the 1987 Constitutional Accord.

22 This was the essence of my submission to the Joint Committee on the impact of the distinct society clause. Joint Committee Hearings, above, note 4, Issue 3:42-71 (W. MacKay). At 8 of my written submission to the Joint Committee I state:

> In conclusion the "distinct society" clause provides a clear illustration of the difficulties in giving effect to the ideals of the Constitutional Accord, 1987. It is left to the judiciary to juggle the various interpretation doctrines. The Constitution is to be interpreted consistently with all the following strands of Canadianism, to name but a few:

To date, judges have not made much use of the interpretation doctrines in dealing with Charter cases. Instead, they have developed judicial approaches to the Charter emphasizing a purposive analysis of rights, to give effect to Charter guarantees, within a free and democratic society.[23] The reference to a "free and democratic society" in s. 1 of the Charter and occasional references to "the supremacy of God and the rule of law" in its preamble,[24] have had much more impact on interpretation than the express interpretive provisions set out earlier.[25] In light of the judges' experiences with the distribution of powers, it is not surprising that they feel more comfortable with references to preambles and judicial doctrines than express constitutional directives on interpretation.

LINGUISTIC DUALITY AND THE DISTINCT SOCIETY: IMPACT ON CHARTER INTERPRETATION

The need for Canadian judges to balance various collective and individual rights is implicit in the Charter of Rights itself, so the Meech Lake amendments will not introduce a totally new dimension. While linguistic duality and a distinct society are not expressly identified in the Charter, judges have been aware of the need to balance the various strands of the Canadian cultural fabric. This point is illustrated by the following excerpt from a speech of Chief Justice Dickson.

> Included in the Charter without any parallel in the American *Bill of Rights* are provisions relating to mobility rights, language and minority education rights, the rights of aboriginal people, equality of the sexes and a general recognition

---

1. Dualism in Canada;
2. A Distinct Society in Quebec;
3. Native rights;
4. Multiculturalism;
5. Equality of the sexes and others;
6. Denominational rights;
7. Educational rights of linguistic minorities.

These doctrines are bound to conflict in individual cases and it will be up to the courts to attach priorities and thereby make important value choices about the nature and shape of Canadian society.

23 *R. v. Big M Drug Mart*, [1985] 1 S.C.R. 295 and *R. v. Oakes* (1986), 50 C.R. (3d) 1 (S.C.C.) are two cases where Dickson C.J.C. elucidates the judicial approach to the Charter.

24 *R. v. Big M Drug Mart*, *ibid.*, is one example of the use of the Charter preamble.

25 *R. v. Big M Drug Mart*, *ibid.*, and *R. v. Edwards Books & Art Ltd.*, [1986] 2 S.C.R. 713, are cases where the Supreme Court of Canada did make use of s. 27's guarantee of multiculturalism in the course of resolving the dispute about freedom of religion. The section was used to buttress freedom of religion.

of Canada's multicultural heritage. These provisions manifest a distinctively Canadian social experience, one marked by a recognition of cultural identity, as well as an awareness of the importance of equality in a multicultural confederation.[26]

Although Senator Lowell Murray originally took the position that recognizing linguistic duality and the distinct society would have no effect on the Charter of Rights,[27] he conceded in his final appearance before the Joint Committee that the distinct society clause would have some impact on the interpretation of Charter rights, as a factor to be considered in the context of reasonable limitations on rights in s. 1.[28]

The crucial shift, for purposes of s. 1 analysis, is away from national standards of reasonable limitation to provincial or even local standards. Frank Iacobucci, Deputy Minister of Justice, is more candid in his recognition of this shift to provincial standards of limitation than Senator Murray.

> To reinforce what the senator said, I think under section 1 of the Charter it is open to the courts to take a provincial piece of legislation and interpret it according to the particular circumstances that relate to that province and that piece of legislation.
>
> To the extent the distinct society clause reflects a reality of Canada, a court will be doing no differently from what it presently could do under the Charter in section 1 and the jurisprudence that has developed.[29]

Two important questions emerge. Does the recognition of provincial standards apply only to Quebec, because of the distinct society clause, or to other provinces as well? Is this really a recognition of what the courts are already doing under s. 1 of the Charter? On the first question, the preamble to the Accord expressly recognizes the principle of the "equality of the provinces", and it could be argued that all provinces have elements of distinctiveness which could justify different limitations on Charter rights from one province to another. It is plausible that courts would adopt such an analysis, and this possibility has alarmed women's groups and minorities who appeared as witnesses before the Joint Committee. Essentially, the courts will be required to reconcile the national standards of the Charter of Rights with the decentralized components of the 1987 Accord, such as a distinct

---

26 R.G.B. Dickson C.J.C., Address (Opening of the Cambridge Lectures, July 15, 1985).

27 Above, note 7.

28 Above, note 8, at 15.

29 *Ibid.* at 16.

society in Quebec and different forms of linguistic duality throughout the country.

The Joint Committee responded to the second question by concluding that courts have recognized the sociological facts of linguistic duality and a distinct Quebec society both before and after the arrival of the Charter of Rights.[30] Linguistic duality was raised before the Supreme Court in *Re A.G. Quebec and A.G. Canada (the Quebec Veto case)*[31] and the distinctiveness of Quebec's society was emphasized by Deschênes J. in *Quebec Assn. of Protestant School Boards v. A.G. Quebec (No. 2)*[32] as a possible justification for limitations on Charter rights to minority language education found in Bill 101. Chief Justice Dickson has also indicated in *R. v. Big M Drug Mart* that Charter rights must be interpreted in their linguistic, philosophical and historical context.[33] In the view of constitutional experts such as Gérald Beaudoin and William Lederman, the effect on s. 1 interpretation will be minimal, as the judges were already heading in that direction.[34]

I think that the constitutional recognition of linguistic duality and the distinct society will add to their weight as a component of the s. 1 balance, and more often tip the scales in favour of the government limitation. Furthermore, I think the express constitutional recognition of provincial standards for s. 1 limits will hasten any pre-existing move in this direction. I also question whether judges at this point have made up their minds about whether s. 1 limitations should be national, provincial or local. The Meech Lake amendments will move them towards a more decentralized approach.

I am also not convinced by Senator Murray, the Joint Committee and the experts upon which they rely, that the recognition of linguistic duality and the distinct society in Quebec will not affect the interpretation of the substantive Charter provisions. Would not fundamental freedoms, mobility rights, minority language education rights and equality rights themselves be interpreted in light of linguistic duality and the distinct society before a court proceeds to s. 1? The situation is far from clear. The guarantee of equality in s. 15 of the Charter has been interpreted as only prohibiting discrimination

---

30 Tremblay and Speyer, above, note 3, at 35-39.
31 (1982), 140 D.L.R. (3d) 385 (S.C.C.).
32 (1982), 140 D.L.R. (3d) 33 (Que. S.C.).
33 *R. v. Big M Drug Mart*, above, note 23, at 344.
34 This was an important component of their submissions to the Joint Committee on the impact of linguistic duality and the distinct society on the Charter of Rights.

between similarly situated groups.[35] The effect of s. 2 of the Constitution Act, 1867 is to recognize that Quebec is not similarly situated
to other provinces. At a minimum, s. 2 can be used to buttress a
reasonable limits argument pursuant to s. 1 of the Charter. Thus
different treatment in Quebec may become the norm, rather than the
exception. National standards such as equality set out in the Charter
of Rights will undoubtedly come into conflict with the decentralizing
thrust of the Accord. While accommodation is possible, the process
will be complex.

A practical example is the protection of the rights of denominational schools in provinces where they exist. The "distinct society"
clause could be used to move away from a Quebec school system based
on religion to one based on language — which would better meet
the needs of Quebec as a "distinct society". Since the guarantees of
denominational rights in s. 29 of the Charter of Rights and s. 93 of
the Constitution Act, 1867 are quite clear, they would not be eliminated
by s. 2, but the latter might affect their interpretation. In light of
the Supreme Court's holding in the *Separate Schools Funding Reference*,[36]
denominational rights are not likely to be reduced, but the position
of other minorities may be less clear.

While the proposed s. 2 of the Constitution Act, 1867 will not
be a limit on Charter interpretation in the way that ss. 33 and 1 of
the Charter are,[37] it will pose a new limitation, either by circumscribing
the definition of the rights themselves or, more likely, as part of the
balancing process in s. 1. It may be that as a matter of extrinsic evidence,
the testimony of Senator Murray and the federal officials before the
Joint Committee will be used to argue that the courts should only
consider linguistic duality and the distinct society at the s. 1 stage
of analysis, where the burden of proof is on the state. However, judges
are not bound by such evidence,[38] which in any event only indicates
the federal view and not that of other signatories to the Accord, such
as Quebec. In this, as in other aspects of the Accord, the final decisions

---

35 *Andrews v. Law Society of British Columbia* (1986), 27 D.L.R. (4th) 600 (B.C. C.A.). Leave
   to appeal to the S.C.C. has been granted (1986), 7 B.C.L.R. (2d) xli (note) (S.C.C.).
36 Above, note 6.
37 Mr. Allmand, a member of the Joint Committee, in questioning Senator Murray suggested
   that there were now three limitations on the Charter of Rights — ss. 33, 1 and 2 of the
   Constitution Act, 1867. This analysis was strongly resisted and Mr. Iacobucci insisted that
   linguistic duality and the distinct society would merely be part of the s. 1 Charter analysis.
   Joint Committee Hearings, above, note 4, Issue 16:48-9.
38 *Reference s. 94(2) of the B.C. Motor Vehicle Act*, [1985] 2 S.C.R. 486.

have been left to the courts, with little guidance from the legislative branch of government.

SECTION 16 OF THE 1987 CONSTITUTIONAL ACCORD: MEANINGLESS OR AN IMPLICIT HIERARCHY OF RIGHTS?

Ironically, the one effort on the part of the architects of the Accord to indicate how the linguistic duality and distinct society clause interact with the Charter of Rights only adds to the confusion. Section 16 of the Accord indicates that s. 2 does not affect ss. 25, 27 and 35 of the 1982 document or s. 91(24) of the Constitution Act, 1867. Thus the Constitution is still to be interpreted consistently with a recognition of the rights of Canada's native people (whatever they are) and multiculturalism. The proposed s. 16 does not give the courts any guidance as to what they should do when the promotion of Quebec as a "distinct society" would conflict with the rights of Canada's native people or the promotion of multiculturalism in Canada. Such conflicts are inevitable, and s. 2 is bound to have some effect on multiculturalism, if it is to have any meaning at all. Quebec's expanded power in respect of immigration is one example where the multicultural rights of refugees or immigrants may have to be limited, so that Quebec can promote a "distinct society" within its province. This example is further complicated by the fact that the immigration provisions are expressly made subject to the Charter of Rights by virtue of the proposed s. 95B(3) of the Constitution Act, 1867. The express inclusion of the Charter in some parts of the Accord leaves the status of the Charter in doubt with respect to the other sections.

The omission of other groups from the proposed s. 16 also causes confusion and uncertainty. There is no reference to s. 28, which guarantees the equality of men and women in Canada. It is amazing that Canada's Constitution builders have, for a second time, ignored the position of women in Canada. Is the principle of sexual equality now secondary to principles of dualism in Canada and the promotion of a "distinct society" in Quebec? There is also no reference to the general guarantee of equality in s. 15 of the Charter. If the different treatment of men and women is necessary to promote a "distinct society" in Quebec, is that constitutionally permissible? The fact that such developments are unlikely with governments of good will is not a substitute for constitutional protection. The fact that ss. 15 and 28 of the Charter of Rights are substantive guarantees and s. 2 of the Constitution Act, 1867 is only a interpretation doctrine would suggest that ss. 15 and 28 should prevail. However, as discussed in the previous section, that does not mean that the interpretation of these rights would be unaffected. The submissions of the various women's groups who appeared before the Joint Committee are compelling on the need for more clearly stated protections for equality in the Accord itself.

A number of explanations were offered for the inclusion of the rights of multicultural people and Canada's aboriginal population in s. 16, and the exclusion of other groups. Senator Murray indicated that the section was included out of an abundance of caution. These groups were included because they refer to collective rather than individual rights and because their protection was also in the form of an interpretive clause.[39] In respect to the exclusion of equality rights for women, Senator Murray adopted the view that sexual equality transcends culture and thus does not need protection.[40]

No one seems happy with s. 16, as even Canada's aboriginal people and people of ethnic groups, other than English or French, do not feel that it adequately reflects their contribution to a distinct Canadian society. Groups representing women want to be included in s. 16, so as not to lose the ground gained in 1982 and 1985.[41] However, to recognize women's claims and not those of smaller, less powerful groups would accentuate the unhealthy hierarchy of rights already implicit in the Constitution. To exempt the whole Charter of Rights from the principles of linguistic duality and the distinct society would be unacceptable to Quebec and cause the whole Accord to unravel.[42]

A compromise solution would be to abandon s. 16 and replace it with a provision which frankly acknowledges that the proposed s. 2 of the Constitution Act, 1867, while not superseding the Charter of Rights, will affect its interpretation. As further guidance to the courts, the new provision could direct judges to take account of the s. 2 principles at the second stage of Charter analysis — the consideration of reasonable limits on rights. This would not only provide clearer guidance for the courts and be consistent with declared federal intentions, but it would also force the state to justify limitations

---

39 Joint Committee Hearings, above, note 4, Issue 2:39 (L. Murray).

40 Joint Committee Hearings, *ibid.*, Issue 16:47-9 (L. Murray).

41 The National Association of Women and the Law argued for the inclusion of ss. 28 and 15 in respect to sexual equality.

42 I think this is a fair assessment of the situation as the net effect of including the whole Charter in s. 16 would be to put Quebec in a worse position than it was before the Accord. This is hardly the basis for a reconciliation.

on rights even if imposed in the name of linguistic duality or the distinct society in Quebec.

CONCLUDING THOUGHTS

The recognition of linguistic duality and the distinct society in Quebec in the proposed additions to the Constitution Act, 1867 is more than a statement of sociological fact. They will limit rights under the Charter, although in what manner and to what degree is not yet clear. Neither the Accord nor the Proceedings and Report of the Joint Committee give the courts much guidance on these complex issues. In its report, the Joint Committee declares great faith in the Canadian judiciary to juggle the various constitutional principles in a way that will benefit all Canadians. While judges have some expertise in deciding rights issues under the Charter of Rights, they have little expertise in delineating the elements of linguistic duality in various parts of the country and the distinct society in Quebec. There is a certain irony in the fact that the distinct society in Quebec will be defined by a predominantly anglophone judiciary.

The real problem with the Accord is not just that it is untidy in the legal sense. A lack of legal symmetry is a matter of concern, but it is not crucial. A certain degree of ambiguity is endemic to constitutional provisions. A more fundamental problem with the Accord is its dishonesty — apparent in the submissions of the federal government both before the Special Joint Committee and in statements to the general public which fail to acknowledge the fundamental value choices being made.

The "distinct society" clause either means something and will have an impact on constitutional interpretation, or it is a hollow promise which will serve to further alienate Quebec within Confederation. Whatever the real intent and impact of the Accord, the politicians supporting it should take responsibility for the important value choices being made and not merely pass the buck to the courts. Given the positive aspects of the Accord, it may be worth the cost, but the federal government and other supporters of the constitutional change should be honest about the potential costs and who is likely to bear them.

The role of courts in Canadian political life, already greatly enlarged by the adoption of the Charter of Rights in 1982, will be further extended by the added task of giving content to the often vague language of the Accord. Greater guidance on the interaction of the Charter of Rights and this Accord should be provided as a minimal level of legislative guidance to the courts. The judiciary is emerging as a significant and powerful national institution, but it should not be left with the whole task. If we are going to leave it to the courts to put together our constitutional jigsaw puzzle, we should at least provide them with pieces that have some definite shape.

The Constitutional Priority of the Charter

Brian Slattery

The Meech Lake Accord[1] is silent on a central question: are the governmental powers it enumerates subject to the Canadian Charter of Rights and Freedoms?[2] Despite some specific references to the Charter in the text of the Accord,[3] there is no provision regulating its overall interaction with the Charter. This is a surprising omission, for the question is one of the most important raised by the Accord. This paper will attempt to provide an answer. But first we need to step back a little, to see the problem in its larger context.

The Constitution Act, 1982, of which Part I is the Canadian Charter of Rights and Freedoms, owes its constitutional status to the fact that it was passed by the British Parliament at Canada's request. In this respect, it resembles older parts of the Canadian Constitution, notably the British North America Act, 1867[4] and its amending statutes (now renamed the Constitution Act, 1867-1975). These are all Acts of the British Parliament passed for Canada, and as such are binding and paramount here. When a statute passed by the Canadian Parliament or a provincial Legislature conflicts with one of the Constitution Acts, it is invalid to the extent of the inconsistency. The Constitution Acts,

---

1 The provisions of the Accord are embodied in the proposed Constitution Amendment, 1987. For convenience, the amendment will be referred to as the Accord. See Appendix 2 to this volume.

2 Being Part I of the Constitution Act, 1982 [enacted by the Canada Act, 1982 (U.K.), c. 11, s. 1].

3 See s. 16 of the Accord, and also s. 3 which adds a new s. 95B(3) to the Constitution Act, 1867 (U.K.), c. 3. These are discussed later.

4 British North America Act, 1867 (U.K.), c. 3 [now the Constitution Act, 1867].

then, make up a legal order superior to ordinary Canadian law.[5]

So much is fairly clear. The more difficult problem is this: what rules determine the relative priority of the various Constitution Acts among themselves? To take the simplest case, where one Constitution Act apparently conflicts with another Constitution Act, which one prevails? Various answers might be given to this question. We will look first at an answer with strong initial appeal, postponing consideration of the alternatives until later. This answer invokes a principle of sequential ordering, which maintains that the priority between constitutional enactments is determined simply by the temporal sequence in which they were enacted.

The principle of sequential ordering is traceable to the rule that arguably governs the interaction between ordinary British statutes. Under the standard version of this rule, no statute is intrinsically superior to any other statute. The relative priority of two statutes, in case of conflict, is determined by their dates of enactment. The later statute takes precedence over the earlier one and repeals or amends any inconsistent provisions.[6] The sequential approach argues that the rule governing the interaction between ordinary British statutes applies also to British enactments passed for Canada, including those of a constitutional nature. Under this rule, the relative priority of the various Constitution Acts among themselves is determined by their date of enactment, with later Acts overriding earlier ones in cases of conflict. Although the rule is British in origin, it arguably passed into Canadian common law upon our independence and continues to govern our basic constitutional instruments.

On this view, the Constitution Act, 1982 and the Charter have priority over the Constitution Acts, 1867-1975 simply because they were enacted later in time. So, for example, the reason why the Charter is taken to limit the broad legislative and governmental powers granted by the Constitution Act, 1867 is not the intrinsic superiority of the Charter as a constitutional instrument, for according to the sequential principle no such superiority exists. The true reason is more conventional. A reading of ss. 1, 32(1) and 33 of the Charter makes it clear that the document sets out to limit the capacity of Canadian

5 For fuller discussion, see B. Slattery, "The Independence of Canada" (1983), 5 Supreme Court L.R. 369, and P.W. Hogg, *Constitutional Law of Canada*, 2nd ed. (Toronto: Carswell, 1985), at 1-49.

6 Of course, it is not always clear whether two statutes genuinely conflict, or whether apparently inconsistent provisions may not in fact be reconciled. Such issues, however, concern the application of the rule, and do not call into question its essential soundness.

governments and Legislatures to affect basic rights and freedoms. This intent conflicts with the scheme of the Constitution Act, 1867. One Act must give way to the other. As the more recent of the two, the Charter will prevail.

This brings us to the main question: how do the Constitution Act, 1982 and the Charter stand relative to constitutional provisions enacted after 1982? In particular, to what extent do they have the capacity to control later amendments? The case in point is the Meech Lake Accord, but the question goes far beyond that particular instrument, and extends to all possible future amendments.

The sequential approach suggests that the relationship between the Constitution Act, 1982 and subsequent constitutional amendments is identical to that obtaining between the 1982 Act and preceding Constitution Acts. There is no intrinsic difference in status between these various constitutional instruments. Their relative priority in cases of conflict is determined simply by their date of enactment. On this view, a constitutional amendment passed after 1982 must be taken to amend or repeal any provisions of the Constitution Act, 1982 that conflict with its terms. How far the later enactment actually modifies the 1982 Act is, of course, a matter of interpretation. But if the terms of the amendment, on their true reading, modify the position obtaining under the 1982 Act, they must be given full effect. What holds true of the Constitution Act, 1982 is equally true of the Charter, which does not occupy any special position within the Act.

Let me give an example of how this approach might operate in practice. Under the current system of Senate appointments, laid down in s. 24 of the Constitution Act, 1867, the Governor General has the power to name qualified persons to the Senate. Although other provisions of the 1867 Act require balanced regional representation in the Senate, the provincial and territorial governments play no formal part in the process of selection. Section 2 of the Accord changes this. It adds a new section to the 1867 Act (s. 25) providing that, where a Senate vacancy occurs, the government of the province to which the vacancy relates may nominate persons to fill the vacancy, and the person chosen by the Governor General must come from among the nominees.

It seems obvious that the Accord has the capacity to accomplish what it explicitly sets out to do: namely, amend the Constitution Act, 1867. Its capacity to do this stems, not from any inherent superiority, but simply from the fact that it is a constitutional instrument equal in status to the 1867 Act and enacted at a later time. The more puzzling question is what relation the amendment bears to the Charter. Is the new appointment system subject to Charter provisions, or does it take priority over them? For example, is the provincial power of nomination governed by s. 15(1) of the Charter, which provides that every individual is equal before and under the law, and has the right to the equal benefit of the law without discrimination?

Suppose that, after the system has been in operation for a number of years, an action is brought against a provincial government alleging that it has systematically discriminated against women in making its Senate nominations and deprived them of the equal benefit of the law under s. 15(1). If the Accord is read literally, as creating an unrestricted provincial power of nomination, it follows on the sequential principle that the provision ousts s. 15(1) of the Charter simply because it was enacted later in time. This interpretation of s. 2 of the Accord is arguably reinforced by the section's silence on the question of the Charter's application. By contrast, s. 3 of the Accord, which adds provisions to the Constitution Act, 1867 concerning federal-provincial immigration agreements, explicitly deals with the matter, providing:

> The Canadian Charter of Rights and Freedoms applies in respect of any agreement that has the force of law under subsection (1) and in respect of anything done by the Parliament or Government of Canada, or the legislature or government of a province, pursuant to any such agreement.[7]

It could be inferred that, in the absence of a parallel provision, the provincial power of Senate nominations escapes the Charter's reach.

On this view, the Accord changes not only the current system of Senate appointments but also its relationship to the Charter. As matters now stand, the various governmental and legislative powers conferred by the Constitution Act, 1867 must be exercised in conformity with Charter standards.[8] In principle, then, the Governor General's power to name Senators under s. 24 of the 1867 Act is controlled by applicable Charter provisions. So, there is the possibility of Charter challenges to Senate appointments for violation of equality rights. By contrast, if the sequential approach is correct, the new system of Senate nominations may fall beyond the Charter's scope.

This example illustrates the general problem of constitutional priority posed by the Accord.[9] But it is not by any means the most

---

7 This provision will be the new s. 95B(3) of the Constitution Act, 1867.

8 See, *e.g.*, *Operation Dismantle Inc. v. R.* (1985), 18 D.L.R. (4th) 481 (S.C.C.).

9 A similar issue is raised by s. 6 of the Accord, which alters the current system of appointments to the Supreme Court of Canada, providing for provincial nominations and federal

important instance of the problem, nor the most difficult. That distinction is reserved for the provisions concerning the linguistic duality of Canada. The Accord adds a new section to the Constitution Act, 1867 (s. 2), which contains a number of interlocking provisions.[10] Although closely related, these provisions in fact perform two quite distinct tasks: first, they set out a new rule for the interpretation of the Constitution of Canada (the interpretive rule); second, they state certain constitutional roles to be played by various Canadian governments (the role-defining provisions).

The interpretive rule is found in the new s. 2(1) of the 1867 Act. It provides that the Constitution of Canada shall be interpreted in a manner consistent with the recognition that the existence of French-speaking and English-speaking Canadians throughout Canada constitutes a fundamental characteristic of the country, and also the recognition that Quebec constitutes within Canada a distinct society. The rule is made applicable to the Constitution of Canada generally, and so covers the Charter.[11]

The interpretive rule is similar in format to an existing Charter provision (s. 27), which states that the Charter "shall be interpreted in a manner consistent with the preservation and enhancement of the multicultural heritage of Canadians". The status of the latter rule is preserved by s. 16 of the Accord, which provides that nothing in s. 2 of the Constitution Act, 1867 affects s. 27 of the Charter. Although the new interpretive rule, like the old, may prove helpful in determining the scope of certain Charter rights and the reasonableness of limits on them, it does not, in my opinion, affect the Charter's operation in a major way.

By contrast, the role-defining provisions may have the potential to do just that. These provisions are embodied in the new ss. 2(2) and 2(3) of the 1867 Act. They recognize: first, the role of the Parliament of Canada and the provincial Legislatures to preserve the linguistic duality of Canada; and second, the role of the Legislature and government of Quebec to preserve and promote the distinct identity

---

appointments. The exercise of the new powers conferred is possibly immune from Charter scrutiny, for the reasons given in relation to Senate appointments. The problem perhaps also arises with respect to Acts implementing the new provisions governing national shared-cost programs found in s. 7.

10 The text of s. 2 is set out in the Appendices found in this volume.

11 See the definition of the Constitution of Canada supplied in s. 52(2) of the Constitution Act, 1982. However, the rule's odd location in the 1867 Act perhaps allows for an argument that the rule's application is limited to the provisions of that Act, or at least is intended to apply mainly to the latter.

of Quebec as a distinct society within Canada. Like the sections dealing with Senate appointments, these provisions can be read as giving governments a fresh constitutional mandate to pursue the goals identified, free of any unspecified constitutional limits. The Accord takes care to state that nothing in the above derogates from existing federal or provincial powers,[12] but no comparable provision preserves the overall position of the Charter.[13] Since the Accord is subsequent in time to the Charter, it arguably takes precedence and amends the Charter accordingly. So, under the sequential principle, governments and Legislatures may be free of Charter constraints in carrying out the roles specified.

Such a conclusion would have far-reaching implications. It would mean that the role-defining provisions provide a separate route for justifying legislation challenged under the Charter, one which eliminates the need to show that the legislation does not unreasonably limit a guaranteed right. So, for example, if Quebec legislation restricting the use of English on public signs is challenged for violating freedom of expression under the Charter,[14] it may be possible for the Quebec government to undercut the Charter argument by showing that the legislation is designed to preserve and promote the identity of Quebec as a distinct society. Since the distinct society clause is drafted in very general terms, it can arguably be pressed into service in a large variety of contexts, relating not only to the linguistic life of the province, but also to the cultural, social, political and religious spheres. In effect, the clause may become a full-blown alternative to s. 1 of the Charter as a way of justifying contested Quebec legislation.

These examples raise questions as to the correctness of the sequential principle, at least in the simple form presented earlier. The principle has some obvious attractions. Most important, it appeals to our traditions concerning the relative standing of ordinary statutes, and so gains plausibility in the constitutional context. Nevertheless, there are difficulties with strict sequential ordering. They are not such, perhaps, as to force us to abandon the principle altogether; but at the least they require its modification.

The first objection to the sequential principle is a specific one.

---

12 New s. 2(4) of the Constitution Act, 1867.

13 Section 16 of the Accord, as just noted, shields s. 27 of the Charter from the impact of the new s. 2 of the 1867 Act, and it does the same for s. 25, which concerns the rights of aboriginal peoples. But it does not cover any other Charter provisions.

14 See *Quebec (P.G.) v. Chaussure Brown's Inc.* (1986), 36 D.L.R. (4th) 374 (Que. C.A.), leave to appeal to S.C.C. granted (1987), 36 D.L.R. (4th) 374n (S.C.C.).

It points out that the relationship between the Constitution Act, 1982 and subsequent constitutional amendments is different from the relations obtaining among the Constitution Acts enacted between 1867 and 1982. The latter Acts are *structurally co-ordinate*, so that it is at least plausible to argue that their relative priority *inter se* is governed by their temporal sequence. By contrast, the Constitution Act, 1982 is *structurally paramount* to subsequent constitutional amendments, so that questions of relative priority cannot be determined simply on a sequential basis. In particular, the validity and effect of constitutional amendments passed after 1982 are governed by the mandatory amending procedure laid down in the Constitution Act, 1982. This is the gist of the argument, which needs to be developed a little more fully.

The Constitution Acts passed between 1867 and 1982 were enacted under a master rule which specified the authority of the British Parliament to legislate for Canada, and the status and priority *inter se* of such enactments.[15] This master rule was at root a matter of common law — initially imperial constitutional law and, after Canadian independence, Canadian constitutional law. It was not embodied in the 1867 Act itself or in any subsequent Constitution Act.[16] It was partially set forth in such British enactments as the Colonial Laws Validity Act, 1865,[17] and the Statute of Westminster, 1931.[18] But these statutes were not the ultimate source of the rule, and indeed their own effect in overseas territories such as Canada was controlled by the common law rule in question. At any rate, the various Constitution Acts passed between 1867 and 1982 were located in the same structural position under the master rule. No one Act controlled the validity and effects of the other Acts.

It is apparent that the Constitution Act, 1982 occupies a different position relative to subsequent constitutional amendments. For it sets out the new master rule governing the enactment of amendments to the Constitution of Canada as a whole. Thus, the Accord has the capacity to modify the Constitution Acts of 1867 and 1982 only insofar as it satisfies the amending provisions of the 1982 Act, embodied in

---

15 Or, more accurately, they were enacted under an *evolving* master rule that changed in status and content when Canada achieved independence. These changes are not, however, relevant here. See the detailed discussion in Slattery, above, note 5.

16 It is implied, nevertheless, in the wording of s. 129 of the Constitution Act, 1867, which assigns a privileged status to Acts of the British Parliament in force in the various provinces at Confederation.

17 (28 & 29 Vict.), c. 63.

18 (22 & 23 Geo. 5), c. 4.

s. 52(3) and ss. 38 to 49. In short, the Constitution Act, 1982 and subsequent constitutional amendments are not instruments of the same constitutional order. The 1982 Act is *structurally paramount* to succeeding amendments.

So far as it goes, this objection is essentially correct. But it seems to require only a small alteration in the sequential principle. Although the Accord clearly owes its validity to certain provisions of the 1982 Act, the latter are basically procedural. So long as a constitutional amendment is passed in the manner specified in the Constitution Act, 1982, it is valid. And further, the relative priority of constitutional amendments enacted after 1982, both *inter se* and in relation to other parts of the Constitution, is governed by their temporal sequence. So, for example, an amendment passed in the year 2000 will take precedence over a 1990 amendment and also the Constitution Acts, 1867-1982. The results then, is a modified version of the sequential principle, which affirms that, within the amending structure provided by the Constitution Act, 1982, the relative precedence of constitutional amendments enacted after 1982 is determined by the sequence in which they were enacted.

A more radical challenge to the sequential principle has recently been advanced.[19] This argues that the Constitution Act, 1982 is paramount to succeeding constitutional amendments not only procedurally but also in substantive ways. In particular, any constitutional amendment passed after 1982 is subject to the Charter and cannot adversely affect the rights guaranteed there, unless it can be justified under s. 1 of the Charter. However, this view leads to the surprising conclusion that the Charter cannot be adversely *amended* at all. For s. 1 does not authorize permanent alterations in the Charter's substantive provisions, but only "reasonable limits prescribed by law" on the rights guaranteed. Where a limitation on a Charter right is upheld as reasonable, the original Charter provision remains intact and continues to govern both the law upheld and any future laws affecting the subject-matter. So if all constitutional amendments that adversely affect Charter rights must satisfy s. 1, they will be valid only if they justifiably limit the rights in question without actually amending the governing Charter provisions.

This proposition has several difficulties. Section 52 of the

---

19 See the reasons of Justice McDonald in *Penikett v. R.*, indexed as *Yukon Territory (Commissioner) v. Canada* (1987), 2 Y.R. 262 (Y.T. S.C.). That decision has been reversed (1987), 21 B.C.L.R. (2d) 1 (Y.T. C.A.).

Constitution Act, 1982 seems to allow for *any* amendments to the Constitution which satisfy the amending formula, and the Constitution is defined in terms that include the Charter. Moreover, s. 1 seems to deal exclusively with the relation between the Charter and inferior forms of law, such as ordinary statutes, regulations, and the common law. It does not address the relationship between the Charter and other parts of the Constitution; much less does it form an essential part of the constitutional amending formula. In light of these difficulties, the argument for the constitutional impregnability of the Charter appears implausible.

I would like to consider now a more moderate objection to the sequential principle. This challenges the supposition that the relative precedence of various Constitution Acts and amendments is unaffected by their *constitutional significance.* The strict sequential approach admits that some parts of the Constitution are of greater importance than others in a political or moral sense, but it holds that this factor is irrelevant in assessing the impact of an amendment on the existing constitutional framework. Here, it is argued, the sequential approach falls into error. The relative priority of co-ordinate constitutional provisions is not governed simply by their sequence of enactment. Regard must also be given to their constitutional weight and the organic relations they bear to one another. This view, then, upholds a principle of organic ordering, which integrates both the sequential and structural principles discussed above, but subordinates them to an understanding of the Constitution as a functioning whole.

The organic approach was endorsed by the Supreme Court of Canada in the recent *Separate High Schools Funding Reference.*[20] At issue was an Ontario Bill that provided full funding for Roman Catholic secondary schools but not for other denominational secondary schools. It was argued that the Bill, in favouring Catholic schools, violated freedom of religion under s. 2(a) of the Charter and also equality rights under s. 15. The counter-argument invoked s. 93 of the Constitution Act, 1867, which guarantees existing rights to denominational schools, and s. 29 of the Charter, which shields a range of such rights from the Charter's impact.[21]

The Bill's detractors maintained that, insofar as s. 93 of the 1867

20 *Re an Act to Amend the Education Act (Ont.)* (1987), 40 D.L.R. (4th) 18.

21 "Nothing in this Charter abrogates or derogates from any rights or privileges guaranteed by or under the Constitution of Canada in respect of denominational, separate or dissentient schools."

Act guarantees preferred treatment for Catholic schools, or at least authorizes it, the section is inconsistent with the Charter. Where two constitutional instruments conflict, the one enacted last prevails. So, the Charter repeals or amends any inconsistent provisions in s. 93 and controls the exercise of the.powers conferred there, unless there is something in the Charter that specifically prevents this result. The only relevant limitation is found in s. 29 of the Charter. On this approach, then, the question ultimately turns on the scope of the latter section. It may be observed how much the overall argument relies on the principle of sequential ordering.

The Supreme Court unanimously rejected this approach in its decision. Madame Justice Wilson, speaking for a majority of the Court, held that the rights granted by the Funding Bill were in fact shielded from Charter scrutiny by s. 29. Nevertheless, she affirmed that this result would have followed even in the absence of s. 29. Mr. Justice Estey, in a separate opinion, took a narrower view of s. 29, holding that it did not cover the rights conferred by the Bill. He too affirmed, however, that they were effectively immune from Charter challenge. Both held, then, that quite apart from s. 29, it would be wrong to think that the Charter overrode the denominational schools provisions of the 1867 Act. The reason given was the importance of these provisions in the political compromise achieved at Confederation.

A passage from the opinion of Wilson J. gives the tenor of the Court's approach:

> I have indicated that the rights or privileges protected by s. 93(1) are immune from Charter review under s. 29 of the Charter. I think this is clear. What is less clear is whether s. 29 of the Charter was required in order to achieve that result. In my view, it was not. I believe it was put there simply to emphasize that the special treatment guaranteed by the constitution to denominational, separate or dissentient schools, even if it sits uncomfortably with the concept of equality embodied in the Charter because not available to other schools, is nevertheless not impaired by the Charter. It was never intended, in my opinion, that the Charter could be used to invalidate other provisions of the Constitution, particularly a provision such as s. 93 which represented a fundamental part of the Confederation compromise.[22]

Wilson J. went on to adopt the words of the majority of the Ontario Court of Appeal in the judgment below: "The incorporation of the Charter into the Constitution Act, 1982 does not change the original Confederation bargain. A specific constitutional amendment would

---

22 Above, note 20, at 60.

be required to accomplish that.''[23]

Estey J. took a similar approach to the question, but indicated more clearly the bearing of the Charter on existing constitutional powers:

> The role of the Charter is not envisaged in our jurisprudence as providing for the automatic repeal of any provisions of the Constitution of Canada which includes all of the documents enumerated in s. 52 of the Constitution Act, 1982. Action taken under the Constitution Act, 1867 is of course subject to Charter review. That is a far different thing from saying that a specific power to legislate as existing prior to April, 1982 has been entirely removed by the simple advent of the Charter. It is one thing to supervise and on a proper occasion curtail the exercise of a power to legislate; it is quite another thing to say that an entire power to legislate has been removed from the Constitution by the introduction of this judicial power of supervision.[24]

The reasoning in these passages subordinates strict sequential ordering to organic considerations. In pondering the relationship between the Charter and s. 93 of the Constitution Act, 1867, the Court took account of the fundamental role that this section played in achieving Confederation, and the overall relationship between the Charter guarantees and the powers conferred under the earlier Constitution Acts. It held that the Charter adds a new layer of norms to the existing Constitution, regulating but not impairing its main existing functions. Insofar as the 1867 Act specifically authorizes or guarantees preferred educational rights, its provisions continue to stand even in the face of apparently conflicting Charter guarantees.

The Court's treatment of s. 29 of the Charter is particularly illuminating. That section, with its explicit saving of certain denominational rights, could be taken to support the view that, absent specific words, the Charter overrides conflicting provisions of the 1867 Act, including provisions conferring specific powers. Why else, it could be said, is the section necessary? But the Court does not see the matter in this light. Rather, it takes s. 29 as visible evidence of a larger ordering principle relating the Charter to the Constitution Act, 1867 — a principle that is partially embodied in s. 29 but has an independent constitutional status, in somewhat the same way that exposed structural beams in one part of a building may serve to suggest the concealed inner structure of the whole.

What significance does the Supreme Court's approach have for

---

23 *Ibid.*, at 61.
24 *Ibid.*, at 27.

our topic? The principle of organic ordering holds that an amendment to the Constitution must be understood as an adaptation of a complex living entity rather than a mere addition to a list of legal propositions. The effect of an amendment cannot be gauged merely by an analysis of its logical content relative to the logical content of existing constitutional norms, whereby contradictions and inconsistencies are detected and eliminated on a strict sequential basis. An amendment must be "placed" within the existing constitutional framework, and understood in the light of the functions performed by various parts of the structure and the relations they bear to one another. An alteration to one part of the structure does not, in the absence of specific indications, change that part's positioning in the overall scheme or alter its mode of interacting with other parts.

It follows that the amendments made by the Meech Lake Accord to the Constitution Acts, 1867-1982 occupy the same position relative to the Charter as the original provisions or institutions that they modify, in the absence of specific words to the contrary. That is, they are "placed" within the existing constitutional framework. On this view, most of the provisions of the Accord are controlled by the Charter, even where this is not specified. The specific references to the Charter in the Accord simply reflect the general principle tacitly governing the relations between the two instruments. So, for example, the provision stating that the Charter applies to immigration agreements articulates what would hold true even is its absence.[25] It does not establish an exception; it illustrates the rule.

What concrete conclusions flow from this analysis? First, it seems clear that the new provisions concerning the appointment of Senators are governed by the Charter to the same extent as the old provisions that they supplement or replace. So, for example, it seems possible that court action might be taken under s. 15(1) of the Charter against a provincial government that systematically discriminated against women in making its Senate nominations. The same general conclusion holds true of appointments to the Supreme Court of Canada. And, most important, where the Accord recognizes the special roles of Parliament and various provincial Legislatures, these bodies are subject to the Charter in fulfilling their mandates. Thus, in preserving and promoting the distinct identity of Quebec, the Quebec government and Legislature are bound to respect the basic rights embodied in the Charter. And the Canadian Parliament is likewise governed by the

---

25 See the earlier discussion of this provision, above, text at note 7.

Charter in acting to preserve the linguistic duality of the country.[26]

The position, however, seems different with respect to the purely interpretive rule embodied in the new s. 2(1) of the 1867 Act. As seen earlier, this is explicitly made applicable to the Constitution of Canada as a whole,[27] and so has the potential to affect the application of some Charter sections. But this potential is a limited one. The provision operates in basically the same manner as the multicultural provision already found in the Charter, which s. 16 of the Accord preserves from the impact of the new interpretive rule. The same section of the Accord shields s. 25 of the Charter, which in turn insulates the rights of aboriginal peoples from the effects of the Charter itself. Considered together, these various sections attempt to ensure that the Charter is applied in a manner that is at once sensitive to Canada's dual French-English character, without impairing the rights of its aboriginal peoples, or affecting the preservation and enhancement of the country's multicultural heritage. If the effect of multiple, confusing directives is generally to leave matters roughly where they were in the first place, it would not be surprising if this happened here.

---

26 These conclusions are tempered by the existing Charter provision found in s. 16(3):

> Nothing in this Charter limits the authority of Parliament or a legislature to advance the equality of status or use of English and French.

27 Subject to the exceptions set out in s. 16 of the Accord, considered earlier.

Part II

National Institutions and the Spending Power

Meech Lake and the Supreme Court[*]

Peter H. Russell

Assessment of any one component of the Meech Lake Accord must address the Accord's overall purpose. The aim of the Accord is to work out terms on which Quebec's provincial leaders can accept the changes made in Canada's Constitution by the Canada Act 1982[1] and approved by the governments of the other nine provinces and the federal government. This is a worthwhile objective, for achieving it will bring Canada closer to living up to the ideal of a constitutional regime based on the consent of the governed. In the spring of 1980, the Québécois, for the first time since being conquered by the British, were directly consulted on their future. By a slight majority they opted to remain in Canada but on the promise of a revised federalism giving Quebec a larger and a special place in Confederation. The 1982 constitutional changes ignored this promise. The Meech Lake Accord is an attempt to come clean on it.

Important as the basic purpose of the Meech Lake Accord is, it is not an objective to be realized at any price. Accommodation with Quebec must not be achieved at the cost of grievous damage to the federation's central institutions of government, such that Canada could no longer function effectively as a viable nation-state providing a reasonable measure of justice, security and well-being for all of its citizens. But accommodation by its inherent nature entails compromise.

---

[*] A somewhat different version of this paper will appear in a special edition of *Canadian Public Policy/Analyse de Politiques* devoted to the Meech Lake Accord (forthcoming, 1988).

[1] Canada Act 1982 (U.K.), c. 11, of which s. 1 enacts Schedule B, being the Constitution Act, 1982, of which Part I is the Canadian Charter of Rights and Freedoms.

The Bourassa government's five demands on which the Meech Lake Accord was built by no means represent the full constitutional aspirations of Quebec federalists. By the same token, those who wish to accommodate Quebec should not insist on perfection in dealing with those parts of the Constitution dear to their own hearts.

By this general standard, I find the Supreme Court proposals acceptable. By constitutionalizing the Supreme Court of Canada, they deal with an item of unfinished constitutional business which has been on virtually every constitutional reform agenda — not just Quebec's — since the 1960s. While this will make it more difficult in the future to make changes in the Court, I do not view the proposed constitutional amendments as leading to undue rigidity. The changes in the method of appointing judges, although not ideal, are not nearly so bad as critics claim. Indeed, with some informal modifications in their implementation, they could be a distinct improvement on the status quo.

CONSTITUTIONALIZING THE SUPREME COURT

For the Fathers of Confederation, a Canadian Supreme Court was only a possibility, not a necessity. Hence s. 101 of the Constitution Act, 1867[2] simply states that "The Parliament of Canada may . . . from Time to Time provide for the Constitution, Maintenance, and Organization of a General Court of Appeal for Canada . . .". The proposed additions to s. 101 mean that the Supreme Court will no longer be merely a creature of the federal Parliament. It will become a creature of the Constitution and receive formal recognition of its status as an essential element of national government.

Constitutionalizing the Supreme Court of Canada involves primarily a symbolic gain. From a practical political standpoint, there was never any danger that the federal Parliament would use its legal power to destroy the court it created in 1875. Still, giving the Court formal constitutional status is important for Canada's national development. As Canada evolves from the English to a more Franco-American style of constitutionalism, the written Constitution comes to serve more as a symbol, a "concise and hallowed expression", to use Murray Edelman's phrase, of what we are and how we are

---

2 (U.K.), c. 3. See relevant sections of the Constitution Acts and the Accord, in the Appendices of this volume.

governed.[3] This symbolic perspective suggests it is high time the head of our third branch of government — the judiciary — is clearly recognized in the Constitution of Canada.

In terms of symbolism, the language of the proposed s. 101A is quite prosaic. It begins with the rather lackadaisical statement that "The court existing under the name of the Supreme Court of Canada is hereby continued . . ." Compare this with Article III of the American Constitution which begins by stating that "[t]he judicial Power of the United States, shall be vested in one supreme Court, and in such inferior Courts as the Congress may from time to time ordain and establish." Chapter III of the Australian Constitution begins with a similar statement. The phrasing of the new section will disappoint those Canadian jurists who have criticized the Fathers of Confederation for being "so lacking in eloquence on the subject of the judicial power".[4] The failure of the architects of the Meech Lake Accord to acknowledge the judiciary explicitly as a third and separate power established by the Constitution indicates that Canadian constitutionalism has not yet been completely Americanized.

Giving formal constitutional expression to the basic features of the Supreme Court may have the practical benefit of reducing, if not overcoming, the confusion created in 1982 by the references to the Supreme Court in the amending formula. The Constitution Act, 1982 put the cart before the horse: rules for amending constitutional provisions concerning the Supreme Court were introduced before the Supreme Court was put in the Constitution. If the Meech Lake proposals are adopted, at least it will be clear that those features of the Supreme Court which are covered in the proposed additions to s. 101 are entrenched and can be changed only by formal constitutional amendment. These features are: the Court's basic function; the number of judges (a chief justice plus eight others); the requirement that at least three of the judges come from Quebec; the qualifications tenure and mode of payment of the judges; and the method of appointment.[5]

---

3 For a discussion of the Franco-American and English approaches see C.H. McIlwain, *Constitutionalism: Ancient and Modern* (Ithaca: Cornell Univ. Press, 1940) and for the symbolic function of Constitutions see M. Edelman, *The Symbolic Uses of Politics* (Urbana: Univ. of Illinois Press, 1970).

4 Jules Deschênes in collaboration with Carl Baar. *Maîtres Chez Eux* (Ottawa: Canadian Judicial Council, 1981) at 13.

5 See William R. Lederman, "Constitutional Procedure and Reform of the Supreme Court of Canada" (1985), *Les Cahiers de Droit* 195. This list appears to cover what Professor Lederman had identified as the "essential" sections of the Supreme Court Act, except for specifying that the Court exercises "exclusive ultimate appellate civil and criminal jurisdiction within

One other item should be added to this list of entrenched features of the Supreme Court: the guarantee contained in s. 133 of the Constitution Act, 1867 of the use of English and French in court proceedings.

By folding s. 42 of the constitutional amending formula into s. 41, the Meech Lake proposals will make it more difficult to make changes in the major institutions of national government, including the Supreme Court. All constitutional amendments concerning the Supreme Court, not just those altering its composition, will as a consequence, require the support of the federal Parliament and all of the provincial Legislatures.

Executive domination of the legislative process in Canada means that the unanimity requirement is not nearly as rigid as it may appear. In the United States, constitutional amendments require the approval of only three-quarters of the state Legislatures. But given the separation of powers in state capitals, a state governor is in no position to deliver the concurrence of the state Legislature. Similarly in Australia, while a proposed amendment need win the support of a majority of voters in only a majority of states, federal and state premiers cannot control that popular process of ratification the way first ministers in Canada control their Legislatures. In Canada, *executive* federalism remains the key political instrument of constitutional change, and it is an instrument which, despite the requirement of provincial unanimity, can make constitutional amendment more accessible then it is in either of Canada's sister federations.

The drafters of the Meech Lake proposals, wisely, have not tried to specify in the Constitution exactly which cases the Supreme Court should hear. Only the Court's general functions are entrenched, and these are described in the original language of s. 101 as "the general court of appeal for Canada, and as an additional court for the better administration of the laws of Canada."

The proposed s. 101E leaves intact Parliament's power to regulate the Supreme Court's jurisdiction so long as it does so in a manner which is consistent with the definition of the Court's basic functions in s. 101A. This probably means that the federal Parliament could not remove a broad category of laws, such as Quebec's civil law, from

---

and for Canada". But apparently there are some lawyers who think that other aspects of the Supreme Court, for instance the qualifications of those appearing before the Court, are affected by entrenchment. See Canada, *The Report of the Special Joint Committee of the Senate and the House of Commons on the 1987 Constitutional Accord* (Ottawa: Queen's Printer, 1987) at 81.

the Supreme Court's jurisdiction. Apparently the demand for recognition of Quebec as a distinct society no longer embraces an interest in having judicial custody of Quebec's distinctive laws in the hands of an all-Quebec court or of a special Quebec-dominated panel of the Supreme Court. Quebec's provincial political elite has joined the English Canadian consensus favouring the integrative benefits which are thought to flow from the Supreme Court's serving as a final court of appeal in all areas of law. From this perspective the Meech Lake proposals on the Supreme Court are a milestone in Canadian nation-building.

Section 101A indicates a second role for the Supreme Court besides its function as the general court of appeal for Canada: the Court is also continued "as an additional court for the better administration of the laws of Canada". This language is used in the Supreme Court Act[6] and has been retained in the Constitution to provide a basis for any residue of original jurisdiction the Court may exercise. But except for reference cases, there is very little of this nor is there likely to be much in the future. The present Court is on record as agreeing with the Canadian Bar Association's Committee on the Supreme Court that, with the exception of reference cases, "The Court should serve only as an appellate court, and should have no original jurisdiction."[7] As for reference cases, they are specifically provided for under the proposed s. 101E. This was probably necessary because in terms of strict legal theory the Court is not acting in a judicial capacity when it answers questions referred to it by government.

The Meech Lake amendments would fix the size of the Supreme Court at nine (a chief justice and eight other judges), with the stipulation that at least three must be from Quebec. The three judges from Quebec rule has long been a statutory requirement and makes some functional sense given the entrenchment of the Court as a final court of appeal in all areas of law, including Quebec's distinctive civil law. It also gives just a touch of symbolic recognition to Quebec's distinctiveness in the constitutional provisions for one of our national institutions. The premiers of the other provinces did not insist that the custom or convention of appointing judges from the various regions

---

6 R.S.C. 1970, c. S-19.

7 "Response of the Supreme Court of Canada "in Canadian Bar Association Committee on the Supreme Court of Canada, *Report of the Canadian Bar Association Committee on The Supreme Court of Canada*, Appendix 1 (Ottawa, Canadian Bar Association, 1987).

of common law Canada be given formal constitutional expression.[8] This is just as well, for as Charter issues displace federalism issues as the politically most significant part of the Court's work, regional balance may have to make room for ideological balance on the Supreme Court bench.

More problematic is fixing the number of judges at nine. The Supreme Court has been increased in size twice: from six to seven in 1927; and from seven to nine in 1949. The highest courts of Canada's sister federations, Australia and the United States, also have increased in size: Australia's High Court from three to seven and the United States Supreme Court from five to nine. But now, unlike Australia and the United States, in Canada a constitutional amendment will be required to increase the size of our highest Court. The Canadian Bar Association's Committee on the Supreme Court believes this will make it too difficult to adjust the size of the Court in the future. It recommends that the number of Supreme Court judges not be fixed in the Constitution and that the guarantee of Quebec representation be expressed as one-third of the Court.

Entrenching the Supreme Court's size does erect a constitutional barrier against a Prime Minister who, like Franklin Delano Roosevelt, might wish to overcome adverse Supreme Court rulings by threatening to expand the Court and to pack it with new appointees sympathetic to his legislative program. But, as the Bar Committee's Report suggests, the danger of such a court-packing scheme is pretty remote in Canada. Besides, the appointing procedure contained in the Meech Lake proposals will put a very formidable check on the federal government's ability to load the Court with judges who conform with its own ideological leanings. Still it is appropriate that the size of an institution so essential in maintaining the federal balance not be amenable to unilateral change by one level of government. In thinking about our national institutions, one must bear in mind that Canada today, in spirit and in principle, is a much more federal country than either Australia or the United States.

Since the United States with ten times Canada's population gets by with a nine-judge Supreme Court, Canada, it may appear, is a long way from requiring any expansion of its Supreme Court. Certainly

---

8 Since 1949 when the Court was expanded from seven to nine, the pattern has been three from Ontario, two from the West and one from the Atlantic Provinces, with only one short deviation from 1979 to 1982 when there were only two from Ontario and three from the West.

in the short run there is not a strong case for expansion. It is true that, under pressure from the new stream of Charter issues, the Court has fallen behind in handling its work load, often taking over a year after the hearing to render a decision. Its annual output of judgments has dropped well below 90 and is about 50 per cent below what it was in the 1970s and 50 per cent below the U.S. Supreme Court's annual output. Still, I would agree with the Canadian Bar Committee that, without any increase in its numbers, the Supreme Court can do much to increase its productivity without sacrificing quality. The introduction in the fall of 1987 of time limits on oral argument is a major step towards the more efficient management of the judges' time.

The ever-growing case-load pressures on the U.S. Supreme Court have been a major source of concern for a generation now.[9] Opportunities for significantly increasing that court's decision-making capacity have long been exhausted. The only way the U.S. Supreme Court can respond to these pressures is to turn away an ever larger proportion of would-be appellants. This has meant, among other things, that differences between the various intermediate courts of appeal just below the Supreme Court often are not resolved, leaving conflicting interpretations of federal and constitutional law in force in different parts of the country. Similarly, the Supreme Court of Canada has become much more stringent in granting leave to appeal. Over the past decade the success rate of those seeking leave to appeal from the provincial courts of appeal and the federal court of appeal has declined from just under 30 per cent to just over 15 per cent.[10] With an annual output of 80 to 90 decisions, the Supreme Court of Canada can review only 1 to 2 per cent of the four to five thousand decisions rendered by the provincial and federal courts of appeal each year. This means that these intermediate courts of appeal become in effect final courts of appeal on many legal issues.

This trend has wider implications in Canada than in the United States. Here, as in the United States, the likelihood of lower courts conflicts in the interpretation of constitutional law or federal law being

---

9 For discussion of the problem, see (1983), 66 *Judicature* 394 (transcript of a panel discussion examining the Supreme Court's work load and what can be done to alleviate it) and (1983), 97 *Harvard Law Review* 307 (addendum on "Of High Designs: A compendium of proposals to reduce the workload of the Supreme Court").

10 For the situation up to 1985 see P.H. Russell, *The Judiciary in Canada: The Third Branch of Government* (Toronto: McGraw-Hill Ryerson, 1985), chapter 14 and for more recent statistics see Appendix 2 of *Report of the Canadian Bar Association on the Supreme Court of Canada*, above, note 7.

left unresolved increases as access to the Supreme Court is reduced. But the Canadian Supreme Court has a wider mandate than its American counterpart: as a general court of appeal, the Canadian Supreme Court is the final court of appeal on all aspects of provincial law. Cases turning solely on issues of provincial law — bear in mind that this category covers Quebec's Civil Code and much of our common law — have felt the impact of the Supreme Court's leave-granting stringency. Fixing the number of Supreme Court justices at nine will make it more difficult to reverse this trend. As a result, provincial courts of appeal will tend more and more to become the final courts of appeal in interpreting the laws of each province and the integrative, unifying role of the Supreme Court will decline.

It is ironic to think of this development in the context of the Meech Lake Accord proposals regarding the appointment of judges. For while these proposals give the provincial governments a primary role in the appointment of Supreme Court of Canada judges, they leave control over the appointment of provincial court of appeal judges, and the judges of the provinces' general jurisdiction trial courts, entirely in the hands of the federal government. Canada is a thoroughly federal country. The Meech Lake Accord confirms that. But what an odd federal country it is!

THE NEW APPOINTING SYSTEM

Most of the public controversy concerning the Supreme Court proposals in the Meech Lake Accord has focused on the new system proposed for selecting Supreme Court judges. Under this system the federal government continues to appoint, but provincial governments take on the role of nominators in the appointing process. The federal government cannot be forced to accept any provincial nominee — but in filling a Quebec vacancy it must eventually appoint a person named by the Quebec government, and for all other vacancies, a person named by the government of a province other than Quebec. Only where a Chief Justice is appointed from within the Supreme Court would the federal government not be required to appoint a provincial nominee.

In a constitutional democracy like Canada which has come to assign such an important role to the judiciary in adjudicating disputes about the powers of governments and the rights of citizens, it is inappropriate for the executive of one level of government to control unilaterally the appointment of judges to the court that heads up the judicial branch. A check and a balance is needed in principle. There is just too much at stake to leave the Prime Minister and cabinet — one group of politicians — with an untrammeled opportunity to load the Court with their political cronies or their ideological soul-mates. Admittedly, in practice, over the past twenty years, despite one-party dominance for most of the period (seven members of the current Supreme Court were appointed by the Trudeau Liberal governments and two by the Mulroney Conservative government), Supreme Court appointments have been neither partisan in the traditional sense nor ideologically imbalanced. Provincial governments, senior members of the judiciary, professional groups and pressure groups have been consulted or listened to by the federal justice minister and Prime Minister in making their selections. But constitutional provisions designed for the long-term future — a future which will see much more political interest in Supreme Court appointments — cannot rely on such benign informal practices.

Provincial governments may seem inappropriate agencies for checking and balancing the federal government in filling Supreme Court vacancies. However, in the future, civil liberties issues arising out of the interpretation of the Charter of Rights, much more than federalism issues, will generate political interest in Supreme Court appointments. These issues cut across federal-provincial lines. Still, provincial governments are the strongest countervailing political force confronting the federal government between elections. In this sense, the provincial governments in Canada serve a function similar to that of the Senate in the United States. Among the provinces there are likely to be governments as opposed to the federal government on civil liberties issues as on federalism issues. Provincial governments are well placed to ensure that there is ideological balance and diversity in the Supreme Court. Ideological pluralism must be the objective — not ideological neutrality. We should not expect men and women to come to the Supreme Court as empty vessels devoid of strong positions on the major philosophical and jurisprudential issues facing the Court. The underlying values and perspectives of judges do make a difference. The support for provincial rights of Mr. Justices Beetz and Pigeon, for example, was an important factor in preventing the centralism of Chief Justice Laskin from dominating the Supreme Court. Today Mr. Justice McIntyre and Madame Justice Wilson seem a long way apart on the Charter of Rights: McIntyre J. inclines towards a fair measure of deference for Legislatures in the limits they attach to rights and freedom whereas Wilson J. is more inclined to treat rights and freedoms as absolutes. Whether the next one or two appointees lean more towards one of these justices than the other can make an enormous difference in the Charter's impact on the country. The United States in modern times has been saved from an ideologically one-sided Court by the swing of the national political pendulum and the frequent failure of Democrats or Republicans to control both the Presidency and the Senate. In Canada, one-party dominance of the national capital has been more frequent and enduring.

Supreme Court vacancies do not occur at regular intervals nor are they co-ordinated with elections. As a result some Canadian Prime Ministers, like some U.S. Presidents, will have exceptional opportunities to have a very long-run influence on the Supreme Court's orientation. Barring death or early retirement, the next Supreme Court vacancy will not occur until 1991 when Chief Justice Dickson reaches the mandatory retirement age of 75 (Meech Lake entrenches compulsory retirement at age 75). A Prime Minister who is in office from 1991 to 1994 might have three vacancies to fill while a Prime Minister fortunate enough to hold office from 1999 to 2003 would be in a position to totally reshape the Court by appointing a majority of its members.

The present Chief Justice of the United States, William Rehnquist, has defended the tendency of American Presidents to use an ideological litmus test in selecting Supreme Court nominees.[11] Rehnquist argues that such a practice ensures that the views of the citizenry who elected the President influence appointments to an otherwise undemocratic branch of government. The trouble with this view is that the President is elected for a term of four years, whereas the judges he appoints may remain in office for decades and the ideology which the President hopes his appointees will bring to bear on the cutting edge of the law represents at best only half of the national political community. Laurence Tribe's recent work on this subject demonstrates how court-packing has enabled several U.S. Presidents to continue to have their point of view imposed on legislative programs long after they have left office.[12] Constitutional provisions that force Supreme Court appointments to reflect a wider consensus provide some protection against this danger.

Under the Meech Lake system, Quebec appointments to the

---

11 W.H. Rehnquist, *The Supreme Court: How It Was, How It Is* (New York: William Morrow, 1987).

12 L.H. Tribe, *God Save This Honorable Court: How The Choice of Supreme Court Justices Shapes Our History* (New York: Random House, 1985).

Supreme Court must be made by a consensus of federal and Quebec governments. Filling the other six positions will give the federal government a little more room for manoeuvring. Consider what might happen when Chief Justice Dickson's place comes open four years from now. The federal government will likely respect the regional representation convention and, since Justice Dickson came from Manitoba, begin discussions with western provincial governments. In the first instance, the federal government, would likely be most interested in finding out whom Saskatchewan and Alberta are considering for nominations as there will be no one from these provinces on the Court, assuming British Columbia's Mr. Justice McIntyre is still serving. Saskatchewan might well be given priority in consideration as it has been unrepresented on the Court for a longer time than Alberta. Saskatchewan and Alberta would put forward some names — likely outstanding members of their (federally-appointed) provincial courts of appeal. The federal government might ask them to consider some additional candidates — for instance, a northern jurist from a territorial court or a prairie son or daughter on the federal court. If neither Saskatchewan nor Alberta put forward names acceptable to Ottawa, British Columbia or Manitoba nominees would likely be considered next. But the political cost of violating the regionalism convention is such that the federal government is most unlikely to thumb its nose at the West and appoint an Atlantic province or Ontario nominee. Thus, when an "Ontario vacancy" is being filled. Ontario's leverage will be almost as great as Quebec's unless, as in 1979, Ontario itself volunteers to set aside its claim.

Previous proposals for provincial participation in Supreme Court appointments contained mechanisms, some of them very complex, for breaking deadlocks between the two levels of government. The absence of such a mechanism from the Meech Lake proposals has attracted a good deal of criticism. It does mean in the case of Quebec vacancies, in particular, that a position on the Court may remain unfilled for quite some time while governments work towards a consensus over the replacement. Nevertheless, the Court's political authority in the country will be best served if its members are appointed on the basis of an intergovernmental consensus.

There is no mechanism for breaking a deadlock in the American system. The recent Senate confirmation hearings of Robert Bork demonstrated how that system, by forcing the President and the Senate to reach a consensus, resulted in the rejection of an ideological extremist. In the United States, Supreme Court vacancies have been left unfilled for as long as five years. It is certainly possible that the need for consensus will delay the filling of positions on the Canadian Supreme Court. But this will not be disastrous. Unfortunately, the Court seldom sits as a full nine-judge Court; five and seven judge panels are the norm. Delay in filling vacancies is a lesser evil than appointing judges who lack the respect of both levels of government.

One factor which will promote federal-provincial convergence in the operation of the new appointing system is that most candidates for Supreme Court positions come from the intermediate courts of appeal. With the exception of Mr. Justice Estey, all of the judges currently serving on the Supreme Court were elevated from either a provincial court of appeal or the federal court of appeal. (Mr. Justice Estey served on the Ontario Court of Appeal before becoming Chief Justice of the High Court of Ontario, the province's superior trial court.) Recruiting Supreme Court justices from the appellate courts just below the Supreme Court has become the prevailing practice in both Canada and the United States. In neither country has it been a legal requirement. Under the Meech Lake amendments it will still be possible to appoint lawyers who have had no previous judicial experience to the Supreme Court. (The last such appointment was that of Mr. Justice de Grandpré who served from 1974 to 1977). Nonetheless, both the provincial and federal governments will, in all likelihood, continue to look primarily to the highest courts of the provinces and the Federal Court of Canada for candidates. It is in these courts that the craft of appellate opinion writing is developed and displayed. Moreover, the opinions of appeal court judges provide a clearer and more salient guide to a prospective appointee's jurisprudential and value orientation than will the record of most lawyers. This primary recruitment pool is, of course, composed entirely of judges appointed by the federal government.

A more logical system of federal-provincial collaboration in appointing Supreme Court judges would be to have the federal government nominate and the provinces confirm. Under the system proposed, no government may feel responsible for conducting a genuine talent search or for carefully considering the functional needs of the Court. The Canadian Supreme Court, as a general court of appeal, has a very diverse jurisdiction — much more diverse than that of the American Supreme Court. Even now with Charter cases streaming up to the Court, cases involving constitutional law account for less than a quarter of the cases it decides. Administrative and criminal law constitute the largest categories of court work, while the Court continues to write opinions on important issues of private law in such areas as personal liability, commercial and family law. From a functional perspective it is far more important to have expertise on the Court in these different areas of law than it is to represent the provinces or regions of the country.

One way in which the new system might be made to work a good deal better is to put in place judicial nominating committees along the lines advocated by the Canadian Bar Association. Since 1967 a national committee of the Bar Association has vetted persons being considered by the federal government for judicial appointments. The Bar committee's role in this appointment process has been entirely passive. It simply reports whether candidates are "highly qualified", "qualified" or "not qualified". Promotions within the federally-appointed judiciary have usually not been referred to the committee. On the basis of an intensive study of the judicial appointment system, the Bar Association has recommended that its national committee on the judiciary be replaced by advisory nominating committees.[13] These broadly-based committees, established in each province, with an additional committee for federal courts, would be constituted by representatives of the federal and provincial governments, appropriate chief justices, representatives of the Bar and the general public. A similar proposal has been put forward by the Canadian Association of Law Teachers.[14] Unlike the present Bar committee, these new committees would be active in recruiting and interviewing candidates as well as performing a screening function.

Broadly-based nominating committees are most urgently needed to improve the quality of appointments to the s. 96 courts of the provinces and the federal court of Canada. The federal government makes, on average, over fifty appointments to these courts each year. The Bar Association study found "political favouritism" had an undue influence in selecting candidates for these positions. If these committees were in place in each province when Supreme Court vacancies came open, they could develop short lists of candidates from which the provincial governments could select nominees. The participation of both levels of government in these committees would reduce the likelihood of deadlocks. But it should be stressed that the point of using these committees as a first step in judicial selection is not to take politics out of the appointing process. Given the enormous role

---

13 Canadian Bar Association Committee on the Appointment of Judges, *Report of the Canadian Bar Association Committee on the Appointment of Judges* (Ottawa: Canadian Bar Foundation, 1985).

14 See J.S. Ziegel, "Federal Judicial Appointments in Canada: The Time is Ripe for Change" (1987), 37 U.T.L.J. 1. The CALT proposes a special committee for Supreme Court nominations.

our courts now have in governing us, that would be both naive and inappropriate. The purpose of the committees is to broaden and balance the professional considerations and political interests which shape the pool of candidates from which politicians make the final selections.

We know far too little about the operation of nominating committees to have them entrenched in the Constitution. But there is much to be gained by setting them up on an informal and experimental basis. The federal government will make more headway with the provinces if, instead of trying to legislate a single format for these committees, it works with individual provinces or perhaps, in the case of the Atlantic provinces, a group of provinces, at designing a committee structure acceptable to the province or region. A number of provinces, in particular British Columbia, have for many years relied extensively on advisory nominating committees in selecting judges to serve on their lower courts. Some of these provinces may well wish to build on this experience. All of the provinces should be interested in working with the federal government on arrangements which will enable them to participate on a more systematic basis in selecting judges to their higher courts.

OPENING UP THE APPOINTMENT PROCESS

While the nominating committees proposed by the Canadian Bar Association might expand the recruitment networks and give more systematic attention to the functional needs of the Court, can they do much to open up the appointment process to public purview? Canadians have watched with fascination the U.S. Senate's judiciary committee cross-examine nominees for the United States Supreme Court under the hot glare of television cameras. This fascination, I suspect, has been tinged with horror. It is doubtful whether many Canadians or many candidates for high judicial office in Canada are prepared for such public exposure of the judicial selection process. A decade ago, when the Canadian Bar Association's Committee on the Constitution recommended that prospective appointees to the Supreme Court be reviewed by a parliamentary committee, the C.B.A. committee stipulated that this review take place *in camera*. This proposal, like others put forward by the Pépin-Robarts Task Force and the MacDonald Royal Commission on The Economic Union, all relied on a reformed upper house to carry out this review function.[15]

---

15 For a summary of these proposals see Appendix 3 of *Report of the Canadian Bar Association Committee on the Supreme Court of Canada*, above, note 7.

As Canadians come to recognize more clearly than they do now the enormous responsibility of our judges — above all the judges who sit on the Supreme Court of Canada — demand for more accountability in the appointing process will increase. If a person is being considered for appointment to such a powerful office in shaping the rights of citizens and the powers of government for years to come, why hasn't the public a right to know something about that individual's qualifications and character, and where he or she stands on the basic principles of the Constitution and the role of the judiciary? Already there are voices raising this question in the popular media and calling for American style confirmation hearings by a parliamentary committee.[16]

Under the appointing system envisaged by the Meech Lake proposals, the federal government could use a parliamentary committee to advise it on provincial nominees. But unlike the American system in which the confirming body, the Senate, considers one nominee at a time, the Meech Lake system is likely to produce a number of provincial nominees for each vacancy, even though there is no requirement that the provinces submit lists of nominees. Thus a parliamentary hearing might degenerate into a popularity contest among candidates ambitious enough to let their names stand. Alternatively, provincial governments, which are the key nominators in the Meech Lake system, might establish hearings before committees of their legislative assemblies as a step in developing lists of provincial nominees.

Instead of using the American legislative confirmation hearing as the model, Canadians would be better advised to increase accountability through the federal-provincial nominating committees discussed above. The membership of these committees would make them better equipped than legislative committees to probe prospective judges' constitutional theories, professional skills and integrity of character. At the very least, the public should know when these committees are meeting to consider candidates for a vacancy. The committees should be open to receiving names for consideration from all quarters and their short lists of proposed nominees should be published. Beyond this, in the more daring jurisdictions, the committees might even experiment with interviewing leading candidates in sessions open to the public.

---

16 A.C. Hutchinson, "Veil of Secrecy on Top Judges should be Lifted" *The [Toronto] Globe and Mail* (6 March 1987) 7; J.R. Finlay, "Cast Off The Cloak of Secrecy" *The [Toronto] Globe and Mail* (22 October 1987) 7.

From the perspective of populist democratic theory, the case for opening up the process of judicial appointments has great merit. But it will not easily move the present generation of Canadian political leaders. They dance to a different democratic tune: they practise elite accommodation within a system of consociational democracy.[17] It was an elite accommodation, an agreement reached in private by first ministers, that produced the Meech Lake Accord. The conflicting streams of public criticism directed at the Accord — too little for Quebec for some Quebeckers, far too much for Quebec for others — suggest how unlikely it is that a constitutional accommodation with Quebec could have been reached at this stage in Canadian history by a more popular form of constitutional politics. In any event, this traditional style of intergovernmental decision-making — the bargaining of federal and provincial leaders behind closed doors — which produced the Accord will also, in the short-term, dominate the judicial appointment system provided for in the Accord.

Alan Cairns has pointed to the discrepancy between Canada's top-down, government-controlled style of Constitution-making and the tendency of the Charter of Rights to generate a more popular sense of constitutionalism.[18] In the future popular constitutional concerns are bound to focus on the process of judicial selection. The distinct society clause in the Meech Lake Accord is a case in point. That clause is pregnant with contradictory possibilities. It might, as the Bourassa government would like its followers to believe and as the Accord's critics fear, give Quebec greater autonomy in pursuing its own cultural policies. On the other hand, it may be essentially symbolic not expanding the legislative powers of Quebec in any significant way. We cannot be sure whether either of these possibilities or something in between will be realized; we can only be sure that it will be judges — most of all the judges on the Supreme Court of Canada — who decide. People whose hopes are dashed or whose fears are fulfilled by the Court's approach to this clause are those who will likely resort to judicial politics more readily than constitutional politics and will attempt to reverse their losses by influencing the judicial selection process. It is then that the arrangements for appointing Supreme Court judges will have their severest test.

---

17 See K. McRae, ed., *Consociational Democracy: Political Accommodation in Segmented Societies* (Toronto: McClelland & Stewart, 1974).

18 See A. Cairns, "The Limited Constitutional Vision of Meech Lake" in this volume at p. 247.

Meech Lake and
the Future of Senate Reform

J. Peter Meekison

This year Canada celebrates another centennial — 100 years of discussion on Senate reform — making this topic the all-time favourite of would-be reformers. In 1887, at the first intergovernmental conference following Confederation, the premiers stated:

> that a leading purpose of the Senate was to protect the interests of the respective Provinces as such; that a Senate to which the appointments are made by the Federal Government, and for life, affords no adequate security to the Provinces; and that, in case no other early remedy is provided, the British North America Act should be so amended as to limit the term for which Senators hold office, and to give the choice, as vacancies occur, to the Province to which the vacancy belongs, until, as to any Province, one half of the members of the Senate representing such Province are senators chosen by the Province; that thereafter the mode of selection be as follows: if the vacancy is occasioned by the death, resignation, or otherwise of a Senator chosen by a Province, that Province to choose his successor; and if the vacancy is occasioned by the death, resignation, or otherwise of any other Senator, the vacancy to be filled as now provided by the Act, but only for a limited term of years.[1]

Their proposals have a very modern ring.

The pressures for reform result from two different and, in certain respects, conflicting perspectives: first, a desire for parliamentary reform and, second, the demand for more effective regional representation. Development of either of these two themes leads Canadians

---

1 "Minutes of Interprovincial Conference held at Quebec, October 20-28, 1877," *Dominion-Provincial and Interprovincial Conferences from 1887 to 1926* (reprinted, Ottawa: King's Printer, 1951) at 21.

down very different paths. Provinces tend to focus on more effective regional representation, while the federal government is more likely to concern itself with parliamentary reform. Their ability to combine both perspectives will test Canadians' willingness to compromise.

What are the components of the Senate reform debate? They are perhaps best reflected in the "Triple E" concept advocated by the Alberta government: equal, elected, and effective. When considering Senate reform, the questions most central to the subject are as follows:

(1.) Equal — Should provinces have equal representation, or should there be some other formula for determining provincial representation?
(2.) Elected — Should senators be elected (directly by the people or by a form of electoral college) or
(3.) Effective — Should the legislative authority of the Senate be equal to or less than that of the House of Commons? Should the Senate have any special responsibilities similar, for example, to those of the United States Senate over treaties and appointments? How should differences between the Senate and the House of Commons be resolved?

One other question should not be overlooked: when a reform proposal takes shape, what will be the possible consequences of the proposed changes for our parliamentary system of Government? One cannot speculate on answers to this particular question until a specific agreement has been reached. At that time, supporters and critics of the agreement can be expected to line up on either side of the question, depending upon what they think may happen. It is difficult enough to speculate on what might emerge as an acceptable model for Senate reform, let alone the consequences of the reform. To be sure, when exploring the dimensions of each question, one cannot overlook the potential effects of proposed changes. But to those advocating a particular position, acceptance of that position is usually more significant than worrying about what might happen if it is accepted. A specific position articulated is a given, while the potential consequences of accepting that position are more in the realm of conjecture.

A similar conundrum arises in the debate over the Meech Lake Accord. One line of reasoning is that, with the changes to the amending formula, Senate reform will be impossible, yet no one can state with *absolute* certainty that this is true. To be fair, the only reasonable position is one based on probabilities, not absolutes.

Outlining the principal issues associated with Senate reform is the easy part. Securing an understanding of the myriad reasons for reform is only the first necessary step to achieving it; at least then individuals and Governments will know why a particular position is being advanced. For example, individuals concerned about situations where the Senate can block a bill approved by the House of Commons will seek solutions which will curb the powers of the upper house. Alternatively, individuals preoccupied with regional issues may be more inclined to concentrate on ways in which House of Commons legislation unwelcome to the provinces can be blocked. Both are equally legitimate objectives, but with diametrically opposed solutions.

SOME CANADIAN PROBLEMS

Each political system has its distinct problems and the Canadian system is no exception. In tackling Senate reform, these problems must be recognized during the debate. This does not mean their resolution must, of necessity, be incorporated into or protected by the suggested changes to the Constitution but, the chances of success increase the more that these idiosyncratic factors can be accommodated.

The first Canadian peculiarity that comes to mind is the position of Quebec. At Confederation it was allotted one-third of the Senate seats. Since then, its share has decreased to slightly less than one-quarter. The principle of equality of provinces (if agreed to) would reduce Quebec's voting strength to one-tenth or less, depending upon territorial representation. Should other provinces be added, the effective weight of Quebec would be further eroded. Would-be reformers cannot overlook this problem. Any solution must, in some way, take into account Quebec's interests. This reality has recently been reinforced by the recognition of Quebec as a distinct society in the Meech Lake Accord.

The second distinct Canadian characteristic is the tremendous disparity between the smallest province, Prince Edward Island, and the largest, Ontario. (I am omitting the even greater discrepancy that would exist between, say, the Yukon and Ontario.) If the principle of provincial equality is accepted, no problem would exist. On the other hand, the magnitude of the disparity makes it the focal point of the debate. I speak from personal experience, when I state that whenever the idea of provincial equality is addressed during discussions on the amending formula, one invariably hears, "But what about P.E.I.?"

The third characteristic has been alluded to earlier. Canada is a federal state with a parliamentary system of government. Changes affecting the dynamics of either of these political structures may have definite consequences for the others. For example, will Senate reform have an adverse effect on the operation of cabinet Government? Will it have an adverse effect on federal-provincial relations? Will it strengthen or erode the position of provincial Governments? Each of these questions has been raised in the past. The direction reform takes will be guided by individual perceptions (perhaps unspoken) of the likely effect on either or both of our two major political institutions.

THE 1987 MEECH LAKE ACCORD

By way of background it should be recalled that the ten premiers at their 1986 annual meeting agreed to limit these constitutional negotiations to Quebec's five items and to begin a further round of negotiations which, among other things, would include Senate reform and fisheries. Some provinces, including Alberta, were concerned that enthusiasm for future discussions might disappear once Quebec's proposals had been adopted. As a result, the premiers added a sixth item to the agenda ensuring a continuation of the process.

How does the Meech Lake Accord affect Senate reform? There are three provisions found in the Accord which relate to the Senate and Senate reform.

The Amending Formula: The amendment to the amending formula incorporates what is now s. 42 of the Constitution Act, 1982[2] into s. 41. Section 42 includes references to the Senate. The effect of this amendment will be to make future changes to the Senate subject to the unanimity clause found in s. 41, as opposed to the clause requiring two-thirds of the provinces representing 50 per cent of the population.

Constitutional Conferences: Section 50 of the Accord provides for an annual constitutional conference. Included on the agenda is the subject of Senate reform. Until reform is achieved, it will be the subject of *annual* debate at this conference.

Interim Appointments: Until Senate reform is a reality, the federal government will appoint members from lists provided by the provinces. This provision is an interim one until the anticipated reform takes place. While what constitutes reform is not specified, presumably this section will be deleted, as will the references to Senate reform on

---

2 Being Schedule B of the Canada Act 1982 (U.K.), c. 11. See relevant sections in the Appendix to this volume.

the agenda of the constitutional conference, when a new constitutional provision is unanimously agreed to.

CONSEQUENCES FOR REFORM

Two of the most frequently expressed criticisms of the Accord as it relates to Senate reform are that the unanimity requirement for change has made reform impossible, and that the provinces will get to enjoy their new responsibilities for nominating senators forever. What was seen as a temporary "reform" will become permanent. Indeed, it has been suggested that provincial appointment is the only reform that will materialize from the Accord. Are these criticisms valid?

I disagree with the view that the prospects for Senate reform are dismal, for a variety of reasons. First, there is the implicit assumption that Senate reform is easy or easier under the amendment provisions of s. 42 than under the proposed changes. Senate reform will be difficult under any formula. In my opinion, the change to the amending formula does not make change any more difficult. It has been argued that neither Quebec nor Ontario will give up their clout in any reformed Senate. If that is the case, the 50 per cent requirement found in the existing formula would not be met, even if eight (not seven) provinces favoured a change. People are too quick to look at the two-thirds rule and ignore the 50 per cent population requirement. I also find it difficult to believe that any federal government would recommend reform of the Senate to Parliament over the strong objections of either Quebec or Ontario.

The proposed unanimity requirement also establishes a different political dynamic than that which operates under the general amending formula. There is no need to form or to seek coalitions or alliances when you have a veto. At the same time, it is very difficult to cast a veto when all around you are seeking a change. The dynamics of intergovernmental negotiations generally force governments to find a compromise solution. That was true of the Meech Lake agreement and it has been true in the past. The myth that unanimity is impossible to achieve is not substantiated historically. The Unemployment Insurance Amendment of 1940 and the amendments affecting pensions in 1951 and 1964 are three examples.

Discussions on Senate reform will not take place in a vacuum. Other subjects will be on the agenda. I assume that governments will enter these future discussions with a view to reaching an agreement or agreements of some kind. A quickly cast veto on Senate reform could lead to rejection of other proposed changes. From my experience, governments are more likely to agree on reforms when a variety of topics are discussed simultaneously, as some recognition and attention must be given to the different priorities and concerns of each government.

All of the foregoing assumes that the House of Commons will accept whatever the provinces and the federal Government agree to. They may or may not. But their position has nothing to do whatsoever with the unanimity rule, since under any formula they must concur.

Nor do I accept the view that provinces will enjoy their temporary responsibility for recommending names of Senators to the Government of Canada so much that Senate reform will be sidelined. It will take a long time before the entire Senate is changed by this means. I predict, also, that the public will grow weary of yet another annual failure as first ministers meet on the topic. That alone should expedite change. The idea of celebrating the bicentennial of Senate reform somehow seems highly unlikely.

In summary, I would argue that pressures for reform will increase because the requirements of an annual conference will eventually force governments to find an acceptable compromise solution. It will be increasingly difficult to explain their inability to resolve this issue. Moreover, without Meech Lake, Senate reform would be less likely to happen. Given Quebec's unwillingness to participate in constitutional discussions, it is very doubtful that the federal Government would seriously pursue substantive changes to the Senate without Quebec's active involvement.

What are some possible solutions for the future? It should be realized that insistence on absolutes will lead to deadlock, and that in turn will lead to failure. As a result, initial discussions will be likely to focus on some of the problems associated with reform and the range of possible solutions. Governments will have to decide whether or not they are more interested in gaining limited objectives on certain elements of reform as opposed to winning everything. Once the landscape has been charted, the more easily agreed upon issues can be resolved. The easiest one on which to gain an understanding is election. To be sure, questions will be raised as to the timing and under whose rules, but there will be few differences on the principle.

The principle of equality, while laudable, will in all probability be modified. Most reform proposals developed to date have recognized that the current distribution is anachronistic and inequitable, leading invariably to recommendations for increased representation from Western Canada. The basis of a compromise will require governments to reduce the inequities and move towards the principle of equality without ignoring the realities of population distribution. To illustrate my point, the following method of distribution accomplishes both objectives:

x seats for 4 million +
y seats for 2-4 million
z seats for 0-2 million

Using the West German method of distributing seats, x would equal 5, y would equal 4, and z would equal 3. An agreement along these lines overcomes the small province problem, while recognizing the population of Ontario and Quebec. Short of accepting equality, this approach (or a variant) has the greatest chance of success.

Offsetting an agreement on this principle is recognition that a reformed and elected legislature will compete with the House of Commons. Accordingly, there will be pressure to reduce the existing legislative powers. The task will be to draw the line between measures requiring an absolute veto, as opposed to a suspensive veto. This approach ensures that for certain matters the will of the House of Commons — with its large number of members from Central Canada — will prevail, and this should reduce the concerns over the diminution of the relative weight of Quebec and Ontario. It would also assist in overcoming possible objections from the House of Commons.

Certain matters may need to be spelled out in greater detail, such as a special role for Quebec on linguistic and cultural issues. Other specific provisions of particular importance to individual provinces might also be considered. In addition, certain special responsibilities, such as screening appointments, might be examined. What is critical here is that individual concerns be addressed and, if possible, reconciled, so that the entire debate does not collapse over a very specific issue. Because of the need for fine tuning, the final structure will likely be more complex than that found in the Constitution of our neighbours to the south.

One finds similar concerns and compromises reflected in the amending formula. It is far more complex and detailed because it was written after the fact. The same dilemma will be confronted by those pursuing Senate reform. Senate reform will not be accomplished over-night, but it can be a reality after the dimensions of the debate are fully understood. Only then can the compromises necessary for agreement be made.

Meech Lake and Federalism:
Accord or Discord?*

Thomas J. Courchene

INTRODUCTION

For many Canadians, the Meech Lake Accord has clearly touched a sensitive nerve. One has to go a fair way back in our history[1] to find the sense of concern, let alone outrage, that has attended the public debate surrounding the Accord. Words such as "dangerous", "catastrophic", "tragedy" and "betrayal" feature prominently in letters to the editor, op-ed features, and indeed in academic writings. Some couch their consternation in more literary terms: for example, "the tree of Canada is being gnawed to pieces by the insects of political expedience."[2] The dominant theme appears to be that the federal

---

* An earlier and expanded version of this paper was prepared for the Special Joint Committee of the Senate and the House of Commons on the Meech Lake Accord. While the substance has remained intact, I have taken the opportunity to incorporate selected aspects of the burgeoning literature on Meech Lake, including the *Report of the Joint Committee of the Senate and House of Commons on the 1987 Constitutional Accord* (Ottawa, Queen's Printer, 1987). It is a pleasure to acknowledge many helpful discussions with my York colleagues, Peter Hogg and Don Smiley and, as always, with my University of Western Ontario colleague Bob Young. Responsibility for what follows rests with me.

1 But not very far "forward" in our history, since the more recent Canada-U.S. free trade agreement has relegated Meech Lake to a distant second place in the public debate. One could also argue that the National Energy Program generated more hostility than Meech Lake. But here the issue involved billions of dollars in rents, profits and labour income, and, unlike the Accord, it pitted premier against premier and the West against Ottawa.

2 D. Birkenheier, "Tree of Canada Gnawed to Pieces," Letter to the Editor, *The* [Toronto] *Globe and Mail* (6 June 1987).

government has sold out to the provinces. Thus the often-quoted refrain: who speaks for Canada?

My view of the Accord is quite different. In general, one can probably group those in favour of the Accord into two camps. First, there are those who have some concern with the detailed provisions, but feel that these concerns are more than offset by having Quebec resume its rightful place as a full participant in Canada's constitutional development. Phrased differently, this position would assert that Meech Lake is not a very high price (some would say a surprisingly low price) to pay for bringing Quebec fully into the Canadian family.[3] Second, there are those who, while recognizing the value of bringing Quebec on-side, also like the detailed substance of Meech Lake. I fall in this latter category although, as will become evident in the analysis that follows, some of the implications of the Accord are far-reaching and will require substantial and probably rather immediate further accommodation or adjustment.

Meech Lake is only the first of what will likely be a series of initiatives and amendments designed to allow Canada to seek and find a new internal balance or equilibrium in response to the provisions of the Canadian Charter of Rights and Freedoms[4] and, more generally, to the Constitution Act, 1982. Regardless of one's view of the Charter, it is nonetheless exercising an "Americanizing" or "republicanizing" influence on Canada because it introduces U.S.-style checks and balances (i.e. the Supreme Court and individual rights) into the former "Parliament-is-supreme" concept of Canadian federalism. Thus, Meech Lake has much less to do with the fact that Quebec was left out of the 1982 arrangements than with the implications of these arrangements for Quebec and, more generally, Canada. But I am getting ahead of my story.

In what follows, I intend to tackle the criticisms of Meech Lake and in the process argue that the Accord is not only a positive, albeit controversial, step in the evolution of Canadian federalism but also a rather inevitable step. My paper begins with some rather general

---

3 Laurent Picard in "L'entente doit être signée" *Le Devoir* [*de Montréal*] (1 June 1987) presents an intriguing analysis of why the Accord must be signed: "No government of Quebec could ever accept an agreement that offered any less than what is now on the table" and "no government of Canada could ever offer any more than what is now on the table" (translated). Picard notes that there are some non-central yet not insignificant changes that might be made to improve the Accord further, but he doubts that the equilibrium can be moved: "By the very nature of negotiating, there can be no further negotiations."

4 Being Part I of the Constitution Act, 1982 [enacted by the Canada Act 1982 (U.K.), c. 11, s. 1].

observations and analysis relating to the interaction between Canadian policy-making and the Constitution. To be sure, the context here is much broader than the specifics of Meech Lake, but it does provide the backdrop necessary for evaluating the various provisions of the Accord. The first part of this section focuses on the degree to which "constitutional architecture" predetermines the way in which Canadians go about resolving the pressing policy issues of the day. Anticipating the analysis somewhat, the suggested answer is "not much" and I think that this will apply to Meech Lake as well. The section then concludes with a subjective interpretation of the manner in which the Charter is altering our political and constitutional landscape. With this as backdrop, the remainder of the paper deals selectively with various provisions of the Accord, beginning with those aspects that relate directly to the earlier discussion of the Charter, namely the "distinct society" clause, the appointment of Supreme Court Justices and Senate reform. A later section will focus on the amending power. A brief conclusion completes the paper.

THE POLICY PROCESS AND THE DIVISION OF POWERS[5]

Constitutional Determinism

I begin with a question that has long intrigued me and presumably others as well. It is generally recognized that in many areas Canada is more decentralized than is the United States. Suppose, however, that in 1776 or, more correctly, in 1787, the U.S. had adopted our Constitution and in 1867 we adopted theirs: would Canada still be the more decentralized federation? This is, of course, a counterfactual question, but my hunch is that even if we inherited the U.S. Constitution in 1867 we would, today, still be more decentralized than the U.S. There is nothing in the U.S. political economy that compares with the power and influence that Ontario wields in Canada. Likewise, there is no U.S. equivalent to Quebec. Moreover, the U.S. homogenization or melting-pot approach to cultural and regional diversity is at odds with our approach to region and culture. To be fair, however, much of what we see in the U.S. could be constitutionally driven.

Nonetheless, this question is all the more interesting because a straightforward reading of our Constitution would suggest that Canada

---

5 This section derives from T.J. Courchene, *Economic Management and the Division of Powers*, MacDonald Commission Studies, vol. 67 (Toronto: University of Toronto Press, 1986) various chapters.

ought to be considerably more centralized than it is. In particular, the residual power would appear, on first reading at least, to reside with the federal government. And this was presumably the intention. After all, our fathers of Confederation, while writing the BNA Act,[6] must have glanced more than once to the south and to the civil war and concluded that they did not want a Constitution that enhanced states' rights or provincial rights to the same extent as the U.S.

Yet we have emerged as the more decentralized federation. One way of rationalizing all of this is that our founding fathers made an enormous mistake. Although they probably intended the residual clause to reside with Ottawa, they also included s. 92 (enumerating provincial powers) in the Constitution. In the U.S., the residual power clearly resides with the states. But since there is no elaboration of state powers, successive judicial interpretations have tended to enhance the powers of the central government. One can almost visualize the process: judges faced with new issues will try to link them to one or another of federal powers. Only if this exercise fails will the residual clause apply. In Canada, however, the potential for the declaratory power or the peace, order and good government (POGG) power to become the residual power was constrained by the fact that there existed an enumerated series of provincial powers. If the authors intended POGG to be all-powerful, why did they include a s. 92? The point can be made in another way. The wording of the U.S. interstate commerce clause is very close to our trade and commerce clauses.[7] Yet the reach of the former is, from a Canadian perspective, astonishingly broad. One of the differences in judicial interpretation of these clauses may be the enumeration of provincial powers in s. 92. This offers at least one explanation for why Canada ended up being a more decentralized federation than the U.S.

However, in addition to constitutional bases, many deep-rooted regional, cultural, geographic and linguistic factors also point in the direction of decentralization. It is possible to become too enamoured with "constitutional determinism", that is, with the proposition that the written constitutional word straitjackets the manner in which a federalism evolves. Two examples to the contrary will suffice. Both examples are central to the operation of Canadian federalism today and neither has any link to the Constitution Act, 1867. Moreover, these features do not play a significant role in the U.S. federation. The first

---

6 British North American Act, 1867 (U.K.), c. 3 [now the Constitution Act, 1867].
7 Found in ss. 91(2) and 121 of the Constitution Act, 1867.

example relates to equalization payments to the have-not provinces. While one can read some equalizing aspects into the original BNA Act (the statutory subsidies contained an element of equalization in the sense that they were per capita grants up to a specified maximum population), this is a far cry from ensuring that provinces have access to "reasonably comparable levels of public services at reasonably comparable tax rates" (the new constitutional provision on equalization). Yet equalization payments have become so much a part of the glue that binds us together as a nation that they were enshrined in the Constitution Act, 1982.[8]

The second example relates to executive federalism — the process by which executives of the ten provinces and the federal government meet to sort out common problems — the apex of which is the first ministers' conference. Safarian has argued that executive federalism is Canada's "contribution to the art of federalism".[9] In order to relate executive federalism to the Canadian context, it is appropriate to step back a bit and focus on alternative federal models. The U.S. is, in the current jargon, an example of intrastate federalism, where the states have their influence on federal government policy-making largely through integration into the political machinery of the centre. In the U.S. context, this is the Senate which, with equal representation by state, is called upon, among other things, to approve presidential nominations to the Supreme Court. More generally, the Senate is the forum where the individual states' interests are brought to bear on policy-making.

Our federalism is typically labelled as interstate federalism, where the interests of the various provinces are articulated through their provincial governments and then, via executive federalism, to Ottawa. The development and sophistication of executive federalism is a rather natural evolution to accommodate the constitutional void relating to the role (or lack of a role) of a provincial presence in decision-making at the centre. To be sure, numerous commentators have described the process of executive federalism as being contrary to the parliamentary system since the elected representatives of both levels of government are, in effect, presented with federal-provincial *faits accomplis*. The Meech Lake Accord falls in this category. Indeed, this constitutes one

---

8 Found in s. 36 of the Constitution Act, 1982.
9 E. Safarian, *Ten Markets or One? Regional Barriers to Economic Activity in Canada* (Toronto: Ontario Economic Council, 1980) at 18.

of the key concerns of those opposed to the Accord.[10] But federal-
provincial compacts are also characteristic of many of the federal-
provincial agreements on the shared-cost and established programs.
And, for that matter, the 1982 constitutional accord probably also falls
in this category.

In any event, the original BNA Act did not constrain the ability
of Canadians to create new processes and even new structures as and
when the need arose. It is probably going too far to claim that the
constitution is endogenous, but it is my view that when it comes to
the evolution of the federation, the constitution is at best conditioning
and not determining. While not denying an important role for the
constitutional structure, I find myself attracted to Carl Friedrich's view
of federalism:

> . . . federalism should not be seen only as a static pattern or design, characterized
> by a particular and precisely fixed division of powers between government levels.
> Federalism is also and perhaps primarily the process . . . of adopting joint policies
> and making joint decisions on joint problems.[11]

In terms of the issue at hand, most aspects of the Accord can
be viewed as contributing to the processes of Canadian federalism
rather than as part of a deterministic constitutional architecture that
is somehow going to alter the fundamental nature of the federation.
This applies to the distinct society clause and to the spending power
provision. There is, however, one aspect of Meech Lake that has
potential for profound change, namely the rather dramatic degree of
Senate reform embodied in the Accord. Later sections of the paper
will elaborate on these points.

The Charter

The Charter is clearly an exception to some of the foregoing
analysis, particularly that relating to constitutional determinism. It
has already had profound implications for the Canadian parliamentary
system. In an important sense, the Charter is very decentralizing, or
"democratizing", to adopt Albert Breton's label,[12] transferring as it
does certain powers and/or processes from legislatures to individuals
and the courts. In terms of the machinery of government, it brings

---

10 This issue will be dealt with in more detail below.
11 C. Friedrich, cited in R. Bastien, *Federalism and Decentralization: Where Do We Stand?* (Ottawa:
    Supply and Services Canada, 1981) at 48.
12 A. Breton, "Supplementary Statement" in Canada, *Report of the Royal Commission on the Economic
    Union and Development Prospects for Canada*, vol. 3 (Ottawa: Supply and Services Canada, 1985)
    486 at 526.

the courts, particularly the Supreme Court of Canada, more directly into the political process and as such adds a check and balance to the powers of legislatures or to again fall back on Breton's terminology, enhances "competitive federalism".[13]

However, the Charter can also be viewed as a centralist, or at least a centralizing, document. As Alan Cairns has noted:

> At a more profound political level . . . the Charter was an attempt to enhance and extend the meaning of being Canadian and thus to strengthen identification with the national community on which Ottawa ultimately depends for support. . . . The resultant rights and freedoms were to be country-wide in scope, enforced by a national supreme court, and entrenched in a national Constitution beyond the reach of fleeting legislative majorities at either level of government. *The consequence, and a very clear purpose, was to set limits to the diversities of treatment by provincial governments, and thus to strengthen Canadian as against provincial identities.* Rights must not be dependent on the particular place where an individual chooses to reside.[14]

More recently Cairns added, "[t]he language of rights is a Canadian language, not a provincial language".[15]

There is a second respect in which the Charter is probably centralizing, namely that the provinces are likely more vulnerable than is the federal government to its provisions. Rights and, to a lesser extent, freedoms tend to fall within the provincial domain. Already the provinces have been strongly affected by decisions under the Charter involving mandatory retirement, Sunday closing, age discrimination in welfare levels, language legislation, parochial schools and the "Rand formula" for the payment of union dues.

In order to assess the role of the Charter in the Canadian federation, it is useful to resort to the concept of "balance" in a federation.[16] Each federation inevitably goes through a long process of internal "co-existence" as it strikes a balance across many fronts: between centralization and decentralization, between the role of markets and the role of governments, between uniformity and diversity. As any review of comparative federalism will attest, this balance is struck at different places for different policies for different countries. Moreover, the balance is clearly time-dependent, as the waves of centralization and decentralization in our own federation demonstrate.

---

13 *Ibid.* at 486.

14 A. Cairns, "Recent Federalist Constitutional Proposals: A Review Essay" (1979), 5 Canadian Public Policy 348 at 354 (emphasis added).

15 A. Cairns, "The Politics of Constitutional Renewal in Canada" in K. Banting and R. Simeon eds., *Redesigning the State: The Politics of Constitutional Change in Industrial Nations* (Toronto: University of Toronto Press, 1985) 95 at 130.

16 Courchene, above, note 5 at 235-238.

Enter the Charter. It has already been and will continue to be a loose cannon on deck as far as the concept of balance is concerned. In one fell swoop, it has effectively destroyed the former balance. It will literally take generations before Canada fully integrates the Charter into its political and governmental machinery and institutions and restores a new balance to the federation. Moreover, without being able to forecast how the Charter will be applied in the future, it is difficult if not impossible to say much about the likely nature of this future balance.

Much of the rationale for Quebec's insistence on becoming a signatory to the Constitution (in spite of the fact that, according to polls, the issue was not high in the minds of individual Québécois) has, I think, to do with the potential for the Charter to undermine Quebec's "collective rights" accomplishments on the socio-economic front. Specifically, the distinct society provision is closely related to the implications of the Charter, as will be elaborated below.

With these general observations as a backdrop, I now turn to the substance of Meech Lake.

THE MEECH LAKE ACCORD

The Distinct Society Clause

The concept of enshrining in the constitution a provision that Quebec is a distinct society is not new, but the impact of the Constitution Act, 1982, and in particular the Charter, created a sense of urgency in Quebec that was heretofore absent. The Macdonald Commission captured the essence of the issue. Under the heading "Quebec as a distinct society", the Commission noted:

> In order to reach a lasting agreement between Quebec and Canada, one which ensures Quebec's place in Confederation and contributes both to the prosperity of the province and to that of the country as a whole, it is essential from the outset to go beyond the traditional clichés about the unique nature of Quebec. In this way, a realistic interpretation will emerge of the facts which apply to Quebec in 1985. However, two specific pitfalls must be avoided. The first mistake would be to seek a cultural homogeneity which embodies Quebec's distinctiveness: if such homogeneity ever existed, it is certainly no longer characteristic of the province. *The second error would be to overlook the collective aspect of the Quebec issue and to view it as a straightforward question of individual rights which could be exercised everywhere in Canada.* Since the matter concerns living, working and thriving in a mother tongue, the collective dimension is not to be underestimated.[17]

---

17 Canada, *Royal Commission on the Economic Union and Development Prospects for Canada*, vol. 3 (Ottawa: Supply and Services Canada, 1985) at 329 (Emphasis added).

Since the Charter has also to do with matters concerning living, working and thriving, the role for a distinct society clause becomes rather easy to rationalize.

It is important to note that the distinct society clause is an *interpretive* clause: the Constitution is to be interpreted in a manner consistent with the recognition that Quebec constitutes a distinct society within Canada. With respect to this clause, the Accord asserts "Nothing in this section detracts from the powers, rights or privileges of Parliament or the Government of Canada, or of the legislatures or government of the provinces, including any powers, rights or privileges relating to language." But not detracting from all parties' existing powers may be consistent with the distinct society clause effectively increasing Quebec's powers in those areas where the substance of the Constitution generates ambiguity.

Needless to say, therefore, the distinct society clause has generated substantial concern, even alarm among non-French-speaking Canadians. Part of this relates to the potential for bestowing Quebec with a special status, constitutionally, compared to the other provinces. Part also relates to the possibility that the distinct society clause will trample the rights and freedoms of Québécois. In terms of the latter, for example, Leonard Shifrin points out in a recent newspaper column that if socio-economic incentives to combat Quebec's low birth rate prove ineffectual, "Discriminatory rules could be introduced to restrict women's access to skills training, for example, in order to discourage them from seeking careers outside the home."[17.1] I think that this and similarly sweeping assessments are wild exaggerations. Of and by itself, the distinct society clause can confer no powers whatsoever on Quebec, since it is interpretive rather than substantive. Moreover, since the distinct society obviously includes both sexes, it is difficult to envisage that it could alter in any way the interpretation of the relevant Charter provisions. Certainly, the Fédération des femmes du Québec are not concerned that their rights will be eroded.[18] Nonetheless, one cannot

---

17.1 L. Shifrin, "How Meech Lake Deal Threatens Women," *The Toronto Star* (17 August 1987) A13.

18 As the Fédération told the Joint Committee:

> . . . we strongly hope that our sisters will not see threats where we feel they do not exist. In answer to the question: Does the concept of a distinct society threaten Quebec women? The Fédération des femmes du Québec answers: No.

The Fédération then adds: "The purpose of the Accord is to bring Quebec into the Constitution, and the protection of the French language, of our culture, our educational system, our network of social services, volunteer organizations, and so on, does not create a situation particularly apt to jeopardize women's rights". Canada, *Report of the Joint Committee of the Senate and the House of Commons on the 1987 Constitutional Accord* (Ottawa: Queen's Printer, 1987) at 64.

dismiss these concerns with 100 per cent certainty, just as one cannot completely rule out the possibility that the Charter could strike down medicare on the basis that it violates the civil rights of physicians. I must confess that I find all this passing strange: to extrapolate with respect to the possibility that the Charter will overturn much of what Canadians hold near and dear is somehow akin to being against motherhood. Even the Macdonald Commission shied away from evaluating the Charter's implications in terms of converting our parliamentary system into some version (as yet unknown) of the U.S. system of checks and balances. Yet, to speculate on the potential downside ramifications of the Meech Lake Accord is not only acceptable, but had become, at least until the free trade agreement came along, Canada's number one indoor sport. Nonetheless, the concerns deserved to be aired and addressed.

The distinct society clause may play a role which derives from why Quebec "wanted in" to the Constitution at this time — the potential role for the distinct society clause is to shield some or all of Quebec's specificity in terms of its social and economic institutions from the sweep of the Charter and more likely from the Charter in tandem with other provisions such as ss. 91(2) and 121 of the Constitution Act, 1867. What I have in mind here are the caisse de dépôt, the Quebec Stock Savings Plan (QSSP) and Quebec's ability to regulate its indigenous financial sector, all of which combined have largely been responsible for Quebec's recent dramatic economic upturn. These institutions or policies have, at one time or another over the past few years, been subject to severe criticism from various quarters and might not survive a rigid application of ss. 121 and 91(2) and the Charter. This would especially be the case if property rights were added to the Charter. For example, the QSSP does fragment the national market for capital. Thus, the federal government refused to allow the other provinces to mount a similar program by means of the tax-credit route because one of the provisions of the Tax Collection Agreements for the personal income tax (to which all provinces except Quebec are signatories) is to preserve the Canadian economic union. With respect to some of these institutions, the distinct society clause may be viewed as an entrenched opting-out or not-withstanding clause. How effective this will prove to be is another matter.[19]

---

19 As noted later, the distinct society clause may also come into play with respect to the new spending power provision. In terms of the potential effectiveness of this clause, those who

It is largely because of this uncertainty as to its likely impact that critics have argued that the meaning of the distinct society should be spelled out in detail. But this is similar to requiring that Peace, Order and Good Government be defined. Any attempt at such definitions would dramatically alter the nature of the clause: included items would tend to become enshrined and excluded items unprotected. Alternatively, the definition would be so broad as to cover everything: La Fédération des femmes du Québec recommended the following definition:

> Our laws, our legal system, our municipal and provincial institutions, our volunteer organizations, our media, our arts, our literature, our education system, our network of social and health-care services, our religious institutions, our savings and loan institutions as well as our language and culture.[20]

Much better, it seems to me, to leave the distinct society undefined since any attempt at definition would have to be at least as sweeping as that enumerated above to satisfy Quebec. As a concluding and somewhat ironical observation in this context, Donald Smiley has noted that in the final analysis the role assigned to the distinct society clause will be in the hands of six common law judges and three civil law judges: i.e., a majority of non-Quebec judges will have the ultimate say as to the meaning of the distinct society clause.

At this juncture, the reader is probably confused by my apparent schizophrenia. I favour the Charter, both because of its individual rights aspects and, relatedly, because of the additional check or balance it brings to the machinery of government. I also favour the distinct society clause, in full recognition that it may increase Quebec's constitutional powers and that part of its rationale is to shield aspects of collective rights against the potential implications of the Charter. I rationalize these apparently inconsistent views as follows. The distinct society clause is, as noted, a sort of enshrined version of the notwithstanding clause. Its potential influence will be to shelter rather than to expand collective rights with respect to Charter decisions, the federal spending power and perhaps other constitutional decisions. Hence, I downplay (but cannot disprove) claims that the distinct society may be used to

---

argue that it will have little impact point out that Quebec cases before the Supreme Court have, where relevant, typically utilized the concept of a distinct society as part of the argumentation. Enshrining the clause will *require* the Court to pay attention to the distinct society, but in the view of some the Court already appeared to accept this line of argument in many cases.

20 Report of the Joint Committee, above, note 18 at 41.

trample upon existing rights and freedoms. Underlying all of this is the notion of balance referred to earlier. Evolution rather than revolution is characteristic of the Canadian way in political economy. The notwithstanding clause and the distinct society clause will facilitate a more measured approach to accommodating any "revolutionary" (albeit appropriate) Supreme Court decisions. However, this does not imply progress will be slow on the individual rights front. Intriguingly, the pace may even be enhanced: without the fallback positions provided by the notwithstanding clause and the distinct society clause, the courts might be much less aggressive in their interpretation of the Charter. Thus, I find no inconsistency in supporting both the Charter and the distinct society clause. I now turn to a related aspect of the Accord — the appointment procedures for Supreme Court Judges.

The Appointment of Justices

Writing in 1981, Donald Smiley clearly foresaw that the provinces would be demanding some say in the appointment of Supreme Court Judges:

> The almost inevitable politicization of the Court as it assumes a more publicly visible role in interpreting the Charter will mean that those who appoint members of this Court will face more vigorous public scrutiny of their choices and, as in the case of the provinces, other groups may demand some influence on these choices.[21]

Smiley's views are consistent with my earlier observation that the Charter set in motion a process of "recontracting" that was, if not inevitable, at least predictable. Thus, Meech Lake is not just about Quebec: it is also about necessary accommodations relating to the integration of the Charter into the machinery of Canadian federalism. The new appointment procedures for Supreme Court Judges fall in this category.

In terms of the new nominating procedures, one can visualize a stalemate developing over the appointment of judges nominated by Quebec, if the appointees are unacceptable to the federal government. Both parties effectively have a veto. This may generate concern from legal and constitutional quarters, but in reality it is just another one of the many areas where Canadians will eventually carve out an acceptable compromise if the situation requires it. The Americans do

---

21 D. Smiley, *The Canadian Charter of Rights and Freedoms* (Toronto: Ontario Economic Council, 1981) 33 at 53.

not have a deadlock-resolution mechanism: with the U.S. Senate's overturning of the Judge Bork nomination, the process must begin anew. The procedures for appointing judges from the other nine provinces are likely to work extremely well. In effect, the provinces will be competing with each other to have their nominees selected. The end result is that the federal government is likely to have an enviable set of choices.

The frequently expressed view is that this is going to lead to further decentralization because the provinces will only nominate persons with a provincial rights approach to the Constitution. To be sure, this will probably occur from time to time, but Ottawa has a veto. More to the point, this centralization-decentralization axis is far too narrow a conception of what will drive the process. Again, Smiley merits quotation:

> There are alternative judicial values that might be brought to bear as the courts give meaning and effect to the provisions of the Charter. In the American context, these alternative values are usually designated as judicial activism and judicial restraint. Another formulation might see a judge of the Supreme Court of Canada in any one of the following roles in his approach to the Charter:
>
> — *the literalist.* The judge's primary cues here are the accepted legal meaning of the words of the Charter and previously decided cases by the Court itself, the Judicial Committee of the Privy Council, and perhaps other courts outside Canada. Because many of the broad terms of the Charter are new to Canadian jurisprudence, this will mean a heavy reliance on the decisions of foreign courts and international or supranational legal tribunals.
>
> — *the crusader.* The judge here is certain enough of himself, his values, and what he believes the Charter to mean to be willing to challenge executives and legislatures in a self-confident and aggressive way . . . For judges who conceive their function in this way, the Charter would of course be a powerful additional rationale for their activism.
>
> — *the policy scientist.* The judge who assumes this stance is primarily guided by the psychological, social, and economic consequences of judicial decisions. Thus he puts a heavy reliance on scientific evidence. For example, in coming to a decision about "cruel or unusual punishment or treatment" the judge might give consideration to the deterrent effects of hanging, when making judgements about the rights to education of official-language minorities he might take into account the fiscal capacity of the local authorities concerned to bear such costs and the psychological consequences to the children involved of such education not being available.
>
> — *the deferentialist.* A judge in this category is very reluctant to challenge either elected legislatures and governments or executive agencies and officials working under the control of those elected bodies. The view here is that on normative

grounds in most circumstances it is inappropriate for courts to substitute their judgments for the judgments of those who are charged with the immediate responsibilities of government. It is likely that this disposition would be combined with a modest appreciation of the actual capacity of courts to effect social change or to protect values and interests challenged by those other organs of government that reflect prevailing opinions and the distribution of power in society more accurately than does the judiciary.[22]

It seems to me that these are the sorts of concerns that will come to bear on the appointments of justices: centralization versus decentralization concerns will not be absent, but they are unlikely to dominate.

I understand, but do not subscribe to, the view that the appointment procedures represent an inappropriate transfer of power or influence to the provinces. Other federations provide for provincial/state input, sometimes via ratification by the upper chamber as in the case of the U.S. Moreover, the role for provincial input is hardly novel. For example, the 1971 Victoria Charter proposals required Supreme Court appointments to be agreed upon by the Attorney General of Canada and the Attorney General of the province, with an arbitration mechanism in case of disagreement. At the other end of the spectrum were the proposals of the 1979 Task Force on Canadian Unity (the Pépin-Robarts Report) which recommended that federal appointments be ratified by a reformed upper house in which the provinces would be meaningfully represented.

Noteworthy in this context is the *Report of the Canadian Bar Association Committee on the Supreme Court of Canada*. As a result of the 1984 "rash of 'political' appointments in the closing days of the federal liberal government (none of them to the Supreme Court of Canada), the Canadian Bar Association established a committee on the appointment of judges, under the Chairmanship of E. Neil McKelvey".[23] The McKelvey Committee recommended the establishment in each province of an advisory committee on federal judicial appointments. Each provincial committee would be composed of the Chief Justice of the province, a delegate of the federal Minister of Justice, a delegate of the provincial Attorney General, two lawyers (one appointed by the Canadian Bar Association and the other by the governing body of the legal profession in that province) and two lay persons. This

---

22 *Ibid.* at 42-44.

23 Canadian Bar Association Committee on the Supreme Court of Canada, *Report of the Canadian Bar Association Committee on the Supreme Court of Canada* (Ottawa: Canadian Bar Association, 1987) at 48.

committee would submit three names for appointment, not only for Supreme Court vacancies, but as well for vacancies in provincial superior, district and county courts, and the expectation would be that the nominee would be chosen from the list. These recommendations were made prior to the Meech Lake Accord. However, the CBA report indicate that they could easily be adapted to the appointment procedures contemplated by the Accord. Specifically, "each province ought to establish an Advisory Committee to recommend to the provincial government the names from which the federal government is obliged to make the appointment".[24]

While the provinces are free to adopt such a procedure under the terms of the Accord (and for those that do, this may enhance the likelihood that their nominees will be selected), I prefer a version of the Pépin-Robarts approach. Specifically, I would recommend that the Parliament of Canada follow the U.S. approach and hold hearings prior to Court appointments where the nominees would be invited to attend. Obviously, nothing in Meech Lake would require compliance with the procedure, nor would the federal cabinet be bound by any such report. However, it should prove a very worthwhile exercise for at least two reasons. First, it would serve to raise the profile of the Supreme Court among Canadians. Despite the growing importance of the Court, I would not be surprised if Canadians were still more familiar with the names of U.S. justices than Canadian justices. Second, the exercise would be inherently valuable: Canadians deserve to have information about the views of those who will preside over the evolution of the Constitution. At first blush, the Senate would appear to be a more appropriate forum than the House of Commons because it is based on representation by region rather than by population. Moreover, under any reform whereby the Senate would end up as a meaningful regional chamber, this task might fall rather naturally in its bailiwick. However, given that the provinces already have a role in the appointment process, it may be that the House of Commons will want to take this on. This will especially be the case if the Senate reform embodied in Meech Lake turns out to be as dramatic as I expect it will.

Now that I have broached the issue of Senate reform, it seems appropriate to turn to it in earnest. Meech Lake has broken the logjam and has ushered in the first significant step in decades toward meaningful Senate reform.

---

24 *Ibid.* at 49.

Senate Reform: The House of the Provinces

Under the provisions of the Accord, when a vacancy occurs in the Senate, the relevant provincial government will submit names of persons to fill the seat, but the person ultimately chosen must be named by, and thus be acceptable to, the government of Canada. Setting aside for the moment the fact that Senate reform is on the agenda for the annual first ministers' constitutional conferences[25] and that this appointment procedure is designed as an interim measure, Meech Lake has in one fell swoop created a "House of the Provinces". To be sure, it may take a while before a majority of Senate members are provincial nominees, but under the Accord it is inevitable.

In this context, I want to second Eugene Forsey's views on the implications of this change:

> The transformed Senate will have all the legal powers of the present Senate, notably the power to reject, absolutely, any bill whatsoever. But it will have a political clout the present Senate cannot even dream of. Its members will take seriously their job of representing provincial and regional interests, and if that makes trouble for the federal government or annoys the House of Commons, what of it?
>
> There would be, in the long run, a shift of power from the elected House of Commons to the appointed Senate. The House of Commons, whose approval is needed to bring the Accord into effect, may not be altogether happy with that.[26]

Hence, I do not understand the concern in the land that the change in the amending formula (from the federal government plus seven provinces with 50 per cent of the population to the federal government plus all provinces) will effectively forestall meaningful Senate reform. Meech Lake gives us profound Senate reform!

Moreover, in terms of any future reform of the Senate, the new amending formula is rather innocuous, except in one instance, to be elaborated later. As Forsey emphasized, the real impediments toward moving to, say, a triple-E Senate are Quebec and Ontario on the one hand (because their relative representation would decrease) and the House of Commons on the other (because it would transfer power to the Senate).[27] But both of these parties had a veto under the old amending formula.

---

25 See s. 50 of the Accord in Appendix.
26 E. Forsey, "A Point by Point Look at Meech Lake" *The Toronto Star* (6 August 1987) A20. These are excerpts from Forsey's presentation to the Special Joint Committee.
27 *Ibid.*

Where I disagree with Forsey is on the issue of further Senate reform. He views the chances as "microscopic". I think that further reform is inevitable. It is true that moving to a Senate that has equal representation by province is probably not in the cards. What is likely, however, is some agreement on the detailed procedures as to how Senators are selected, including their length of time in office and perhaps some move toward more equal distribution by province. Let me elaborate a bit. Suppose that instead of submitting names for a Senate vacancy, Alberta holds province-wide elections for the vacancy and submits the name of the winner to serve for a five-year term to the federal government. Ottawa will have a very difficult time saying no to this procedure, since Canadians in all provinces will probably applaud the process. Hence, what I see as likely is the provinces agreeing among themselves to some mutually acceptable procedures, like the election route, that will serve to enhance the Senate's political acceptability among Canadians and, therefore, enhance its moral authority to take on the very substantial powers it does have under the Constitution Act, 1867. Given that the Senate appointments are going to come from provincial lists in any event, Canadians are likely to insist that the election route, with a time limit, is preferable to some combination of federal-provincial patronage.

There is no question in my mind that Senate reform is the most dramatic and far-reaching aspect of the Accord. And there is also no question that this poses substantial problems in terms of the role of the House of Commons. Prior to turning to this issue, it is appropriate to focus briefly on the enshrining of executive federalism in the constitution.

First Ministers' Conferences

Meech Lake adds a new Part XII to the Constitution Act, 1867 which would require the Prime Minister to convene once a year a first ministers' conference on the Canadian economy and such other matters as may be appropriate. Again, one can raise the spectre of more *faits accomplis* hammered out away from the elected assemblies. Yet, in effect, this is little more than just enshrining what has become an accepted feature of the federation in recent years. Indeed, as Watts et al point out:

> To make these conferences part of our normal and regular political process will reduce the political gamesmanship which has often characterized the calling of meetings and will provide in future an opportunity for legislatures and interest

groups to inject their views into the process prior to the intergovernmental meetings.[28]

At one level then, this amounts to enshrining and making more predictable a part of the machinery of our federation that has come to play an increasingly important role in the governing process. At a deeper level, some concerns are warranted with respect to the manner in which the federation appears to be evolving in terms of accommodating the provinces' role in decision-making. To this I now turn.

Interstate Plus Intrastate Federation: Whither the Commons?

It is somewhat disconcerting that the combination of Meech Lake and the Constitution Act, 1982 appears to be an embracing of U.S. intrastate federalism (checks and balances with increasing provincial representation at the centre) while at the same time a confirming of interstate federalism (enshrining the first ministers conferences). One would normally expect that the shift toward intrastate federalism would eventually erode the power of provincial premiers since provincial and regional interests would now have representation at the centre. For this reason, I have never quite comprehended why Premier Getty is so intent on a triple-E Senate. Clearly, there is genuine concern, if not solid evidence, that regional interests get short shrift from time to time in federal government decisions. But over the long haul, a triple-E Senate would surely usurp part of the premiers' authority and power. It may well be that this is the conceptual underpinning for the enshrining of first ministers' conferences: it will serve to perpetuate the process of executive federalism in the face of an increasing provincial presence and influence at the centre. It may also be the case that the provinces, if and when they come to realize this, may themselves not push as hard as one might otherwise expect for further Senate reform. This is yet another area where Canada will eventually evolve toward a new "balance".

What all of this means, however, is that the House of Commons is in for some serious soul-searching. Prior to Meech Lake it may have been possible simply to abolish the Senate. But the combination of provincial input into Senate appointments and the new amending formula makes this virtually impossible. (Here is one area where

---

28 R. Watts et al., "Strengthening the Federation," a submission to the Special Joint Committee on the 1987 Constitutional Accord (Department of Political Studies, Queen's University, 1987) [mimeograph].

moving to unanimity will make a difference. Abolishing the Senate may no longer be possible now that it has become a source for provincial, rather than federal, patronage). Over the next decade or so, the House of Commons will have to confront and accommodate provincial influences at two levels: first ministers' conferences (and what this can imply with respect to *fait accompli*) *and* the growing provincialization of the Senate or, more appropriately, the House of the Provinces. There is no easy way out for the House of Commons; moving to an elected Senate, for example, may curtail the role of executive federalism, but only at the expense of increasing the power of the Senate.

One alternative might be for the House of Commons to undermine the potential future influences of executive federalism by extending further the recent changes that have enhanced the role of House of Commons' committees. However, to be fully effective, this would probably require a substantial reduction in party discipline and, hence, a much greater distinction than at present between the cabinet and the House of Commons (i.e. between the executive and legislative functions). Phrased differently, the principal reason why executive federalism works in Canada is that we have responsible government. The U.S. President and the 50 governors may well be able to agree on a given initiative, but it hardly represents a *fait accompli* because there is no guarantee that the governors, or even the President, can deliver their respective legislatures. Under responsible government, the eleven Canadian first ministers *can* deliver their legislatures. Thus, one way of countering the influence of executive federalism is to move away from responsible government — hardly an appealing prospect for Canadians, although in his memoirs, René Lévesque proposed such a checks-and-balances system for Quebec.[29] Nonetheless, some further moves in this direction are, in my view, inevitable given the increasing erosion of the effective powers of the House of Commons.

This brings me to the likelihood of Senate reform. The popular view, expressed earlier, that the House of Commons is a bulwark against Senate reform because it will not voluntarily enhance the role of the upper chamber now falls by the wayside in light of the fact that Meech Lake invigorates the Senate. (Actually, the crunch has already come with the drug-patent bill. In this case the Senate obviously felt that it represents an important constituency — the elderly, the poor and the provinces — and, therefore, had the "moral authority"

---

29 R. Lévesque, *Attendez que je me rappelle . . .*, Montréal, Québec, Amérique, 1986.

to exercise fully its considerable powers. Under Meech Lake this "moral authority" will, to a large extent, come from the appointment procedures themselves). The range of possible trade-offs is fascinating: for example, the accommodation of certain provincial demands in return for a Senate with more limited powers than would likely evolve out of the Accord.

The related key issue is why Ontario and Quebec would willingly reduce their influence in any reformed Senate. One answer is that without Senate reform, they may not be able to exercise their 60 per cent share of the population and, therefore, of the House of Commons, in the face of an obstructive Senate. The fact that Quebec and Ontario almost have a majority of Senate seats may not count for much if these senatorial appointments arose from previous administrations, both federal and provincial. Thus, it seems to me that both the need and the incentives for Senate reform are now present. Since the nature of the Senate will alter only gradually, it might be argued that the House of Commons need not worry about the Senate over the near term. But time is not really on the House of Commons' side here. What is possible now may not be possible a few years down the road, if even one of the provinces comes to appreciate the manner in which the Senate is evolving. Thus, it would be surprising indeed if, when Senate reform comes on the agenda of the forthcoming first ministers' constitutional conferences, as it must under the provisions of the Accord, the provinces are the only ones to come forth with reform proposals. In order to increase the likelihood of Senate reform, it might be appropriate for the House of Commons to recommend that the Governor-in-Council not act on the provincial lists submitted in response to Senate vacancies until meaningful reform is in place. Carried to the extreme, this approach would, over time, effectively abolish the Senate although it would run counter to the spirit, if not the letter, of Meech Lake.

The Amending Formula

Much has been made in the public debates about the manner in which Meech Lake has altered the amending formula. As a matter of fact, not all that much has changed, although some of the implications may be substantial. In order to introduce this subject, it is appropriate to review what exactly has transpired.

First, Meech Lake maintains the current general amending formula set out in s. 38 of the Constitution Act, 1982, which requires the consent of Parliament and two-thirds of the provinces representing at least 50 per cent of the population.

Second, under the Constitution Act, 1982, a province has the right to opt out of any amendment that transfers legislative jurisdiction of a provincial responsibility to Parliament. If the amendment concerns education or other cultural matters, the federal government is required to provide reasonable compensation to any opting-out province. Meech Lake extends this provision by guaranteeing reasonable compensation *in all cases* (not just education and culture) when a province opts out of an amendment transferring provincial jurisdiction to Parliament.

Third, the Constitution Act, 1982 required unanimity (Parliament plus the ten provinces) for amendments on the following matters: the office of the Queen, the Governor General and the Lieutenant Governor of a province; the right to a number of members in the House of Commons not less than the number of Senators by which the province was represented in 1982; the provisions concerning the use of English or French that apply to Parliament, the Government of Canada and all the provinces; the composition of the Supreme Court of Canada; and the amending formula itself. Meech Lake leaves all of this intact.

Fourth, the general amending formula (Parliament plus two-thirds of the provinces, representing 50 per cent of the population) also applied to the following areas: the principle of proportionate representation of the provinces in the House of Commons; the powers of the Senate and the method of selecting Senators; the number of Senators for each province and their residence qualifications; the Supreme Court of Canada; the extension of existing provinces into the territories; and the establishment of new provinces. Under Meech Lake, this fourth category will henceforth require unanimous consent of Parliament and the ten provinces. The expressed rationale for this is, in part, that since the provinces cannot opt out of this fourth category of amendments, they ought to require the unanimity rule for amending purposes.

In general, I favour these changes. It would be a peculiar federation indeed that could, for example, alter the number of Senators for Prince Edward Island over its objection. In essence, all provinces will now have a say in any changes in our national institutions. To the extent that Meech Lake can be viewed as decentralizing, the claim applies most appropriately to the amending formula. In effect, it is a decentralization at the provincial level. Under the Constitution Act, 1982, Ontario and Quebec, together, could veto any constitutional change. But no other two provinces could; in fact, no other three provinces could. Under Meech Lake, all provinces are treated equally. In my view, this is a step in the right direction, although some would prefer the regional veto proposed in the Victoria Charter. Part of the ingenuity of the Quebec position through all of this was that, apart from the distinct society clause, any special privileges the province obtained through the constitutional bargaining process were granted to other provinces as well. And as noted earlier, even the distinct society clause may in the long run increase the options available for the other nine provinces.

One major criticism of this extension of the unanimity clause is that it may now make the incorporation of new provinces more difficult. I agree with this. However, while one has to be sympathetic to the aspirations of the residents of potential new provinces, I am not particularly sympathetic to the underlying argument. First of all, there is no way, politically, that Canada could incorporate new provinces without Quebec becoming a signatory of the Constitution. Second, it seems appropriate that all provinces should agree to the creation of a new province. This is particularly the case for the smaller, "have-not" provinces, since they may have the most to lose in terms of the creation of new provinces. Consider equalization, for example. Even though the concept is now enshrined in the Constitution, the fact remains that introducing a northern province may strain the federal government's ability to finance the increased demands on the equalization formula. This is not an argument against new provinces. Far from it. It is, however, an argument that states that the three traditional "have" provinces of the federation (Ontario, British Columbia and Alberta) ought not to have a veto on new provinces if the three "have-not" Maritime provinces do not have a veto, particularly if the level of equalization payments is at stake.

Again, the real problem here is the Constitution Act, 1982. Prior to 1982, the federal government had full power to create new provinces, as long as existing provincial boundaries remained intact. Unanimity may, in practice, be more constraining than seven provinces with 50 per cent of the population, but the real constraint was subjecting the creation of new provinces to the general amending formula in 1982.

CONCLUSION

Canadians and their provinces still have to pass judgment on the specifics of the Meech Lake Accord. I believe that Meech Lake represents a positive step in the evolution of our federation. However, it is likely only the first step of what will be a series of accommodations and initiatives as the Canadian federation wrestles to strike a new internal balance. The major piece of unfinished business of the Accord relates to Senate reform. Both the Meech Lake provisions and the current House of Commons–Senate impasse suggest to me that further Senate reform is inevitable. In conclusion, therefore, I support the substance of the Accord and, to reverse the typical argument of those in favour of Meech Lake, as an added bonus in all of this, Quebec will now become a full member of the Canadian constitutional family.

The Meech Lake Accord and the Bonds of Nationhood

A. W. Johnson

The purpose of a Constitution is to proclaim and define nationhood. It is to proclaim and define the rights and freedoms of the citizens of the nation, and to establish a system of governance which will contribute to the flourishing of the nation, its citizens and its "identities". Lying behind these constitutional provisions is the manifest objective of affirming and strengthening the bonds of nationhood.

The Meech Lake Accord addresses itself to this latter objective: its purpose and intent is to strengthen the bonds of nationhood as they are felt in the Province of Quebec. I take this to mean the strengthening of the bonds of nationhood as they are felt by the people of Quebec; clearly, it is their feeling for Canada which finally determines the strength of nationhood in that province.

The Accord, however, addresses itself not to the people of Quebec, but to the government of that province. As it turns out, its concern is to meet the demands of the Government of Quebec that the powers of the federal government be diminished in that province (in certain particulars), and that the powers of the Government of Quebec be increased correspondingly. The fathers of Meech Lake reasoned that, if this concern is met, the Government of Quebec would be persuaded to become a signatory to the Constitution of Canada — which was the objective of Meech Lake in the first place. And that is what happened, of course.

However, if I am right about the bonds of nationhood — that they depend upon the sense that a *people* feels for the nation as a whole

— then the fundamental question about the Meech Lake Accord is its underlying assumption concerning the place of citizens in the drafting of constitutions, as opposed to that of governments. The Accord clearly seems to assume that the feeling of the people of Quebec for Canada will be enhanced if the powers of the Government of Quebec are increased, and the powers of the Government of Canada are correspondingly reduced. On the basis of this assumption, the Government of Canada was prepared to strengthen the powers of *all* the provincial governments, and to weaken its own powers correspondingly, in order to achieve the desired results in Quebec.

The validity of this assumption — a more powerful Quebec government will increase the sense of Canadianism on the part of individual Québécois — is at least open to question. What effect will the Meech Lake Accord have upon the identification of Québécois, and of all Canadians, with Canada? In my judgment, the bonds with the nation, and with the national government of Canada, will almost certainly be weakened.

First, the Accord weakens the potential for Canadians to come to share certain common privileges and benefits of citizenship, wherever they live in Canada. The Accord brings this about by reducing the future capacity of the Canadian Government to initiate certain nation-wide programs or public services which, while lying within provincial jurisdiction, have come to be seen by Canadians generally as being important to a decent and dignified life for all Canadians.

Second, the sense of affinity and association — even esteem — which Canadians feel, or may reasonably come to feel, for their national governmental institutions is weakened. The Accord brings this about by the provision which will, in future, give to a provincially-nominated Senate — an appointed, not an elected one — the power to veto or amend any decision the elected arm of the government may reach. The relative representation of the smaller provinces in the Senate is to remain unchanged, short of unanimous agreement on the part of all the premiers.

These two bonds of nationhood have been weakened by the Meech Lake Accord — at least in my view. I will examine both of them, in turn.

SHARED RIGHTS AND BENEFITS

The question of shared rights and benefits is one which individual Canadians deeply and intuitively understand. They *know* they enjoy the rights and the freedoms which the Charter now guarantees, and they know that, beyond this, they enjoy other rights and benefits which their national *cum* provincial governments have conferred upon them. I'm talking about medicare, hospital care, old age security pensions and disability allowances, accessibility to higher education, even the Trans-Canada Highway — *all* of which were established or made national in scope as a result of the actions of the national, the *federal*, government. In every one of these cases, save for post-secondary education where only federal finances were involved, one of two courses of action was pursued to make the shared public service possible: either a federal-provincial shared-cost program was established, with the provinces administering the programs in accord with nationally-established criteria or principles (like medicare and hospital care), or a constitutional amendment was passed to enable the federal government to undertake the program itself (such as unemployment insurance and old age security).

Simply to reflect upon the history of Canada's social security programs, or indeed of other programs, is to perceive the importance of these two constitutional means to Canada's development. Parliament used its spending power to provide conditional grants to the provinces for the purpose of establishing medicare, hospital care, and the Canada Assistance Plan; and it sought and obtained constitutional amendments to enable it, alone, to undertake unemployment insurance, old age security pensions, and the Canada Pension Plan. Even the Trans-Canada Highway was built, as I have said, because Parliament offered to give the provinces financial support if they would build it.

The point is clear: one of the distinguishing features of nationhood in Canada — the sharing across the country of certain common public services — has been made possible by these instruments of the Constitution. The fathers of Meech Lake, however, have not recognized this point. Whether this is because they have forgotten Canada's history, or because they simply do not believe the country will, in the future, need new or revised national public services, we do not know. But what they have done is clear. They have adopted provisions which will seriously attenuate the future potential for amending the Constitution to give the Government of Canada the power to establish new nation-wide programs. They have adopted provisions which will seriously attenuate Parliament's capacity to influence the provinces to establish new nation-wide programs — that is to say, provincial programs which are consistent or congruous with one another — by using federal spending power in particular ways. In both cases, this has been done by endowing the provincial governments with the right to "opt-out" of the amendment, or of the federal-provincial program, with federal compensation.

THE SPENDING POWER

Under the Meech Lake provisions, the Government of Canada could not have enacted medicare as we know it today — at least, so it seems to me. It could not have incorporated into the law the five principles which now bind the provinces in their medicare plans, and under which extra-billing was ended. All the Government of Canada could have done, had Meech Lake been in effect, would have been to declare in the law the "national objectives" it hoped to achieve. That, unhappily, is a long way from the principles as we know them today. An "objective", after all, has to do with "the object of an action" (Oxford), while a "principle" is a "fundamental attribute, an essential characteristic" (also Oxford) — which is why the word "principle" was used in the first place in medicare.

More than this, the provinces are effectively told by Meech Lake that they would not have been obliged, had the Accord been in effect, to enact similar, or mutually consistent medicare plans, in order to qualify for federal money. All they would have been required to do would have been to "carry on" plans or initiatives which were "compatible" with the federal objectives. Now, it is true that in English the word "compatible" may mean "accordant, consistent, congruous", as well as "capable of existing together" (Oxford). But in the French language, "compatible" means only "capable of existing together" (Robert).

So there it is. Under Meech Lake, the only power our national government will have in the future, in establishing federal-provincial programs, is the power to finance provincial programs which are "capable of existing together", in the achievement of certain specified "national objectives". This is surely to return to the "hodge-podge" federalism of the past, in respect of future national programs — be they in the field of home services for the elderly and disabled, or legal aid, or child care, or any other public program under provincial jurisdiction — where the public may believe there should be nation-wide levels of service, but where some provincial governments do not. Some argue that the Meech Lake Accord is not as bad as I have portrayed it. For example, they say that "objective" might be interpreted as meaning "principle", or that "compatible" might be interpreted as meaning "consistent" or "congruous". If that is so, why were these words not chosen in the first place? It must surely have been because one or more of the premiers didn't want the more precise words: they wanted the door left open to the literal and less limiting (for them) interpretations I have mentioned.

Another argument advanced by the advocates of Meech Lake in support of the spending power provision is that even with the worst-case interpretation of the new limitations on the spending power, the changes are not as serious as they are being made to appear. All that is required in the future, they argue, is the same imaginative approach to the development of new policy instruments to achieve national goals, as has been evidenced in the past. For example: in 1968, medicare was started by the substitution of "principles" in a federal statute, for the much criticized "conditions" in a shared-cost agreement; in 1967, federal financing of post-secondary education was extended by the use of unconditional grants to the provinces, instead of direct grants to universities and colleges, but with the grants being calculated by reference to the operating expenditures of universities and colleges (and hence indirectly to the level of provincial support for these institutions). By the use of this kind of imagination in the future, governments might be brought to use grants to persons and institutions, where opting-out is not a problem, instead of shared-cost grants to the provinces, where it is a problem, or to find new means for achieving unanimity among the provinces, in order to avoid the opting-out provisions of the Meech Lake Accord.

The essence of this proposition, I take it, is that the weakening of the federal powers in the Meech Lake Accord is acceptable because the new limits can be circumvented. A curious argument, I should have thought, but one which is assailable on purely objective grounds: the substitution of unknown for known means in order to achieve an agreed constitutional objective is scarcely good constitution-making. Certainly it is not good enough to reassure Canadians about the limiting of the spending power.

OPTING-OUT AND CONSTITUTIONAL AMENDMENTS

The real question is whether or not the fathers of Meech Lake agreed that provincial opting-out of proposed nation-wide programs is a good thing. The answer is to be found in the fact that the opting-out principle was introduced not once, but twice into the Accord: once in respect of the spending power and shared-cost programs, and once in respect of any future constitutional amendments which might transfer powers from provincial governments to the federal government.

The opting-out provision in respect of constitutional amendments is even more enfeebling to national initiatives than is the one having to do with the spending power. What the Accord says, in essence, is that when a constitutional amendment has been agreed upon, which transfers some legislative power from the provincial legislatures to the Parliament of Canada, and where there are provincial governments which continue to dissent from the amendment after it has been passed, these provinces will be entitled to "reasonable compensation" from the Government of Canada.

What this means, in practice, can be seen in a simple illustration. Suppose the Government of Canada were to seek an amendment to the Constitution enabling it to regulate all private pension plans in the country, in order to achieve wider coverage of the labour force, and to assure the portability of private pension plans. (Such a reform would be desirable since it would relieve the pressure on governments to use the public sector to provide more adequate retirement incomes.) Say the Government of Canada and eight provinces agreed to the amendment, but two did not, persisting in their rejection of the amendment even after the eight provinces had agreed. These two dissenting provinces would be entitled, under the Accord, to "reasonable compensation" from the Government of Canada — whatever that may come to mean. No limits are placed upon how or where the "reasonable compensation" may be used by the recipient provinces.

What this provision implies for future amendments to the Constitution is clear. It provides a positive incentive to provincial governments *not* to agree to a constitutional amendment (presuming the required seven provinces will agree), particularly so where the newly proposed program involves large expenditures. And it provides a disincentive to the federal government even to set out on the tortuous course of seeking a constitutional amendment.

In short, the future for nation-wide programs in areas which lie in provincial jurisdiction is very bleak indeed — particularly when one recalls that it has been federal, not interprovincial, action which has led to the extension of particular provincial programs across the whole of the nation.

NATIONAL INSTITUTIONS

This weakening in the powers of the federal Government to take national initiatives is exacerbated by the changes brought about in governmental institutions. The fathers of Meech Lake have decided, in effect, that the elected institutions of the national government shall be constrained in the exercise of their powers by empowering provincial governments or their delegates to interpose their views at strategic points in the decision-making process. This comes about in three steps.

First, the federal-provincial conference of first ministers' (CFM) is accorded constitutional status in the Meech Lake Accord and is empowered to discuss, once a year, "the state of the Canadian economy and such other matters as may be appropriate". I take this to mean economic and other policy matters which fall in the domain of the Government of Canada: obviously the governments of the provinces already possess the power to discuss provincial matters together.

As it is, the CFM already exercises a considerable influence over federal policy-making by reason of the platform which is afforded to the premiers and their views by televised federal-provincial conferences. Indeed, a good many Members of Parliament — who were *elected* to influence national policy-makers — would argue that the premiers have more influence on federal policy than they do. To give the CFM constitutional status alongside the elected House of Commons is to legitimize, and thus surely to increase, the role of the "first-ministers-in-conference", relative to that of the elected Commons. Conversely, it is to diminish the position of the MPs — who were elected to represent the public's views on national issues.

Step two of the constraint of the Canadian Government is the transformation of the Senate into a "house of provincial delegates". In future, the senators will be nominated by the premiers of the provinces, not by the Prime Minister, and they will continue to enjoy plenary authority to veto or amend any legislation put before them. What this suggests seems clear: if the Prime Minister won't listen to the provincial governments' views in federal-provincial conferences, then he may be forced to do so by the premiers' delegates in the Senate. Checkmate the Government of Canada; checkmate, too, the House of Commons, despite the fact it is an elected body, while the Senate is to remain an appointed one.

Checkmate, finally, the electorates of the provinces. Not only are the people still disenfranchised in the naming of their senators;

in the case of the smaller provinces, they are being told that there is little hope that their relative powerlessness in the Parliament of Canada will be alleviated. For Saskatchewan, to take the case of my native province, this means they must look forward, indefinitely, to a situation where they have only 14 elected Members of Parliament out of 282 (in today's terms), and where their relative representation in the Senate is not much better. This is powerlessness; this is the stuff of Western alienation.

Step three in limiting the federal government's powers is a provision that will make it extremely difficult to reform the Senate in the future — whether to increase the representation of particular provinces, or to cause the senators to be elected, or to limit the plenary powers of the new house of provincial delegates. The fathers of Meech Lake have decided that any and all of these constitutional amendments will, in future, require the approval of *all* the provincial governments, not just seven representing a majority of Canada's population. This means that any single premier, or any single legislative assembly may, from Meech Lake on, block Senate reform.

The supporters of the Accord — to do them justice — point out that the Accord is not this stark. In the first place, the Senate won't become a full "house of delegates" until all of the present senators have reached 75 years of age. That is true, though it does not alter the intent of the Accord, nor its future effect. This can be seen already, as even today's Senate has begun to flex its legislative muscles. Second, we are assured — on what basis, we do not know — that the new amending formula will not stand in the way of early Senate reform; indeed there is to be a constitutional conference (of first ministers) every year, beginning next year, and that Senate reform is to be on the agenda. That, too, is true: this is explicitly provided for in the Accord. But what does that tell us about the possibility of reform? Not much: one is left wondering, indeed, whether it is not an egregious error in constitution-making to make it more difficult to reform the Senate before setting out to do so.

A QUESTION OF BALANCE

These, then, are the limitations which have been made in the powers of the national government in order to gain the assent of the Government of Quebec to the Constitution Act, 1982.

One is forced to ask two questions. First, even given the emphasis the fathers of Meech Lake have attached to the reconciliation of government interests in constitution-making, as opposed to citizen interests, have they found the right balance between meeting Quebec's demands, on the one hand, and protecting the ability of the national government to meet the needs of Canadians at large, on the other? This, surely, is a question which ought to have been debated. That it has not been is a measure of the belief of Canada's leading politicians that constitution-making ought to be the preserve of governments, and not of citizens. It was the Prime Minister, and the ten premiers, and the two opposition leaders of the House of Commons who unanimously agreed that the Meech Lake Accord ought to be approved without any effective public debate.

The second question which needs to be asked has precisely to do with this question of constitutions for citizens *versus* constitutions for governments. Is it not possible that if the citizens of Quebec and of the whole of Canada had been consulted on the balance which had to be struck at Meech Lake, they would have come to a quite different conclusion than did the politicians? Would they have been as determinedly opposed to the use of the spending and amending powers for the creation of nation-wide programs as were the politicians? Would they have rejected the notion of an elected Senate which would give the citizens of Canada's several regions a larger and more direct voice in the national government? Would the citizens, in short, not have employed a "citizens' calculus", rather than a "governments' calculus", in determining what arrangements should be made to bring the Government of Quebec to become a signatory to Canada's Constitution?

Herein lies the root of the flaws in the Meech Lake Accord, as I see them. Both in the process by which the fathers of Meech Lake reached their conclusions about the Constitution, and in the conclusions they reached, the citizens and their perspectives were excluded. This may well have been acceptable — even necessary — in Charlottetown in 1864; it is not so today. A broad and unconstrained debate on the Meech Lake Accord is called for, if the citizens are to bring *their* judgment to bear on the question of how to strengthen the bonds of nationhood.

Analysis Of The New Spending Provision (Section 106A)

Peter Hogg

BACKGROUND

The Parliament of Canada has the power to spend the money that it raises through taxes, borrowing and other means. Curiously, this spending power is nowhere explicit in the Constitution Act, 1867,[1] but must be inferred from some or all of the powers to legislate for the peace, order, and good government of Canada (s. 91 opening words), to levy taxes (s. 91(3)), to legislate in relation to public property (s. 91(1A)), and to appropriate federal funds (s. 106).[2]

Federal spending power is the basis for the establishment by the government of Canada of national shared-cost programs. These programs are designed and established by the Canadian government, but are only partially funded by that government. The federal contribution to the funding of the program in a particular province is made conditional upon the provincial government contributing a share of the cost. The largest of the shared-cost programs is the health care program. Initially, this was established as two separate programs, one for hospital services which came into force in 1958, and the other for physicians' services which came into force in 1968. Now both programs have been amalgamated by the Canada Health Act.[3] Under this Act, the federal government makes contributions to provincial

---

1 Constitution Act, 1867 (U.K.), c. 3. See the Appendix to this volume.

2 P. Hogg, *Constitutional Law of Canada*, 2nd ed. (Toronto: Carswell, 1985) at 123-126.

3 S.C. 1983-84, c. 6.

health care plans, which are plans covering the provision of hospital and physician services. The provincial health care plans are each established by provincial legislation, medical services being a provincial responsibility. However, the Canada Health Act stipulates conditions for a province to qualify for a full federal cash contribution to its health care insurance plan. The province's plan must satisfy criteria coming under five heads, namely: (1) public administration; (2) comprehensiveness; (3) universality; (4) portability; and (5) accessibility. Included under the last head is the controversial ban on extra-billing by doctors. If a provincial health care plan does not satisfy the federal conditions, the Act makes provision for the withholding or reduction of the federal cash contribution.

Provincial participation in a national shared-cost program is voluntary. In practice, however, there is substantial pressure to participate because a refusal to participate would deny to the province the federal grant that represents the federal contribution to the program. Once a province decides to participate, it is committed to the funding of a program that the province neither designed nor established. Many of the programs — the health care program is again the most important example — are within provincial legislative jurisdiction, and require provincial legislation for their implementation. The national shared-cost programs thus exercise a heavy influence on provincial spending and legislative priorities.

In 1969, the federal government issued a White Paper that acknowledged criticism by the provinces to the effect that federal shared-cost programs forced upon the provinces changes in their priorities. The White Paper suggested that, in future, shared-cost programs should be subject to two requirements: (1) a program within provincial jurisdiction should not be established until there existed "a broad national consensus in favour of the programme"; and (2) each province should have the right not to participate in the program without "fiscal penalty".[4] While the federal government never publicly adopted these two principles, they probably did become federal policy. After 1969, no new programs have been established or even publicly suggested that would violate the principles of the 1969 White Paper. At the very least, the federal government would be subject to intense political pressure to structure any new shared-cost program in such a way that a province could opt-out of the program without fiscal penalty.

---

4 P.E. Trudeau, *Federal-Provincial Grants and the Spending Power of Parliament* (Ottawa: Queen's Printer, 1969) at 36.

The new s. 106A that is to be added to the Constitution Act, 1867 imposes a constitutional restriction on the power of the federal government to establish a new national shared-cost program in an area of exclusive provincial jurisdiction. Section 106A will impose on the federal government a constitutional obligation to provide "reasonable compensation" to the government of a province that chooses not to participate in the program, provided that the province carries on a program that is "compatible with the national objectives." The various elements of s. 106A are analyzed in the text that follows. For present purposes, it suffices to point out that s. 106A reflects the political reality that the federal government must respect provincial autonomy when it develops federal policies in areas of exclusive provincial jurisdiction.

CLARIFICATION OF FEDERAL POWER

The explanatory commentary to the Meech Lake Accord, issued by the federal government, says that the purpose of s. 106A "is not to define or extend the spending power of Parliament".[5] Nevertheless, s. 106A assumes that the federal Parliament possesses the power to establish and fund a "shared-cost program" in an area of "exclusive provincial jurisdiction." It also assumes that the federal Parliament can attach conditions to its grants to the provinces, because it assumes the existence of a "national shared-cost program", and cost-sharing contemplates, I think, grants that are conditional at least in the sense that (1) they must be applied by the province to the shared-cost program, and (2) they must be matched by some level of provincial contribution. Finally, s. 106A assumes that there can be "national objectives" in an area of exclusive provincial jurisdiction. In my view, all of these propositions accurately state the present constitutional law.[6] But the present law is not entirely clear, and so the new s. 106A constitutes a clarification of the breadth of the federal spending power.

Subsection (2) of s. 106A provides that: "Nothing in this section extends the legislative powers of the Parliament of Canada or of the legislatures of the provinces." But subs. (1) makes sense only in the light of the assumptions about the existence of the extensive federal spending powers described in the previous paragraph. So subs. (2) must be saying, in effect, that the federal power to spend and impose

---

5 Canada, *A Guide to the Meech Lake Constitutional Accord* (Ottawa, 1987) at 6.
6 Hogg, above note 2, at 123-126.

conditions in areas of exclusive provincial jurisdiction has always existed.

RESTRICTION ON FEDERAL POWER

The ostensible purpose of s. 106A is to impose a restriction on the federal spending power by conferring on each province a constitutional right to opt-out of any future "national shared-cost program" established by the Parliament of Canada, and to receive reasonable compensation for opting-out. The present constitutional position is that the federal Parliament need not compensate provinces that choose not to participate in a national shared-cost program established by the Parliament of Canada. However, as noted earlier, the federal Parliament would probably be constrained by political considerations to permit opting-out with reasonable compensation.

NATIONAL SHARED-COST PROGRAM

The constitutional restriction on federal power that is imposed by s. 106A applies only to "a national shared-cost program that is established by the Government of Canada." Any federal policy, including a spending program, that does not take the form of a national shared-cost program is unaffected by s. 106A.

What is a national shared-cost program? There is no definition in s. 106A, but the essential elements can be inferred from s. 106A itself and from the characteristics of existing programs, such as the program of health care. A "national" program is one "established by the Government of Canada", as s. 106A explains. The program would take the form of an offer of cash, or tax points, by the federal government to the provinces for the purpose of partially funding the provision of federally-defined services in each province. The offer would be conditional upon each province (1) applying the federal grant for the stipulated purpose, (2) contributing a share of the cost of the services in that province, and (3) enacting any legislation that was required for the provision of the services and that was within the exclusive competence of the provincial legislature.

If the federal offer was accepted by a province, and if the province satisfied the conditions, then the national program would operate in that province. If the federal offer was not accepted by the province, or if the province failed to satisfy the conditions, then the national program would not operate in that province and the province would not be entitled to the federal grant. In the latter situation, the effect of s. 106A would be to require the Government of Canada to pay "reasonable compensation" to the province, provided that the province establishes a program of its own compatible with the national objectives of the federal program.

Even a national shared-cost program is only caught by s. 106A if two limiting conditions apply. The first condition is that the program must be established "after the coming into force of this section." Thus, s. 106A applies only to new programs, not to existing ones. The second condition is that the program must be established "in an area of exclusive provincial jurisdiction." Thus, s. 106A would not apply to a shared-cost program in an area of exclusive federal jurisdiction, such as "Indians" (s. 91 (24) of the Constitution Act, 1867). Nor would s. 106A apply to a shared-cost program in an area of concurrent federal-provincial jurisdiction, such as "Agriculture" or "Immigration" (s. 95 of the Constitution Act, 1867.).

NATIONAL OBJECTIVES

The obligation to provide reasonable compensation arises only if the non-participating province "carries on a program or initiative that is compatible with the national objectives." It is unfortunate that the phrase "national objectives" was not given clearer definition in the constitutional text. However, in the context of a provision dealing with "a national shared-cost program", it seems plain that the national objectives are the objectives of the national shared-cost program.

How are the objectives of the national shared-cost program to be ascertained? Again, the context suggests an answer. Since the national shared-cost program is "established by the Government of Canada", it seems plain that the objectives established by the Government or Parliament of Canada would be accepted by the courts as the objectives of the program. If Parliament was foolish enough not to articulate the objectives in the legislation establishing the program, then obviously the objectives would have to be inferred from the details of the program. If, as is more likely, Parliament did articulate reasonable national objectives in the legislation establishing the program, then a court would accept that articulation as the national objectives. I say "reasonable" national objectives, because the courts will undoubtedly review Parliament's assertion of the national objectives to be sure that there is an intelligible national rationale for each. The courts will not uncritically accept every picayune point that is asserted in federal legislation as a national objective.

A national objective will always be a rather general proposition, but it may carry detailed specific implications. Take the Canada Health Act as a hypothetical example. (It is hypothetical because s. 106A has no application to shared-cost programs that are already in existence.) If the universal accessibility of free health care were accepted as a national objective, then the ban on extra-billing would seem to be an essential element of any plan that conformed to the national objectives. In other words, a plan established by a non-participating province that did not include a ban on extra-billing would not be compatible with the national objectives.

COMPATIBILITY

Section 106A requires reasonable compensation to be paid to a province that "carries on a program or initiative that is compatible with the national objectives." What does "compatible" mean in this context?

The word "compatible" is defined in the Shorter Oxford English Dictionary as follows:

1. Sympathetic.
2. Mutually tolerant; capable of existing together in the same subject; accordant, consistent, congruous.

The only meaning that makes sense in the context of s. 106A is "sympathetic". The obvious purpose underlying s. 106A is to extend funding to provinces that are pursuing programs with objectives that are sympathetic to, that is similar to the objectives of the national program.

If compatible were given a broader meaning, as including anything not directly inconsistent with the national objectives, s. 106A would lack an intelligible purpose. If a national day-care program were established by the federal government, it would make no sense to pay reasonable compensation to a non-participating province that wanted to put the money into public libraries, for example. Such a use of the funds would leave day-care unsupported in the non-participating province, and would apply federal funds to an objective which, even if it is "national" in some sense, had never been approved by the federal government, which has the responsibility for disbursing funds raised from all across the country.

I conclude that a provincial program would be "compatible" with the national objectives only if the provincial program pursued essentially the same objectives as those of the national program. What is permitted by s. 106A is some variation in the means by which those objectives are to be achieved. For example, if a national day-care program were established by the federal government, and if it called for assistance to profit-making as well as to non-profit day-care centres, a non-participating province might want to limit its program to non-profit day-care centres. That is a variation in the means of delivering day-care that might suit the conditions of the province and the ideology of its government better than the national plan. It seems likely to me that the province's plan would be "compatible" with the national objectives of the national plan.

REASONABLE COMPENSATION

What form must "reasonable compensation" take?

Cash is obviously acceptable. Reasonable compensation could therefore take the form of a cash grant from the federal government to the non-participating provincial government.

What about tax points? This is more difficult, because tax points are no more than potential provincial revenue. A grant of tax points to a non-participating province means a lowering of federal tax rates for the residents of the non-participating province so as to make possible an increase in provincial rates. Tax points are now used to adjust revenues between the federal government and the provinces, and are used to compensate Quebec for opting-out of existing shared-cost program. I think "reasonable compensation" will be interpreted against the backdrop of established Canadian federal-provincial fiscal mechanisms, and would be held to include tax points.

Note that s. 106A stipulates that reasonable compensation be provided "to the government of a province". This would preclude the federal government from providing compensation in the form of benefits to individuals. Payments to the residents of the non-participating province, or tax deductions or tax credits for the residents of the province, would not qualify as reasonable compensation.

How much compensation is "reasonable"? If the non-participating province is operating a program that is equivalent in cost to the national program, presumably reasonable compensation would consist of whatever the province would have been entitled to had it joined the national program. If the province's program is more costly than the national program, the compensation would still be the same: the discretionary choice to put more provincial resources into a program should not entitle the province to extra federal aid. If the province's program is less costly than the national program, then I think this would react on the amount of compensation that had to be provided. In that case, a lesser sum would be "reasonable." Otherwise, federal funds earmarked for particular national objectives would become available for general provincial purposes.

Political Meaning And Social Reform

Keith Banting[*]

The federal spending power provisions in the Meech Lake Accord cry out for definition. Section 106A is replete with words that admit of diverse meanings, and the result has been characterized as a section of "massively indeterminate language."[1] It is hardly surprising that this aspect of the Accord is subject to widely different interpretations, with some observers predicting a dramatic strengthening of federal power and others pronouncing with equal confidence on its imminent emasculation.

Action, especially collective action, does not proceed on the basis of complete uncertainty. Any initiative inevitably proceeds within some broad frame of reference which structures the terrain, providing a cognitive map or definition of the context. This definition need not be comprehensive. As March and Simon pointed out long ago, "choice is always exercised with respect to a limited, approximate, simplified model of the situation."[2] Nevertheless, some operational definition is a prerequisite for action, and those who interpret new situations also structure the range of responses that will be actively considered.

The operational definition of s. 106A is unlikely to emerge from judicial decisions, however. Governments have carefully avoided legal certainty about the precise scope and limits of the federal spending power throughout this century, preferring political resolutions of the

[*] A somewhat different version of this paper will appear in a special edition of *Canadian Public Policy/Analyse de Politiques* devoted to the Meech Lake Accord (forthcoming, 1988).

[1] J.D. Whyte, "Submission to the Special Joint Committee of the Senate and the House of Commons on the 1987 Constitutional Accord" (mimeo, August 20, 1987) at 17.

[2] J. March and H. Simon, *Organizations* (New York: Wiley, 1958) at 139.

conflicts inherent in the existing constitutional silence on the subject. The negotiated has always seemed safer than the litigated.

There is little likelihood for change in governmental preferences in an era governed by Meech Lake. Admittedly, the dangers inherent in a judicial determination would be lower. At the moment, the basic principle of the spending power might be at risk in a legal challenge, whereas judicial interpretations of s. 106A would deal solely with the terms and conditions of its exercise. These remain issues of critical importance to governments, however, and political leaders would undoubtedly seek to avoid litigation, especially in the case of the first programs developed under the new rules. Indeed, it is conceivable that an authoritative judicial interpretation of the section might never emerge.[3]

As a result, if the Accord is ratified, we should anticipate a political, rather than a judicial, definition of the meaning of the section, especially in the early years. This is not to argue that the legal text is unimportant. The range of plausible judicial interpretations would constitute a set of boundaries within which political conflict and bargaining would proceed and more specific political definitions of the meaning of the clause would emerge. In this context, the best indicators of the operative definition of the section are to be found in the political incentives embedded in the legal text, and the set of understandings and expectations about its meaning held by governments themselves. Concern about the legal meaning of the section thus needs to be balanced by a closer examination of the political dynamics that would be set in motion.

THE POLITICAL MEANING OF MEECH LAKE

The Meech Lake Accord represents a powerful affirmation of the collaborative model of federalism, and s. 106A reflects this ethos clearly. In operational terms, the section is more about procedure than jurisdiction. It represents a constitutional injunction to intergovernmental negotiation in the development of future shared-cost programs, and an attempt to eliminate unilateralism and the *fait accompli* from the arsenal of the federal government. In effect, the Accord identifies the federal-provincial conference as the central planning mechanism

---

3 It is possible that legal certainty might be thrust on governments as a result of private legal challenges. Whether private interests would be likely to challenge the details of the spending power when the underlying principle is entrenched remains an open question, however.

for future developments in important sectors of Canadian social policy.

Each government would enter into negotiations over proposed programs armed with a new bargaining chip. The federal position would be strengthened because Meech Lake would formally entrench the federal spending power in the Constitution. Historically the constitutional status of the spending power has been ambiguous, and successive provincial governments, especially in Quebec, have battled against its unrestricted use. Moreover, during the 1980s, legal challenges to the constitutionality of the federal spending power were mounted by private interests. The Meech Lake Accord would eliminate these problems by establishing an explicit constitutional basis for the spending power. The right of the federal government to mount a shared-cost program in any area of exclusive provincial jurisdiction, and to attach conditions relating to national objectives, could no longer be challenged.

The negotiating position of the provincial governments would also be strengthened. Each province would enjoy the constitutional right to opt out of a national program, and to receive reasonable compensation if it carries on a program or initiative that is compatible with the national objectives. Provinces have always had the absolute right to ignore a shared-cost program, but this was a difficult position to sustain indefinitely. Citizens of a province exercising this right still had to pay federal taxes to support the program elsewhere in the country, and the provincial government tended to come under pressure to join from opposition parties and the electorate. The guarantee of "reasonable compensation" would make it easier to opt out and to mount a separate program.

The recent debate over these twin elements of s. 106A dramatically highlights the two solitudes of Canadian political discourse. While critics in Quebec fear that the proposal would strengthen the federal role, critics in English Canada foresee precisely the opposite result. In large part, these conflicting predictions reflect a concentration on different aspects of the proposal, and they underline the importance of examining the implications of both the entrenchment of the spending power and the terms governing opting-out.

Entrenchment and Centralization

Debate about s. 106A within Quebec has concentrated on entrenchment. Such a step would clearly strengthen the federal spending power in both legal and political terms. Admittedly, the legal significance of this step can be debated, since legal challenges to the federal spending power over the years have been unsuccessful. In the words of the special parliamentary committee on the Accord:

> Canadian courts in the last 30 years have shown little or no hesitation in "recognizing" the federal spending power, even in the case of conditional payments in areas of exclusive provincial jurisdiction.[4]

Nevertheless, some constitutional ambiguity remains, since the Supreme Court itself has never ruled on the use of the spending power in such circumstances. The Meech Lake Accord would resolve the question definitively.

The key issue, however, is the political significance of entrenchment. The unanimous agreement of eleven governments to entrench the spending power and to specify rules governing its exercise would undoubtedly confirm the political legitimacy of the shared-cost mechanism. Indeed, such a collective political affirmation would strengthen the spending power far more than a favourable ruling of the Supreme Court ever could.

For Quebec, this step is highly symbolic. In effect, the provincial government would be declaring a truce in its long war against the principle of the spending power, and for critics such as Jacques Parizeau, this represents "un grotesque retour en arrière". As he emphasizes:

> Pour la première fois dans l'histoire, un gouvernement du Québec acceptera donc formellement le droit du gouvernement fédéral d'intervenir dans des champs de compétence provinciale exclusive et fera enchasser ce droit dans la Constitution.[5]

Parizeau fears that, in time, a growing portion of the resources of the government of Quebec would be consumed by the provincial share of federal shared-cost programs, and that the broad priorities of the province would increasingly be set by federal political currents, rather than those of Quebec society. "M. Lesage doit se retourner dans sa tombe," Parizeau concludes. In a similar vein, Andrée Lajoie and Jacques Frémont describe the provision as "un véritable cheval de Troie au sein des compétences législatives exclusives du Québec," including such sensitive areas as education, culture and language. The result could

---

4 Canada, *Report of the Special Joint Committee of the Senate and the House of Commons on The 1987 Constitutional Accord* (Ottawa: Queen's Printer, 1987) at 72.

5 *Le Devoir [de Montréal]* (May 6, 1987). Also reprinted in *Le Québec et le Lac Meech* (Montreal: Guérin littérature, 1987) at 177-179.

be the gradual relegation of provinces to the status of municipalities.[6] From this perspective, Meech Lake represents the new face of centralism.

This argument assumes that the legitimacy of a policy instrument is critical to the extent of its use. In the future, federal authorities contemplating a new shared-cost program would not have to grapple with the political controversy that currently surrounds the spending power. The fact that fiscal constraints would limit the immediate prospects for such initiatives is irrelevant. The constitutional and political right of the federal government to act would be clear and, as the argument concludes, in the long term the number and scope of such programs would grow in a future governed by the Accord.

There are several reasons for questioning this line of argument. The uncertain legitimacy of the spending power does not appear to have dramatically constrained the scope of the existing shared-cost domain. Admittedly, the interwar years were populated with federal politicians who often hesitated to launch social programs and cited the division of jurisdiction as a reason for inaction. When attention shifts to the postwar period, however, it is difficult to identify major social programs to which the federal government was committed that were not established because of the political sensitivity of the spending power. Federal initiatives may have come more slowly and incrementally than they would have otherwise. But the most significant influence of the uncertain status of the spending power was probably on the stringency of the conditions attached to shared-cost programs in this country, as opposed to the United States for example, rather than on the number of programs established.

If constitutional uncertainty exercised, at best, a mild restraint on federal authorities in the past, there is little reason to assume that the enhanced political legitimacy inherent in s. 106A will significantly increase the use of the shared-cost technique in the future. Moreover, any expansionist potential of this sort might be offset by other tendencies. If the consensual spirit of Meech Lake were to fade, and if the establishment of national shared-cost programs were to prove politically unrewarding for Ottawa, federal politicians might well look to their own jurisdiction when responding to new social needs, relying more heavily on income-security programs and the tax system rather than shared-cost initiatives. The tax-transfer system, after all, provides

---

6 *Le Devoir* [*de Montréal*] (May 11, 1987). Also reprinted in *Le Québec et le Lac Meech, ibid.*, at 170-173.

a flexible instrument that establishes a direct contact between the federal government and individual citizens in all regions.

The scope of the shared-cost domain in a Meech Lake world is clearly open, to be shaped by the balance of political forces in years to come. On balance, however, it seems unlikely that the new rules would lead to a significantly more rapid expansion than would otherwise have occurred.

Opting-Out and Decentralization

Critics in English Canada have tended to ignore the implications of the entrenchment of the spending power, and to focus exclusively on the nature of the programs that might develop in the future. The controversy here concerns the right of any province to opt-out and to receive reasonable compensation if it carries on a program or initiative that is compatible with the national objectives. Critics worry that the federal government's capacity to establish national standards would be eroded fatally, and that the guarantee of reasonable compensation would effectively constitute positive encouragement to opt-out.

The substantive — as opposed to symbolic — impact of this provision depends heavily on the terms governing the opting-out provision. Quebec opted-out of the Canada Assistance Plan in 1965, for example, but this proved to be of marginal significance, since the province agreed to continue to meet CAP program standards. The question is whether the requirement in the Meech Lake Accord that provincial programs be compatible with national objectives would produce similar constraints.

This is unlikely. The most plausible interpretation is that the Accord would lead to greater regional variation in social service programs developed in the future. Federal authorities would likely seek to minimize the number of provinces choosing to opt-out of a scheme by allowing for considerable regional variation within the national program itself. This emphasis on flexibility would pervade both the national objectives and program design.

The national objectives of a new shared-cost program would be shaped by the ethos of joint planning implicit in the Accord. In the words of Senator Murray:

Obviously, extensive negotiations would have to take place between both levels of government. And it would be wiser if both the federal and provincial governments agreed beforehand on the program's national objectives.[7]

The formulation of a new shared-cost program would begin with the federal government suggesting a set of national objectives, and canvassing provincial reactions. If there was general agreement on objectives, then negotiations could proceed to questions of program design. If, on the other hand, there was no consensus on objectives, federal authorities would presumably negotiate with the provinces concerning alternative formulations which might command more general agreement. While the federal government could legally establish national objectives independently, such unilateralism would presumably anger provinces and maximize the extent of opting-out and the possibility of legal challenges, both of which federal authorities would want to avoid.

In effect, the ethos of the Accord suggests that national goals and federal goals are not synonymous, and the formulation of truly national objectives should be a joint activity. Such a dynamic would incline new programs towards very general objectives, and perhaps even a more diverse set of objectives than would have emerged otherwise.

A similar pressure towards flexibility would govern issues related to program design. The history of the negotiations over the Accord suggests that national objectives will not be seen as national standards. While a legal case might be made for the proposition that national objectives could be so specific as to approximate standards, a proposal involving national "standards" was explicitly rejected during the negotiations. The initial proposal on the table included a requirement for prior provincial consent for the launching of any new shared-cost program.[8] Once accepted, however, such programs would have been subject to national standards.

This proposal was rejected, largely because of concern from Atlantic Canada and Manitoba about the requirement for prior provincial consent. The essential trade-off within the process was the

---

7 Canada, *Minutes of Proceedings and Evidence of the Special Joint Committee of the Senate and the House of Commons on the 1987 Constitutional Accord*, Issue No. 2 (Ottawa: Queen's Printer, August 4, 1987) at 59.

8 The initial federal proposal, which was adopted from the policy document of the Quebec Liberal Party, assumed that the establishment of a shared-cost program was, in effect, a change in the division of jurisdiction between governments, and should therefore be approved through a procedure similar to the constitutional amending formula. See Policy Committee of the Quebec Liberal Party, *Mastering Our Future* (Montreal) 1985 at 14-15, 50-51.

elimination of the consent requirement in exchange for a softening of the language of national standards to that of national objectives. As a result, during the formative early years at least, participants in the process can be expected to draw a distinction between the broad objectives of a program, on the one hand, and the means of achieving those objectives and the modalities of its design, on the other.[9]

Thus regional diversity would flow from the natural incentive for the federal government to minimize the extent of opting-out from future programs, and from the broader understandings of the parties to the agreement itself. The Accord would nudge new initiatives towards the model of the Canada Assistance Plan, with a general umbrella agreement containing relatively few conditions and broad flexibility to accommodate provincial preferences.[10]

Regional diversity would also be emphasized because some provinces would opt out anyway. Quebec would perhaps do so as a matter of principle. Other provinces might be tempted to follow, although much would depend on the formula for calculating reasonable compensation. For example, a formula based on average national costs would discourage provinces with above average costs from opting-out but create an incentive for those with below average costs to do so.

It is important to emphasize that if the national program provided for substantial flexibility from the outset, the additional degrees of freedom gained by opting-out might prove limited, indeed negligible. As long as the "spirit" of Meech Lake pervades the negotiating process, a decision to opt out would be largely symbolic.

In short, the dynamics that would be set in motion by the Accord point to a more regionally diverse pattern of social service initiatives in the future. There is no reason to assume that the total resources being dedicated to social policy generally would necessarily vary more among regions, but Canadians crossing provincial boundaries would notice greater variation in program design than they would otherwise have done.

---

9 From this point of view, Senator Murray's suggestion that the concepts of national objectives and national standards, conditions or criteria are more or less interchangeable, seems curious. See the discussion of his comments in Canada, *Report of the Special Joint Committee*, above, note 4 at 73-75.

10 This prospect was not lost on national social groups. The leaders of the Canadian Day Care Advocacy Association, for example, feared that in the course of intergovernmental negotiations national objectives might "become so watered down and bare-bones minimal just in an effort to keep everyone." Canada, *Minutes of Proceedings and Evidence of the Special Joint Committee of the Senate and of the House of Commons on the 1987 Constitutional Accord*, Issue No. 7 (Ottawa: Queen's Printer, August 13, 1987) at 18-19.

MEECH LAKE AND THE FUTURE OF SOCIAL POLICY

An agreement as complex as the Meech Lake Accord can be evaluated according to a variety of criteria. Most assessments focus on the twin pillars of the Canadian political system, federalism and democracy. Some judge the Accord according to competing models of an ideal federal system, examining its impact on the relationships between levels of government and the political integration of Quebec into the larger political system. Others evaluate the Accord according to principals of democratic governance, holding the process of its creation and ratification up to scrutiny, or examining its impact on human rights in general and the Charter in particular.

Equally central to any comprehensive evaluation of the Accord is its implication for the development of social policy in Canada. Certainly any evaluation of s. 106A cannot turn solely on competing models of federalism or democracy. The capacity of the Canadian state to respond effectively to emerging social needs in the decades to come is also critical.[11]

The relationship between federalism and the welfare state has long been debated in this country and elsewhere. During the 1930s, many commentators argued that the decentralized nature of the Canadian federal system was a conservative force in welfare politics, which inhibited the development of essential social programs. Certainly the significant expansion of the federal role that did take place during and after the Second World War facilitated the establishment of major social programs during the following quarter century.

Section 106A does not represent such a draconian limitation of the spending power as to return Canada to the paralysis of the 1930s. However, another proposition about the impact of federalism on social policy is relevant to the ethos of Meech Lake. This argument insists that the fragmentation of power inherent in federal structures constrains the scope for bold action on a national level, and condemns the political system as a whole towards an incremental process of policy change.

---

11 While the implications of the spending power for future social programs had been an important issue at the outset of the debate over the Accord, it clearly began to fade later on. Indeed, in the final appearance of Senator Murray and his officials before the special parliamentary committee, the subject was hardly mentioned. See Canada, *Minutes of Proceedings and Evidence of the Special Joint Committee of the Senate and of the House of Commons on the 1987 Constitutional Accord*, Issue No. 16 (Ottawa: Queen's Printer, September 1, 1987). In their supplementary comments in the report of the committee, the Liberals returned to the issue, but the NDP did not (*The 1987 Constitutional Accord*, at 152-157).

This is particularly the case with a collaborative or consensual model of federalism. A central role for federal-provincial negotiations diversifies that range of ideologies and interests that are brought to bear on major issues. While regional interests are stoutly defended by provincial champions, partisan and ideological differences also flow into federal-provincial channels. An emphasis on consensus among governments representing diverse regional and ideological complexions saps boldness, since consensual mechanisms inevitably favour those least interested in change. In this, as several commentators have observed, the intersection of federalism, regionalism, and ideology generates a pattern of policy change similar to what one would expect in a unitary state from a large coalition government.[12]

The Meech Lake Accord, with its celebration of collaborative federalism, would reinforce this incremental dimension of policy change in Canada. The injunction to make the federal-provincial forum the central planning instrument of future initiatives in the social services, the emphasis on general objectives capable of accommodating the varied preferences of ideologically diverse governments, and the greater flexibility in program design would incline the Canadian welfare state to a more piecemeal, incremental pattern of change. To minimize the extent of opting-out, national programs would have to be sufficiently flexible to accommodate the aspirations of the most conservative as well as the most adventuresome government at the table. The locus of initiative, innovation and boldness would be lodged more firmly at the provincial level, and new ideas would spread more slowly through demonstration effects rather than federal direction.

None of this is to suggest that the Accord would stop social progress. Nevertheless, progress would come along a more diverse set of provincial pathways and, for the country as a whole, the pace would be slower. Such a system undoubtedly has benefits in terms of policy experimentation and diversity at the provincial level. It also has costs. And those costs would be borne primarily by the poor and the vulnerable in those provinces that chose to go less far than they would have done under stronger federal direction.

SUMMARY REFLECTIONS

Concern about the diverse theoretical possibilities inherent in the

---

12 For an elaboration of this argument, see K. Banting, *The Welfare State and Canadian Federalism*, 2nd ed. (Kingston and Montreal: McGill-Queen's University Press, 1987) ch. 11.

imprecise language of the Accord needs to be balanced by an appreciation of the political incentives and understandings that would define its operational meaning, especially in the early years when the critical political — as opposed to legal — precedents would be created.

In the case of s. 106A, the essential political imperatives are reasonably clear. The constitutional injunction to intergovernmental bargaining, the concern to avoid litigation, and a federal concern to limit the extent of opting-out would shape the future of shared-cost programming.

This is not to argue that judicial as opposed to political responses to constitutional uncertainty are inherently preferable. If the cost of avoiding recourse to the courts did prove to be excessive incrementalism in policy development, however, litigation might prove essential to the social responsiveness of the Canadian state.

The Federal Spending Power and Meech Lake

Andrée Lajoie

The most important transfer of powers envisaged by the Meech Lake Accord is probably found in s. 7, pertaining to the spending power of the federal government. It would add s. 106A to the Constitution.[1] In ascertaining the impact of this particular proposal of constitutional modification, as of any other, one must first look at the law as it reads before amendment. It is not superfluous either to start with a given conception of federalism or at least with an idea of the minimum conditions that a Constitution must meet in order to qualify as federal.

THE LAW AS IT STANDS

My personal position is that the exercise of a federal spending power in fields of exclusive provincial legislative jurisdiction, especially conditional spending, is no part of Canadian constitutional law as it now stands. The question of the constitutionality of the spending power is, in fact, still open for want of a Supreme Court decision, and the direction the Court would take if confronted with the problem is quite uncertain since two of its members are on the record with conflicting views on the subject.

In fact, in the thirties, the Court had favourably commented on the constitutionality of the spending power in the *Reference Re Unemployment Insurance*, but it has not been confirmed on that point by the

---

1 Constitution Act, 1867 (U.K.), c. 3. See the Appendix to this volume for relevant sections and the text of the Meech Lake Accord.

Privy Council which, in the same case, held a different view:[2]

> But assuming that the Dominion has collected by means of taxation a fund, it by no means follows that any legislation which disposes of it is necessarily within Dominion competence.

Such a statement left the question expressly open, and Professor La Forest, as he then was, acknowledged that it still remained so as late as 1981,[3] even though he is the member of the Supreme Court who favours the constitutionality of the spending power.[4] Since the *Unemployment Insurance Reference*, other tribunals have rendered decisions without settling the question, either because they skirt it or because they are not binding.

Both the *Central Mortgage and Housing*[5] and the *Porter*[6] cases followed the Supreme Court decision in the *Unemployment Insurance Reference*, which, as noted, was not upheld by the Privy Council. These two decisions and that in *Angers*,[7] were on the record when La Forest wrote in 1981. La Forest nevertheless concluded that the question was still open, probably because of the ruling of the Privy Council in the *Unemployment Insurance Reference*, as well as the fact that these decisions did not emanate from the Supreme Court. He went as far as to refute the *ratio* in *Angers*, which based the spending power upon the residual legislative competence of Parliament.[8]

Three other decisions skirt the issue. In *Lofstrom*,[9] the Saskatchewan Court of Appeal decided that no individual right derives from federal-provincial agreements, because only governments are parties to them. Therefore, the status of beneficiary is for the provinces to define, a position confirmed by the Supreme Court decision in *Alden*.[10] But in that case, Mr. Justice Ritchie stopped short of any pronouncement on the constitutionality of the agreement, as did Mr. Justice Le Dain in the recently decided case of *Finlay*.[11]

---

2 *Reference Re Unemployment Insurance (Employment and Social Insurance Act)*, [1936] S.C.R. 427, not affirmed on this point (*sub nom. A.G. Can. v. A.G. Ont.*), [1937] A.C. 355 at 366 (P.C.).

3 G.V. La Forest, "The Allocation of Taxing Power Under the Canadian Constitution" (1980-1981), 65 *Canadian Tax Papers* 50.

4 See below, at 5.

5 *Central Mortgage & Housing Corp. v. Co-operative College Residences Inc.* (1974), 44 D.L.R. (3d) 662 (Ont. H.C.), affirmed (1977), 71 D.L.R. (3d) 183 (Ont. C.A.).

6 *Porter v. R.*, [1965] Ex. C.R. 200 (Ex. Ct.).

7 *Angers v. M.N.R.*, [1957] Ex. C.R. 83 (Ex. Ct.).

8 La Forest, above, note 3 at 80.

9 *Re Lofstrom and Murphy* (1971), 22 D.L.R. (3d) 120 (Sask. C.A.).

10 *Alden v. Gaglardi*, [1973] S.C.R. 199.

11 *Finlay v. Canada (Minister of Finance)*, [1986] 2 S.C.R. 607.

Finally, there are two pronouncements from the Alberta and Saskatchewan Courts of Queen's Bench, both in the context of declaratory actions. The first[12] deals with the provincial spending power as applied to matching grants for international aid, a subject the court considered to be within federal legislative jurisdiction over external affairs. The court concluded however, that appropriation bills passed by the Saskatchewan Legislature authorizating such expenditures were *intra vires*. The *ratio* of the decision, supported by two precedents,[13] seems to be that the Legislature did not purport, in such an appropriation, to exercise control or to regulate activity beyond its legislative competence. Without going into the question of whether the attribution of such grants falls within federal legislative jurisdiction to begin with,[14] it must be noted that the grants were unconditional, and therefore did not qualify as an exercise of legislative power. Consequently, the effect of such a decision, even if it emanated from a higher court, would not extend to conditional grants made to provincial governments, the issue with which this paper is concerned.

In contrast, the last of these two decisions[15] confronts directly the question being dealt with here. In a declaratory action, a judge of Alberta's court of first instance found the federal Income Tax Act[16] to be *intra vires*, even though the money it raised was transferred to provinces under the authority of a number of other federal statutes imposing conditions on the recipient provinces, and was to be used for provincial programs in health, welfare and post-secondary education, all matters within exclusive provincial legislative authority. Mr. Justice Medhurst characterized all of this legislation as being, in pith and substance, in relation to the federal purpose of raising money by taxation, the monies not being specifically levied for provincial purposes. The whole issue being one of characterization, the relevant questions are whether the characterization was correct and whether it should be permissible to do indirectly what the Constitution directly prohibits. At any rate, despite its thorough treatment of the question,

---

12 *Dunbar v. A.G. Sask.* (1984), 11 D.L.R. (4th) 374 (Sask. Q.B.).

13 *Dow v. Black*, [1875] L.R. 6 P.C. 272, and *McMillan v. City of Winnipeg* (1919), 45 D.L.R. 351 (Man. K.B.).

14 Some international activity falls within provincial powers, when it is related to a matter within its exclusive legislative jurisdiction. See J.Y. Morin, "La personnalité internationale du Québec" (1984), 1 *Revue québécoise de droit international* 265.

15 *Winterhaven Stables Ltd. v. A.G. Can.* (1986), 29 D.L.R. (4th) 394 (Alta. Q.B.).

16 S.C. 1970-71-72, c. 63.

this isolated decision from a court of first instance in one province is far from binding.

Given these decisions, it then still appears to be true that no case yet has settled the question of the federal spending power, unless one is ready to consider Mr. Justice Pigeon's pronouncement in the *Reference Re Agricultural Products Marketing Act*,[17] where he declared unconstitutional even unconditional federal expenditures in a provincial field of jurisdiction. The statement is part of the *ratio* of a majority opinion, but it has gone unnoticed in the spending power debate because it was pronounced in a case that, although concerned with spending, did not deal with a shared-cost program. One is then left wondering whether the Supreme Court would confirm that precedent if confronted now, in the present state of constitutional law before it is amended, if at all, by the Meech Lake Accord, with a case dealing directly with the constitutionality of federal conditional spending in the context of such a program. The answer would depend on whether the Court would be rallied by Mr. Justice La Forest or Mr. Justice Beetz, assuming both of them still hold to the views they respectively expressed in the sixties while professors of law.[18] Their opinions diverge as to whether federal authorities are constitutionally empowered to spend the product of the taxes they levy by whatever means and for whatever purposes comprised within provincial legislative jurisdiction.

It is of course superfluous to mention that federal spending in federal jurisdiction is not in question here, nor are unconditional equalization payments since the adoption of s. 36(2) of the Constitution Act, 1982.[19] Indeed, most constitutional experts would agree that the reference to a federal commitment to the principle to make equalization payments to provinces, in that section has the effect of constitutionalizing such payments even though they transgress the constitutional division of legislative jurisdiction as it stood before the 1982 Act. This result follows because there is no proviso reserving federal and provincial legislative jurisdiction as it stood before that amendment.[20] Where disagreement exists, however, is on the question

17 [1978] 2 S.C.R. 1198.

18 G.V. La Forest, "The Allocation of Taxing Power under the Canadian Constitution" (1967-68), 46 *Canadian Tax Papers* 40; J. Beetz, "Les attitudes changeantes du Quebec à l'endroit de la Constitution de 1867" dans P.A. Crépeau et C.B. MacPherson, éds., *The Future of Canadian Federalism/L'avenir du fédéralisme canadien*, Toronto and Montreal, University of Toronto Press and Presse de l'Université de Montréal, 1965, at 113.

19 Being Schedule B of the Canada Act 1982 (U.K.), c. 11. See Appendix to this volume.

20 This is true *only* of equalization payments, governed by subs. (2) of s. 36. The promotion

of federal spending in a provincial field of jurisdiction, when the spending depends on the provinces meeting certain conditions, which are then equivalent to constraints in the exercise of their legislative jurisdiction.

On this question, Mr. Justice La Forest has affirmed the constitutional validity of such spending.[21] His reasoning is founded on the federal legislative jurisdiction regarding public property, found in s. 91(1A) of the *Constitution Act, 1867*. According to his interpretation, the product of federal taxation, raised by whatever means, can be spent at the discretion of the federal government even for provincial purposes since the monies are federal public property. As long as the provinces voluntarily adhere to federal conditions, they are not constrained by compulsory regulations nor is their legislative jurisdiction invaded.

Mr. Justice Beetz[22] sees things differently. For him, federal spending in the provincial sphere invades, by its very existence, the provincial autonomy defined by the Constitution, even when the payments are unconditional,[23] because the mere fact of spending for provincial purposes deprives the provinces of resources that they themselves need to act autonomously, in the same way or otherwise, in that field or in another, when they feel like it, at their discretion. One could not find a more eloquent articulation of the view that sovereignty in a jurisdiction entails the choice of legislative and executive priorities in that field and between all fields of jurisdiction attributed to that authority.

In my view, the problem with the contrary opinion, very well expounded by Professor La Forest, as he then was, and often taken up again in decisions,[24] is the contestable characterization of the nature of conditional federal spending in provincial fields and the misconception of the constitutional division of executive powers. It is

---

of "equal opportunities", through conditional grants or otherwise, covered by s. 36(1), remains subject to the division of legislative authority as it read in 1982, given the introductory clause of that section: "Without altering the legislative authority of Parliament or of the provincial legislatures, or the rights of any of them with respect to the exercise of their legislative authority . . ." See Appendix in this volume.

21 La Forest, above, notes 3 and 18.

22 J. Beetz, above, notes 3 and 18. Translation, however incompetent, is mine.

23 *Ibid*. It must be noted that this text was of course written before the Constitution Act, 1982 was enacted and that Mr. Justice Beetz might now want to make an exception for equalization payments, given the effect ascribed to s. 36(2) of the Act; see text above, and note 20.

24 The last and most complete being *Winterhaven*, above, note 15.

colourable to characterize legislation authorizing federal expenditures, without referring to its real purposes, as legislation related in pith and substance to public property and not to education, health or whatever other matter of provincial jurisdiction for which the proposed expense is intended. With regard to the powers of the executive, the opinion favouring the constitutionality of the spending power assumes that executive powers are divided differently between federal authorities and the provinces than their respective legislative powers. This view requires further assessment.

The Constitution Act, 1867 does not provide much guidance. However, its general economy and the exceptional specific attributions of executive powers to federal authorities (for example, in relation to treaty making and expropriation for defense purposes) speak in favour of an implicit division along the lines of legislative powers unless an exception is expressly stated. The courts have confirmed this view, even when executive powers are derived from the prerogative power. This view was expressed in *Maritime Bank*,[25] a decision of the Privy Council which was approved twice in the last five years by the Supreme Court:[26]

> Their Lordships do not think it necessary to examine, in minute detail, the provisions of the Act of 1867, which nowhere profess to curtail in any respect the rights and privileges of the Crown, or to disturb the relations then subsisting between the Sovereign and the provinces. The object of the Act was neither to weld the provinces into one, nor to subordinate provincial governments to a central authority, but to create a federal government in which they should all be represented, entrusted with the exclusive administration of affairs in which they had a common interest, each province retaining its independence and autonomy. *That object was accomplished by distributing, between the Dominion and the provinces, all powers executive and legislative, and all public property and revenues* which had previously belonged to the provinces; so that the Dominion Government should be vested with such of these powers, property, and revenues as were necessary for the due performance of its constitutional functions, *and that the remainder should be retained by the provinces for the purposes of provincial government.* [Italics mine][27]

The same view concerning the division of executive powers was expressed by the Privy Council in *Bonanza Creek*:[28]

> The result had been to establish wholly new Dominion and provincial

25 *Liquidators of the Maritime Bank of Canada v. Receiver General of New Brunswick*, [1892] A.C. 437 (P.C.).
26 *Re Resolution to Amend the Constitution (Patriation Reference)*, [1981] 1 S.C.R. 753, and *Re Manitoba Language Rights*, [1985] 1 S.C.R. 721.
27 Lord Watson in *Maritime Bank*, above, note 25 at 441-442.
28 *Viscount Haldane in Bonanza Creek Gold Mining Co. v. R.*, [1916] 1 A.C. 56 at 579-581.

Governments with defined powers and duties, both derived from the statute which was their legal source, the residual powers and duties being taken away from the old provinces and given to the Dominion. *It is to be observed that the British North America Act has made a distribution between the Dominion and the provinces which extends* not only *to legislative but to executive authority* . . .

. . .

The effect of these sections of the British North America Act is that, subject to certain express provisions in that Act and to the supreme authority of the Sovereign, who delegates to the Governor-General and through his instrumentality to the Lieutenant-Governors the exercise of the prerogative on terms defined in their commissions, *the distribution under the new grant of executive authority in substance follows the distribution under the new grant of legislative powers.* [Italics mine]

Some have contended, however, that s. 36 of the Constitution Act, 1982 has changed the constitutional division of legislative and executive powers alike, specifically with regard to the spending power. The language of the section is that of international agreements between contracting parties and not that of unilateral imperative prescriptions or attributive dispositions. Subsection (2) acknowledges a commitment by federal authorities to make equalization payments and, as I have previously observed, insofar as the Constitution recites this commitment, one can infer that payments made in compliance with it are not unconstitutional. But where the promotion of equal opportunities, by conditional grants or otherwise, is concerned, the provincial and federal authorities are committed to this goal by s. 36(1), subject to the proviso that this has to be done "*without altering* the legislative authority of Parliament and the provincial legislatures". In other words, the provinces and the federal authorities cannot alter the constitutional division of powers by a mere agreement about a shared-cost program; whatever jurisdiction Parliament lacked before 1982, it cannot bestow on itself merely by contracting with the provinces for the purposes mentioned in s. 36(1). Consequently, if I am right in thinking that the federal government did not then have the power to limit provincial jurisdiction through conditional grants, it has not acquired it since.

In these circumstances, I fail to see how one can justify, under present Canadian constitutional law, federal spending in the provincial field, especially when the spending is conditional. I may, however, be wrong in favouring the opinion of Mr. Justice Beetz and holding that conditional federal spending in provincial fields of jurisdiction is no part of Canadian constitutional law. If so, one must be ready, I believe, to go as far as to deny that the Canadian Constitution has a federal character.

MINIMAL REQUIREMENTS OF FEDERALISM

Most constitutional scholars are not very prolific, to say the least, on the subject of the theory of federalism,[29] and especially on the differences between federalism and administrative decentralization within a unitary state. They all agree,[30] however, on a threshold below which there may be no real federalism: that line is drawn when local authorities are subordinate to central authorities[31] or where their independence from the central authority is not constitutionalized.[32] Some even mention that local authorities must have sufficient fiscal powers to guarantee their independence.[33]

In this light, if Canadian constitutional law were to allow a subordination of provincial legislative jurisdiction to the discretionary spending power of the federal executive, one would conclude that the Constitution was not of a federal character. This is especially so in view of the recent restatement by the Supreme Court, in two landmark cases,[34] of the federal principle in the very words used by Lord Watson in *Maritime Bank*:

> The object of the Act was neither to weld the provinces into one, nor to subordinate provincial governments to a central authority, but to create a federal government in which they should all be represented, entrusted with the exclusive administration of affairs in which they had a common interest, each province retaining its independence and autonomy.

> The federal principle cannot be reconciled with a state of affairs where the modification of provincial legislative powers could be obtained by the unilateral action of the federal authorities. It would indeed offend the federal principle that "a radical change to . . . [the] constitution [be] taken at the request of

---

29 With the exception of H. Brun et G. Tremblay, *Droit constitutionnel*, Cowansville, Éditions Yvon Blais, 1982, who devote a long chapter to this important question.

30 The exception is G. Rémillard, *Le fédéralisme canadien*, t. 1, "La Loi constitutionnelle de 1867", Montréal, Éditions Québec/Amérique, 1983 at p. 48. He centres his discussion on the differences between federations and confederations and is silent on the basic requirements of federalism.

31 P. W. Hogg, *Constitutional Law of Canada*, 2nd ed. (Toronto: Carswell, 1985) at 230; Brun et Tremblay, above, note 29 at 294; A. Tremblay, *Précis de droit constitutionnel*, Montréal, Thémis, 1982 at 88; François Chevrette et H. Marx, *Droit constitutionnel*, Montréal, Les Presses de l'Université de Montréal, 1982 at p. 219; N. Finkelstein, *Laskin's Canadian Constitutional Law*, 5th ed., vol. 1 (Toronto: Carswell, 1986) at 16; G.-A. Beaudoin, *Le partage des pouvoirs*, 2ᵉ éd., Ottawa, Éditions de l'Université d'Ottawa, 1982 at 11; J. E. Magnet, *Constitutional Law of Canada* (Toronto: Carswell, 1983) at 1.

32 A. Tremblay, *ibid.*, at 88.

33 J. Whyte and W. Lederman, *Canadian Constitutional Law*, 2nd ed. (Toronto: Butterworths, 1977) at 1-29.

34 The *Patriation Reference* and the *Manitoba Language Rights* cases, above, note 26.

a bare majority of the members of the Canadian House of Commons and Senate."[35]

THE PROPOSED AMENDMENT

The problem, then, with the amendment embodied in the proposed new s. 106A is precisely that it implies subordination of the provinces in the exercise of their legislative jurisdiction to the federal executive authorities. Quebec has thus tried in vain to amend the draft of s. 106A so that it would contain the same proviso as s. 36(1) of the Constitution Act, 1982 which reads: "Without altering the legislative authority of Parliament or of the provincial legislatures, or the rights of any of them with respect to the exercise of their legislative authority . . ."[36] Such a proviso was of course inconsistent with the rest of s. 106A, to the point of making it meaningless and uninterpretable, since the section empowers the federal government to establish "national objectives" for programs in "fields of exclusive provincial legislative jurisdiction". This is an obvious curtailment of provincial jurisdiction and an important shift in the distribution of powers.

Some constitutional commentators admit that this is the case, but favour this political option because they hold a centralist view of federalism or because they see it as the only realistic way to obtain compensation for provinces wishing to opt-out from shared-cost programs. Others have contended that the above interpretation does not represent the true effect of the proposed s. 106A. Some hold that subs. (2) of that section, which states that "Nothing in this section extends the legislative powers of the Parliament of Canada or of the legislatures of the provinces," has the effect of maintaining the integrity of the legislative jurisdiction of the provinces because the legislative jurisdiction of Parliament has not been extended, and legislative jurisdiction is a finite entity exhaustively divided between Parliament and the provincial legislatures. Those who rely on this argument do not take into account the possibility of the constitutional test ascribing power directly to the executive and removing it entirely from legislative competence. They might have failed to notice that this text,

---

35 *Maritime Bank*, above, note 25 at 441-442.
36 Québec, Assemblée Nationale, Journal des Débats, Commissions parlementaires, 1ère session, 33e législature, *Commission sur les Institutions*: C.I. 2177-2257 (microfiche), at p. 2234, Gil Rémillard, Ministre des Affaires intergouvernementales: "Si on ajoutait: Sous réserve des compétences législatives du Parlement et des Législatures et le droit de les exercer, [comme] pour le libellé de l'article 36 — je fais une hypothèse — quelle serait votre réaction?"

by expressly mentioning only legislative powers, does not purport to maintain the purview of executive powers as they previously stood but, on the contrary, allows for the extension of federal *executive powers* at the expense of provincial *legislative jurisdiction*.

A somewhat different expression of the same argument — also grounded in the principles of parliamentary democracy — claims that since all government expenditures must be authorized by Parliament, if the legislative powers of Parliament have not been extended, Parliament will not then be able to legislatively authorize grants on conditions that would bind the provinces within their jurisdiction. The answer is that although parliamentary democracy postulates legislative authorization for public expenditure by the executive, it does not require that a specific detailed purpose be approved for each disbursement. Parliament could very well appropriate large sums of money for compensation owing to provinces opting-out of a program, and leave the definition of national objectives to the executive, who could then couch them in the agreement only, thus avoiding not only legislation, but even regulations.

Others still claim that when Parliament authorizes expenditures related to compensation for opting-out provinces and sets national objectives that must be met by the programs carried out by these provinces, it is not adopting mandatory legislation in the fields of exclusive provincial jurisdiction either because objectives have a somewhat less restricting effect than norms and standards, or because provinces may escape its binding effect if they are ready to forgo the compensation.

In my opinion, neither of these arguments holds water. For one thing, the Supreme Court has very recently stated that there is no authority in Canada for applying the doctrine which distinguishes between mandatory and directory statutory provisions to constitutional law, even if that distinction has any ascertainable basis in statutory law.[37] Furthermore, in this view, objectives would not be "not binding" because they would bind in less detail than norms and standards. I contend that they would only be somewhat less restricting, but that their aim would still be to bind in the full scope of their object. Whenever a provincial legislature must contain its legislation within the purview of objectives dictated by an external authority, it is bound to that extent. To be bound in less detail is certainly not equivalent to having complete legislative sovereignty.

---

37 *Re Manitoba Language Rights*, above, note 26 at 740-741.

As for reading a legislative condition as "not binding" because a province can evade it by foregoing compensation, that view rests on a very narrow understanding of what regulation means, and one that has been refuted by Roderick MacDonald.[38] It postulates that loss of compensation, expressly imposed by the Constitution, would be a less severe or important sanction than a pronouncement of legislative invalidity by a court. The least that can be said for such a statement is that legal realists would not agree with it — nor would most taxpayers.

I consequently remain convinced that the adoption of s. 106A as it is now proposed would empower the federal executive authorities, merely by entering into an agreement with some provinces, to impose discretionary conditions that would translate into constraints on the exercise of provincial legislative jurisdiction and thereby modify the constitutional distribution of powers. The net result will be a transfer of powers from provincial legislatures to the profit of the federal executive.

As if this transfer of powers to the federal executive were not sufficient, the amendment also would have the effect of vesting even more powers in the judiciary, already somewhat burdened by the increase in constitutional control effected by the Charter. The interpretive problems raised by the spending power provisions of the Meech Lake Accord are numerous and have been discussed elsewhere in this collection of essays. I have one further question, however: should we also expect the judges, after they have interpreted all of the vague and open terms of s. 106A, to tell us not only what constitutes a "distinct society", but also how a society is going to be able to maintain its distinctiveness when its education, health and other social policies are imposed from the outside, through national objectives defined by another society, distinct of course, by definition, from the "distinct" one?

It is in the light that one must read the proposed s. 106A. No wonder it states that the legislative powers of Parliament are not extended: executive power will suffice, with a little help from the Supreme Court. As for provincial jurisdiction, no one in his or her right mind would think it could be extended by such an amendment. Wasn't the question, however, that it should not have been diminished?

---

38 R. A. MacDonald, "Pour la reconnaissance d'une normativité juridique implicite et inférentielle" (1986), 18 *Sociologie et Sociétés* 47 at 59.

Meech Ado About Nothing?
Federalism, Democracy and the Spending
Power

*Andrew Petter**

I find myself in an uncomfortable position. Like Professor Trudeau in 1957, my stance on the federal spending power places me "in disagreement with my friends and with people whose ideas I usually find congenial".[1] To make matters worse, Mr. Trudeau, whose opinions on this subject helped to shape my own, has renounced his earlier constitutional vision.[2]

Yet, despite the discomfort, I remain unrepentant in my views. The partisan pronouncements of Trudeau, the politician, fail to undermine the trenchant teaching of Trudeau the academic. Today even more than thirty years ago, the federal spending power — the power assumed by Ottawa to spend funds on matters beyond its legislative jurisdiction — represents a threat to federalism and to democracy. If Canadian federalism is to survive as a dynamic form of democratic government, the spending power must be curtailed.

This does not imply that I am especially enthusiastic about the

* I would like to express my appreciation to Rod Haley, Peter Hogg, John Kilcoyne, Jim MacPherson, Patrick Monahan and Murray Rankin for their helpful comments and suggestions. I would also like to thank the British Columbia Ministry of the Attorney General for providing research assistance for this and a larger project on the spending power.

1 P.E. Trudeau, "Federal Grants to Universities" (*Cité Libre*, February 1957), in *Federalism and the French Canadians* (Toronto: MacMillan of Canada, 1968) at 79.

2 Renunciation in deed came with the Trudeau government's sponsorship of the Canada Health Act, S.C. 1983-84, c. 6. Renunciation in word can be found in P.E. Trudeau, "Nothing Left but Tears for Trudeau," *The [Toronto] Globe and Mail* (May 28, 1987) A7.

qualification to the spending power proposed in the Meech Lake Accord. Under s. 7 of the Accord, provinces are to be given a limited right to receive compensation for opting-out of national shared-cost programs. In my opinion, this provision is not nearly radical enough. At best, it represents a tentative first step in the direction that I favour. At worst, it could do more to confirm the legitimacy of the federal spending power than to curb its exercise.

In order to explain my position more fully, I will address the underlying values of the Canadian Constitution and their relationship to the spending power.

CONSTITUTIONAL VALUES

There are many values which find voice in the Constitution but, in terms of the structure of democratic institutions, the two most fundamental are federalism and responsible government. Federalism has many forms but, at root, it implies a division of legislative and executive responsibilities between two orders of government, neither of which is subordinate to the other.[3] Responsible government is a system of representative democracy in which the head of state acts upon the advice of an executive that, in turn, is directly answerable to a democratically elected legislature.

Federalism and the spending power

The underlying rationale for federalism is a belief that while some matters are better decided by the national political community, others should be left to regional political communities. Implicit in this belief

---

3 Some writers have posited visions of federalism that deviate from this norm. However, as Peter Hogg notes, in doing so "they have so eroded the concept of federalism that it has become too vague to be useful": P.W. Hogg, *Constitutional Law of Canada*, 2nd ed., (Toronto: Carswell, 1985) at 81. Moreover, whatever the merit of these visions in conceptual terms, it is clear that they have little application to the vision of federalism represented in the Canadian Constitution. Sections 91 and 92 of the Constitution Act, 1867 (U.K.), c. 3, divide political powers between Parliament and the provincial legislatures in a manner that seeks to avoid the possibility of overlapping jurisdiction. Under s. 92, the provinces are given the power to "exclusively make Laws in relation to Matters coming within the Classes of Subject next hereinafter enumerated", while, under s. 91, Parliament is given authority to make laws "in relation to all Matters not coming within the Classes of Subject assigned exclusively to the Legislatures of the Provinces." It is true that the Constitution Act, 1867 provides for a few areas of concurrency, but these stand out as narrow exceptions to the general pattern of division in ss. 91 and 92. See E.R. Black, *Divided Loyalties: Canadian Concepts of Federalism* (Montreal: McGill-Queen's University Press, 1975) at 7-8.

is a view that, with respect to certain matters, regional governments can more adequately reflect the political attitudes and aspirations of citizens.

In a country like Canada, it is not hard to see why this might be the case. Given the country's size and diversity, the opinions and priorities of Canadians in one region may well differ from those of Canadians in other regions. A system of regional governments is more likely to be responsive to these regional variations than is a single central government. This is so not only because regional governments have more extensive knowledge of local conditions and preferences, but also because such governments depend for their existence upon regional constituencies. While a central government can afford to ignore the preferences of a particular region of the country (and may have to do so in order to garner voter support in other regions), a regional government cannot afford to do so.

In this way, federalism is a democratizing force. It provides citizens greater influence over policies that are assigned to regional governments than they would have if those same policies were assigned to a central government. To put it another way, it ensures that the preferences of a greater number of citizens are reflected in government policies. As Albert Breton and Anthony Scott have stated:

> An increase in the number of governmental units increases the probability that any person living in any jurisdiction will be a member of a majority able to secure for him or herself the quantity and quality of public policies that he or she (and others of his or her group) prefer.[4]

The problem with the spending power is that, by enabling the federal government to use fiscal means to influence decisions that fall within provincial jurisdiction, it allows national majorities to set priorities and to determine policies within spheres of influence allocated under the Constitution to regional majorities. Thus, both by design and effect, the spending power runs counter to the political purposes of a federal system.

Supporters of the federal spending power have sought to finesse this concern by contending that conditional grants are provided on a voluntary basis, and that those to whom they are offered are free to reject them. However, this argument is unconvincing. Even those writers who have stressed the voluntary nature of such grants have

---

4 A. Breton and A. Scott, *The Design of Federations* (Montreal: Institute for Research on Public Policy, 1980) at 15.

been forced to concede their coercive impact upon provincial decision-making. Peter Hogg, for example, has noted that provinces find it "very difficult" to refuse conditional grants, particularly since refusal "wears an aspect of taxation without benefit".[5]

The suggestion that conditional grants are voluntary also ignores the relationship between spending and taxation. The impact of such grants upon provincial decision-making is a function not only of the carrot of federal spending, but also of the stick of federal taxation. The extent to which funding for such grants is derived from the imposition of federal taxation is the extent to which provinces are denied potential tax revenues. The point here is not simply that refusal of such grants would subject residents of a province to taxation without benefit; it is that federal occupation of the tax field for provincial purposes diminishes the tax room available to provinces, thus restricting the capacity of provinces to raise revenues in support of policies that they favour. In this way, federal spending that derives from federal taxation has a coercive impact upon provinces as well as provincial taxpayers.

Responsible government and the spending power

An even more powerful objection to the federal spending power concerns its impact upon responsible government. The organizing principle of responsible government is political accountability: accountability of the executive to the legislature and of the legislature to the electorate. It is this thread of accountability that transforms what would otherwise be a despotic system of government into a democratic one.

Thus for responsible government to function in a federal state, citizens must have a definite understanding of the powers and responsibilities of each order of government. An electorate that is unable to attribute political responsibility to one order of government or the other lacks both the ability to express its political will and the assurance that its will can be translated into action. As Mr. Trudeau put it when he was still a philosopher and not yet a king:

> Since the same citizens vote in both federal and provincial elections, they must

---

5 This is because "residents of the non-participating province would still have to pay the federal taxes which finance the federal share of the programme in the other provinces": Hogg, above, note 3 at 120.

be able to determine what government is responsible for what; otherwise democratic control of power becomes impossible.[6]

By allowing the federal government to use fiscal means to influence provincial policies, the spending power compromises political accountability and thereby weakens the ability of electors to exercise democratic control over government. The point has been expressed most succinctly by Donald Smiley:

> [T]here is an increasing number of important public functions for which the federal authorities assert the provinces have the primary responsibilities but on behalf of which federal financial assistance is available. In these circumstances it is almost impossible to enforce accountability, and no satisfactory answer can be given to the broad question of whether the provinces have in fact been delinquent in providing adequate support for particular services or, alternatively, whether some or all of them could not reasonably be expected to do better in the light of existing distribution of tax sources, revenues and functional responsibilities. Further, if we were to assume that the federal government has *some* direct responsibilities in relation to particular provincial programs, it is almost impossible to gauge whether their level of support for these activities has been satisfactory.[7]

An illustration

An illustration of the above concerns is provided by the Canada Health Act.[8] Under the terms of that Act, funds are made available to provinces that establish hospital insurance and medicare programs in accordance with federally stipulated criteria. Provinces that fail to adhere to these criteria are denied full federal funding. The purpose of the Act is to influence provincial policy with respect to the provision of public health insurance. The extent to which it achieves this purpose is the extent to which decisions assigned under the Constitution to regional political communities have been effectively transferred to the national political community. Moreover, the diffusion of political responsibility serves to weaken the ability of either community to attribute political responsibility for the strengths and deficiencies of the public health care system.

Suppose, for example, that a majority of citizens in a particular province came to believe that medical user fees should be imposed

---

6 Trudeau, above, note 1 at 80.
7 D.V. Smiley, *Conditional Grants and Canadian Federalism: A Study in Constitutional Adaptation* (Toronto: Canadian Tax Foundation, 1963) at 54.
8 S.C. 1983-84, c. 6.

upon higher income earners in order to finance a preventive health care initiative aimed at school-age children. Under the Act, the imposition of such fees would produce reductions in federal transfers to the province with no commensurate reductions in federal taxation. The political pressure created by the combined threat of declining federal grants and continued federal occupation of the tax field would make even the most sympathetic provincial government balk at implementing a policy of this kind.

Some may say that the solution is for citizens who favour such a policy to organize at the national rather than the provincial level. The first thing to note about this suggestion is that it qualifies as a "solution" only if one is prepared to abandon the political purposes of assigning health care to provincial control in the first place. The problem, however, runs much deeper than that. Even if the citizens, by organizing nationally, were able to convince the federal government to endorse their proposal, that government would be forced to rely solely upon fiscal measures to implement the reform. While such measures could probably be structured so as to compel provincial acquiescence with federal requirements, they could not give the federal government direct regulatory control over the policy. Thus the policy, although well conceived at the federal level, could suffer from incompetence or lack of political support on the part of the provincial authorities charged with its administration.

What the above example shows is that the spending power does not simply shift political responsibility from one order of government to the other; it intersperses responsibility between both orders. The result is to require those advocating a particular reform to fight a battle on two fronts. At the same time, it becomes virtually impossible for citizens to determine which order of government to hold accountable for policies that fail or, for that matter, for ones that succeed.

In short, reliance upon the spending power to overcome legislative limitations in a federal system of responsible government creates the worst of all possible worlds. It imposes upon citizens the costs and incovenience of supporting two orders of government while denying them the benefits of local control. In addition, it creates a situation in which political power is so diffused that citizens possess less ability to influence and control government decision-making than they would even in a unitary state.

REALPOLITIK

The discussion thus far has centred around constitutional principles. Yet, as the debate over the Meech Lake Accord has shown, those who support the federal spending power are concerned less with theory than with realpolitik. Many seem to fear that, without the spending power, politics in Canada would regress: regional disparities would increase; there would be a lack of revenue for social programs; political advances on behalf of women and other disadvantaged groups would grind to a halt. These are the myths, but what are the realities?

Political myths

One of the strongest political claims made on behalf of the federal spending power is that the power is required to promote the principle of equalization. This argument takes a number of forms. Its most common version maintains that conditional grants promote equalization both by guaranteeing all Canadians equal access to a minimal level of social services and by redistributing tax revenues from richer to poorer parts of the country.

The problem with the argument is that it makes an unwarranted link between the principle of equalization and the need for federal interferences in the delivery of specific social programs. If the federal government is concerned about the need to equalize the position of citizens across the country, it can achieve this goal through unconditional grants.[9] Given that the goal of equalization can be met through unconditional payments, equalization cannot provide the rationale for conditional grants. Conditional grants are necessary only if the federal government wishes to influence the way in which equalization payments are spent — in other words, if it wishes to use equalization as a pretext for influencing policy-making at the provincial level.

A second argument commonly made in support of the federal spending power suffers from similar deficiencies. According to this claim, the spending power is necessary because the provinces lack the

---

9 Given that equalization of wealth among regions is a discrete function that falls beyond the scope of provincial legislative power, a federal law whose purpose is limited to equalization should be sustainable on the basis of the national dimensions component of the peace, order and good government power. Moreover, since 1982, the Constitution has explicitly acknowledged the right of the federal government to make "equalization payments to ensure that provincial governments have sufficient revenues to provide reasonably comparable levels of public services at reasonably comparable levels of taxation": Constitution Act, 1982 [enacted by the Canada Act 1982 (U.K.), c. 11, s. 1], s. 36.

financial capacity to fund social programs themselves. Yet how can this be so? If a province's incapacity to fund social programs stems from regional disparities, these disparities can be redressed through unconditional equalization grants. On the other hand, if that incapacity stems from an absence of taxable revenues, then this absence should inhibit the delivery of federal programs as much as provincial ones. It is true that provinces can levy only direct taxes but, given that income taxes are direct, this fact does not pose a major constraint on provincial revenue-raising.

Of course, it may well be that there is insufficient tax room *at present* to allow provinces to assume the full cost of funding existing shared-cost social programs. But this is simply because the federal government is generating revenues to fund provincial programs. In the words of Professor Trudeau, Ottawa is violating its duty "to ensure that it does not collect taxes for that part of the public interest not within its jurisdiction".[10] If the federal government were to relinquish the tax room it currently requires to fund initiatives within provincial legislative competence, that room would provide the same revenue-raising capacity to the provinces.

A third argument commonly made on behalf of the federal spending power is that such power is necessary to promote new, and to protect existing, social initiatives on behalf of women and other disadvantaged groups in society. Underlying this claim is an assumption that the central government is better trusted with the social welfare of Canadians than are provincial governments.

There are two responses to this argument. The first is to question the relationship between the assumption and the solution. If it is true that the central government is more trustworthy, surely the solution is to seek a constitutional amendment transferring jurisdiction to the central authorities. The use of the spending power to overcome jurisdictional shortcomings is a poor alternative. As shown above, the spending power provides federal authorities limited control over the programs it funds, while compromising the ability of both regional and national majorities to influence policy and to hold governments politically accountable.

The second response is to challenge the centralist assumption on which the argument is based. Why should it be that the central government is more trustworthy in terms of social policy? The national electorate, after all, is simply the sum of the regional electorates. What

---

10 Trudeau, above, note 1 at 87.

reason is there for believing that voters, when they enter a federal polling booth, possess different attitudes about questions of social welfare than when they enter a provincial polling booth? Perhaps there is a view that central Canadians, who comprise the bulk of the national population, are more enlightened in their attitudes to social welfare than their Atlantic or western counterparts. If so, there is no evidence to support this view. On the contrary, David Poel's statistical study of the diffusion of legislation among the Canadian provinces shows that, in the period from 1945 to 1975, Saskatchewan was by far the most innovative province in terms of initiating social welfare programs.[11] Besides, even if it were true that the population of central Canada is more strongly dedicated to a particular vision of social justice, what political justification would this provide for requiring that view to be imposed upon those in other regions who embrace a different vision?

Another ground for questioning the centralist assumption concerns the structure of national and provincial politics. In a country as large and varied as Canada, national politics is necessarily preoccupied with mediating among competing regional, cultural and linguistic interests. It is within the less diverse provincial units that economic and social issues are more likely to occupy political centre stage. Further, regional differences make it more difficult to develop a national consensus around any given social issue. Absent a strong unifying force such as depression or war, it is generally harder to mobilize the national electorate in favour of a new social initiative than it is a provincial electorate. Thus it is no coincidence that Canadians tend to identify with their provincial government first and their national government second.[12] Provincial governments are inherently more responsive to demands for innovation than their national counterpart.

There is also the question of numbers. Provinces provide special opportunities for social innovation simply because there are ten of them. Even in conservative times, at least one or two provincial governments have been sympathetic to a reformist agenda. And, assuming a reform is successful, adoption by one provincial regime inevitably fuels political demand for its implementation elsewhere. As Breton and Scott have noted, federalism permits creative provincial

---

11 D.H. Poel, "The Diffusion of Legislation among the Canadian Provinces: A Statistical Analysis" (1976), 9 Can. J. Pol. Sci. 605.

12 See K. Norrie, R. Simeon and M. Krasnick, *Federalism and Economic Union in Canada* (Toronto: University of Toronto Press, 1986) at 166.

governments to undertake "pilot projects" for the rest of the country while avoiding the political risks "implicit in large or national projects".[13]

This is a phenomenon that is familiar to most Canadians. Hospital insurance, medicare, labour codes, human rights codes, even bills of rights were pioneered by innovative provincial regimes before gaining political acceptance across the country. The same pattern continues today with initiatives such as public auto insurance, gay rights and pay equity. The implementation of public auto insurance in Saskatchewan fueled demand for a similar scheme in Manitoba; the example set by the two prairie provinces paved the way for voter acceptance of government plans in British Columbia and Quebec; and the track record of these four provinces has bolstered campaigns for public auto insurance in Ontario and elsewhere. Similarly, the move to amend human rights codes to prohibit discrimination on the basis of sexual orientation began in Quebec and has since spread to the Yukon, Ontario and Manitoba. The example set by these provinces will undoubtedly encourage other provinces, and eventually the federal government, to follow suit. The same process is likely to occur with respect to pay equity. Ontario's enactment of pay equity legislation applying to the provincial private sector is already placing pressure on other provincial governments to undertake similar initiatives.

The point is not that provincial politics is invariably preferable to national politics. There are many problems that, for a variety of reasons, may demand national as opposed to regional resolution. Moreover, just as provincial political units are more amenable to calls for social reform, they are also more responsive to pressures for political retrenchment. The recent British Columbia experience with labour legislation and abortion stands as a stark reminder. The point is simply that, for those concerned with social progress, there is nothing inherently reactionary about provincial politics. On the contrary, there is much to recommend provincial politics as a staging ground for social reform. As Professor Trudeau put it to Canadian socialists in 1961:

> Federalism must be welcomed as a valuable tool which permits dynamic parties to plant socialist governments in certain provinces from which the seeds of radicalism can slowly spread.[14]

---

13 Breton and Scott, above, note 4 at 18.
14 P.E. Trudeau, "The Practice and Theory of Federalism" (*Social Purpose For Canada*, 1961), in *Federalism and the French Canadians*, above, note 1 at 127.

Political realities

Having confronted the myths, it is time to deal with some political realities. One such reality is that, like it or not, we live in a country that for the past forty years has built its political system around the assumption of a federal spending power. To simply terminate that power would pull the rug out from a myriad of grants, subsidies and tax expenditures. For example, the constitutionality of federal health grants, student loans and child tax credits would be undermined. Any reform that fails to incorporate mechanisms to minimize the risk of such political dislocation will be doomed before it starts.

A second reality is that Canada is no longer the same society that it was at Confederation. Problems that were of local concern one hundred years ago attract national interest today. New issues have emerged that require innovative solutions or that fall between the cracks in the constitutional order. These changes require constitutional adjustment and, in many cases, the spending power has served as a tool for such adjustment. If that tool is now to be taken away, mechanisms for formal constitutional amendment must be made more flexible.

THE MEECH LAKE ACCORD

Section 7 of the Meech Lake Accord would add s. 106A to the Constitution Act, 1867. This section guarantees a provincial government "reasonable compensation" for opting-out of future national shared-cost programs, provided it establishes a provincial program "compatible with the national objectives." In this way, the Accord seeks to limit the power of Ottawa to use conditional grants as a mechanism for dictating the details of programs that fall within provincial legislative jurisdiction.

The limits of section 106A

The problem with s. 106A is that it does not go nearly far enough. First, it applies only to future shared-cost programs, not to existing ones. Second, while purporting to guarantee a measure of provincial control over the details of such programs, s. 106A does not impede the ability of the federal government to set spending priorities or to dictate general program objectives. Indeed, by giving formal recognition to Ottawa's power to set "national objectives", it could actually encourage the federal government to tighten the conditions it imposes on certain shared-cost programs.[15] Third, s. 106A does nothing to curb federal spending outside the context of shared-cost programs. Thus if Ottawa wished to avoid the new limits on shared-cost programs, it could establish spending programs of its own. Alternatively, it could seek to use the device of tax expenditures to avoid limitations imposed upon.it by the proposed amendment.

At best, therefore, s. 106A might marginally enhance provincial autonomy over policies falling within provincial legislative jurisdiction. At the same time, it will do little if anything to strengthen political accountability. Because political responsibility is left diffused between two orders of government, voters will continue to be left in doubt as to whether the deficiencies of a shared-cost program — even a provincial program — lie in the provincial or federal aspect of its design and implementation.

A more radical approach

What is needed is a more radical and comprehensive approach. Conditional transfers between governments should be constitutionally prohibited, and the tax room required to fund such transfers given over to the government with legislative jurisdiction. Moreover, federal and provincial governments should commit themselves to a joint initiative aimed at eliminating the use of other conditional grants, loans and tax expenditures for the promotion of policies that fall outside their respective legislative jurisdictions.

Let us consider each of these proposals in turn. The first is directed at eliminating the spending mechanism that is most destructive of provincial autonomy and political accountability: the conditional transfer from the federal to provincial governments. Such transfers are particularly pernicious because they do not use federal spending to address social conditions directly; rather, they use it to influence the exercise of regulatory authority by the other level of government. The disruptive potential of eliminating these grants would be great if not accompanied by specific guarantees ensuring the continuity of the programs that they fund. However, this danger would be substantially reduced if the federal government were required to turn over

---

15 An example of this tendency is provided by a recent *Globe and Mail* editorial which relied upon the wording of s. 106A to argue that Ottawa ought to attach conditions to the block funding it currently provides provinces for post-secondary education: Editorial, *The [Toronto] Globe and Mail* (November 5, 1987) A6.

to the provinces the tax room currently occupied to fund such grants. As a further hedge against political disruption, provinces should be required to continue programs in accordance with federal conditions until after a provincial election. This would ensure electors an opportunity to express their views before any provincial government decided to abandon or substantially alter an existing program.

The second proposal seeks to place some political limits on the use of other conditional spending initiatives. It would entail the establishment of a specialized political agency to prevent both federal and provincial governments from employing such initiatives as a means of influencing policies beyond their respective legislative jurisdictions. Such an agency, for example, would require the phasing out of federal student loans and provincial foreign aid. Again, to minimize political disruption, the funding government would be obliged to transfer the necessary tax room to the government with legislative jurisdiction. In return, the latter would be required to assume responsibility for the program and to continue it in its present form until after a general election.

Why should this agency be political rather than judicial? The answer lies in the complexity of current fiscal arrangements and in the difficulty of distinguishing between spending that is aimed at a legitimate federal or provincial purpose and that which is not. Unlike conditional transfers, which invariably flow from the federal government and which relate to a discrete group of policy initiatives, other conditional spending initiatives comprise a complex web of federal and provincial grants, loans and tax expenditures. The task of disentangling this web requires political sensitivity and skill. It is a job that must be given to an agency that is capable of comprehending the complexity of the task and possesses the means to respond in a constructive and sophisticated fashion.

Moreover, while programs funded by means of conditional transfers have been generally recognized as falling under provincial legislative jurisdiction, the jurisdictional pedigree of many other spending initiatives is problematic. This is especially true of tax expenditures. Is a particular expenditure aimed at promoting tax equity or a social policy unrelated to the purposes of taxation — or is it aimed at both? In many cases, the answer turns purely upon political judgment. To leave determinations such as these to a detached indicative agency with limited remedial powers would invite ongoing political instability and disruption. The only practical solution is to entrust the decision to a body that fully understands the practical implications of its actions and has the ability to make decisions and recommendations that will produce jurisdictional disentanglement at minimum political cost.

These two proposals would go a long way to restoring provincial autonomy and political accountability to Canadian federalism. But there is more to be done. If governments are to be deprived of spending as an informal means of constitutional adjustment, it is essential that the formal procedures be made more flexible. In this respect, the Meech Lake Accord represents a step backwards. First, it imposes a unanimity requirement for changes to national institutions.[16] Second, by expanding opportunities for compensation to provinces that opt-out under the general formula, the Accord makes it politically more difficult to obtain the required measure of consent for other constitutional amendments.[17] The inevitable impact of embracing such constitutional rigidity will be to increase the pressure upon governments to resort to spending and other expedients to overcome jurisdictional barriers.

CONCLUSION

The thesis of this short paper can be simply stated. It is that the spending power compromises both the federal and the democratic character of the Canadian state. I have therefore criticized the Meech Lake Accord for not going far enough and have made some proposals of my own. But criticism is cheap. Pierre Trudeau spent much of his academic career criticizing conditional grants and much of his political career conferring them.[18] Those who signed the Meech Lake Accord, with all its deficiencies, have at least served constitutional notice that they acknowledge a problem with the spending power. In doing so,

---

16 Section 9 of the Accord would amend ss. 41 and 42 of the Constitution Act, 1982 to require unanimous provincial consent for amendments relating to: the principle of proportionate representation of the provinces in the House of Commons; the powers of the Senate and the method of selecting Senators; the Supreme Court of Canada; and the establishment of new provinces. Under current arrangements, such amendments require only two-thirds of the provinces representing 50 per cent of the population.

17 Section 9 of the Accord would amend s. 40 of the Constitution Act, 1982 to require the federal government to provide "reasonable compensation" to provinces that opt out of constitutional amendments that transfer legislative powers from provincial legislatures to the Parliament of Canada. Such compensation is currently required only with respect to amendments "relating to education or other cultural matters."

18 To be fair, Trudeau in his first decade as Prime Minister did make efforts to curb the coercive effect of conditional transfers to provinces. The enactment of the Canada Health Act in 1984, however, represented a complete change in direction and an implicit repudiation of his academic views.

they have taken a first, tentative step along the road toward more meaningful reform.

This, in turn, suggests that the significance of s. 106A depends less upon its immediate effects than upon its influence on subsequent constitutional developments. If the section provides the impetus for further reform, it may yet be regarded as an important constitutional milestone. If, on the other hand, it serves as the last word on the scope of the federal spending power, future commentators will rightly dismiss the current controversy over s. 106A as "Meech ado about nothing".

Section 106A and
Federal-Provincial Fiscal Relations

J. Stefan Dupré

Section 106A responds to a Quebec demand for limitations on the federal spending power that is as old as the agony of constitutional reform this country has suffered since the mid-1960s. In this brief paper I shall examine s. 106A in the light of the following perspectives: (1) the art of federal-provincial compromise; (2) its potential for judicializing federal-provincial fiscal relations; and (3) its long-term impact on the conduct of these relations by our eleven first ministers and their ministers of finance.

Two preliminary observations are in order. First, if anyone did cheer the Constitution Act of 1982,[1] I was not among them. As far as I am concerned, Keith Banting and Richard Simeon could not have chosen a more appropriate title for the collection of essays they edited on the subject.[2] To me, a Constitution deemed in part illegitimate by the bipartisan resolution of the Quebec National Assembly has been a symbolic monstrosity. In that s. 106A, along with the rest of the Meech Lake/Langevin Accord, may yet receive the approbation of Canada's eleven parliamentary assemblies and thereby purge the constitutional landscape of this monstrosity, its passage into constitutional law will receive my standing applause.

If my first observation brands me as a biased constitutional observer, my second may brand me as an incompetent constitutional forecaster. Given that so many of the means of remedying the symbolic

---

1 Constitution Act, 1982 [enacted by the Canada Act 1982 (U.K.), c. 11, s. 1].
2 K. Banting and R. Simeon, eds., *And No One Cheered* (Toronto: Methuen, 1983).

monstrosity of 1982 found our eleven governments shackled by the unanimity chains of s. 41, I was confidently predicting, as recently as March of 1987, that the youngest freshman in my class would reach the age of mandatory retirement from judicial office by the time we got our constitutional house in order. As I delightedly stand on the brink of being proved wrong on this score, I gladly live with whatever skepticism this invites concerning the validity of my forecast of the impact of s. 106A on fiscal federalism.

SECTION 106A AND THE ART OF FEDERAL-PROVINCIAL COMPROMISE

Stripped to its bare essentials, and therefore of the textual uncertainties I shall examine in the next part of this paper, s. 106A(1) creates a constitutional obligation whereby the federal government must compensate a province that chooses to opt-out of a future national shared-cost program in an area of exclusive provincial jurisdiction. To trigger this obligation, the opting-out province must undertake a measure that is compatible with the program's objectives. Section 106A(2) adds that the federal-provincial division of jurisdiction, as we have come to know it, is not thereby affected.

Viewed as an exercise in the art of federal-provincial compromise, s. 106A is a masterpiece. The federal spending power has been derived from s. 91(3) "The Raising of Money by any Mode or System of Taxation" and s. 91(1A) "The Public Debt and Property" of the existing division of jurisdiction.[3] These two sections have come to mean that the federal government, having applied its tax powers under s. 91(3) to the raising of monies paid into the Consolidated Revenue Fund that is the Public Property of s. 91(1A), can dispose of those monies in any manner it chooses, even though the object served comes under provincial jurisdiction. Such monies can be disbursed in the form of federal transfers, conditional or unconditional, to individuals, institutions or provincial governments.

David M. Cameron and I have characterized the federal spending power as the "single most dynamic element of Canadian federalism." In our words:[4]

---

3 Constitution Act, 1867 (U.K.), c. 3. See the Appendix to this volume for relevant sections and the text of the 1987 Constitutional Accord.

4 D. M. Cameron and J. S. Dupré, "The Financial Framework of Income Distribution and Social Services" in S. Beck and I. Bernier, eds., *Canada and the New Constitution: The Unfinished Agenda*, vol. I, (Montreal: Institute for Research on Public Policy, 1983) at 340.

The manner in which the spending power has been applied in different ways at different times has been a source of centralization and decentralization, of symmetry and asymmetry, of unity and disunity in Canadian federalism — all of these without ever altering so much as a comma in the text of the (Constitution Act of 1867). In the process the spending power has made nonsense of the allegedly "water-tight" compartments into which the [Constitution] Act divides federal and provincial jurisdiction. "Water-tight" compartments are not "money-tight."

In the annals of federal-provincial fiscal relations, the spending power has spawned federal payments to individuals (e.g. family allowances, adult training allowances), to institutions (universities, municipalities) and to provinces (from categorical conditional grants through the unconditional equalization payments now enshrined in s. 36 of the Constitution Act, 1982 to the umbrella shared-cost grants of the Canada Assistance Plan). It has also come to be hedged by various limitations. Some of these limitations have been the outcome of explicit compromise, e.g. provincial configuration of family allowances; provincial (Quebec) opting-out of various shared-cost programs in the 1960s. Other limitations have been bred by the sheer political force of provincial opposition. I have long been fond of making the point that interposition, the eminently American state practice historically invoked in that country against the enforcement of Court decisions, was successfully invoked in Canada by Premier Duplessis against the federal spending power — in this instance, federal payments to universities. Indeed, it can be observed that:

> the legacy of the university grants episode has severely circumscribed the application of the federal spending power to universities, municipalities, and other institutions under provincial jurisdiction. For practical purposes the scope of the federal spending power has increasingly been limited to the making of payments to individuals and to provincial governments.[5]

The point, as Cameron and I summed it up, is that "Politics can effectively inhibit what the Constitution permits."[6]

It is from the perspective of this well-known history that I view s. 106A as a stunning expression of the art of compromise. It is silent on the matter of federal payments to institutions which are under provincial jurisdiction. As such, it implicitly recognizes the effectiveness of the political limitations on such payments, while leaving their future configuration to coming generations of politicians and citizens. It is silent on the matter of federal payments to individuals: the Victoria

---

5 *Ibid.* at 341.
6 *Ibid.* at 341.

Charter's flirtation with a constitutional limitation on adult training allowances was not rekindled. Accordingly, the most visible and politically potent manifestations of the federal spending power are uncurbed. And as for what s. 106A addresses, it creates a federal obligation towards an opting-out province, rather than a limitation on the application of the spending power to federal-provincial shared-cost programs. One searches s. 106A in vain for any of the limitations with which past products of the constitutional reform industry sought to hedge the initiation of shared-cost programs by Ottawa. I refer to the generic idea of requiring the registration of consensus by a substantial majority of provinces, either through their premiers or through a provincially instructed upper house before a shared-cost program can be launched. Section 106A leaves this idea to gather dust on the same library shelves as stock the federal White Paper of 1969, the Quebec Beige Paper of 1980 and the intervening products of the constitutional reform industry. Finally, s. 106A features a *quid* for the *quo* of the constitutional obligation it imposes on the federal government vis-à-vis an opting-out province. Its explicit reference to shared-cost programs with national objectives in areas of exclusive provincial jurisdiction shifts the legitimation of these manifestations of the federal spending power from judicial *obiter dicta* to the black letters of constitutional text.

In summary, I discern in s. 106A what is indeed a masterpiece of compromise. It bypasses federal payments to institutions that are effectively confined by the political process. It equally bypasses federal payments to individuals and therefore brooks no limitations on future federal recourse to this politically potent spending instrument. What is left are shared-cost programs, and here a federal constitutional obligation vis-à-vis an opting-out province is exchanged for the explicit legitimation of federally conditioned payments to provinces in areas of exclusive provincial jurisdiction. That Quebec's longstanding demand for limitations on the federal spending power can be met to its satisfaction through this minimalist approach can only be called a triumph in the art of "getting to yes."[7]

SECTION 106A AND THE JUDICIALIZATION OF FEDERAL-PROVINCIAL FISCAL RELATIONS

It is one thing to describe the content of s. 106A in the everyday

---

7 R. Fisher and W. Ury, *Getting to Yes* (Boston: Houghton Mifflin, 1981).

language I have used so far. It is quite another to reflect upon its formal wording. The text of s. 106A is awash with uncertainties and ambiguities that can only be definitively resolved by the Supreme Court of Canada. To be sure, there will have to be recourse to the courts before s. 106A produces a judicialization of federal-provincial fiscal relations. Before addressing the likelihood of this eventuality, textual analysis is in order. In my mind, untutored in the law but schooled in the fiscal relations that the text of s. 106A addresses, the following questions arise.

(1) What is a "shared-cost program"? The answer may be that it is any provincially-administered program financed in part by a province, in part by the federal government. The vocabulary of federal-provincial fiscal relations, as developed by the ministers and officials who conduct these relations, has suggested a narrower definition: a shared-cost program involves a predetermined federal share (percentage) of program costs whose level is annually set by provincial spending decisions. Thus we were told at the time established program financing was initiated in 1977, that shared-cost programs in the fields of post-secondary education, hospital and medical insurance would be replaced by block funding. Henceforth, provinces would no longer dictate federal spending by determining the rate of increase in the federal obligation to share a set proportion of the costs incurred. Subsequently, through the Canada Health Act,[8] block funding was reconditionalized through federal recourse to fiscal penalties against provinces that violate a federally prescribed code of conduct.[9] Does block funding geared to a code of conduct constitute a shared-cost program?

(2) What is a *national* shared-cost program? Presumably what is invited is a distinction between what in the practitioner's lexicon is a bilateral federal-provincial program tailor-made to the needs of a particular province and a multilateral federal-provincial program offered on like terms to all (most? several?) provinces. Is there a point at which a series of bilateral federal-provincial shared-cost initiatives such as those spawned pursuant to the alphabet soup of DREE, DRIE and ERDA could be taken as constituting a national shared-cost program in an area of exclusive provincial jurisdiction (which DREE, DRIE and ERDA do not likely occupy)?

---

8 S.C. 1983-84, c. 6.

9 J. S. Dupré, "Reflections on the Workability of Executive Federalism" in R. Simeon, ed., *Intergovernmental Relations*, MacDonald Commission Studies, vol. 63 (Toronto: University of Toronto Press, 1985) at 19.

(3) What is an area of exclusive provincial jurisdiction? Before taking refuge in the comforting words of s. 106A(2), we should remind ourselves of Claude Morin's observation that the federal-provincial relations carried out under ss. 91 and 92 are littered with claims and counterclaims that seek to distinguish or confound urban affairs and municipal institutions, training or research and education, the economy or employment and anything.[10]

(4) What is the "program or initiative that is compatible with the national objectives" that an opting-out province is supposed to carry on? Is an "initiative" less than a program and, if so, does the national shared-cost program constitute a shopping list for provincial initiatives any one of which, if implemented, would offer grounds for federal compensation? The umbrella nature of a shared-cost program like the Canada Assistance Plan is a strong reminder that this question is pertinent. As for what constitutes "compatibility" with the "national objectives" (the objectives in the federal legislation or the federal spending estimates or such portion of these objectives as might be deemed "national"), questions abound. And then there is the matter of what, if anything, distinguishes objectives from conditions or criteria or codes of conduct.

(5) What is the "reasonable" compensation to which an opting-out province may be entitled? Perhaps this compensation is to be "reasonable" in relation to the share of costs that the federal government pays in other provinces. Perhaps this compensation is to be "reasonable" in relation to the fiscal effort which the opted-out province, given its fiscal capacity, and need, must exert in order to mount its compatible program or initiative. Who knows?

Who knows indeed? I have raised these illustrative questions to establish that s. 106A is a showcase of uncertainty. I will now argue that this very characteristic leads me to discount its potential for judicializing federal-provincial fiscal relations.

Why have federal-provincial fiscal relations been virtually exempt from governmental recourse to the courts in the past? It is well to remember that these relations have been conducted over more than half of a century by governments of widely different political persuasions. The co-operative phases of these relations have been generously interspersed with the most conflictual episodes in the annals of Canadian federalism. If governments avoided head-to-head litiga-

---

10 C. Morin, *Quebec versus Ottawa* (Toronto: University of Toronto Press, 1976) at Chapter 5 and *passim*.

tion over the spending power even when their relations were at their most acrimonious, this must be because they perceived that the disadvantages of court-dictated resolutions outweighed the advantages.

Again and again, negotiated solutions have enabled governments to avoid definitive court rulings that could be as damaging from a federal perspective as from a provincial one. That the Supreme Court might deem a particular set of conditions as disguised federal legislation in a field of provincial competence has posed a risk which federal governments have been loath to run. That it might, on the other hand, legitimize detailed conditions or the federal financing of universities has posed an equally unpalatable risk from a provincial perspective. Meantime, federal and provincial finance ministers, with their joint concerns for the revenue and debt positions of government and their capacity to achieve financial tradeoffs quantified in tax points or cash, have had their own stake in avoiding judicial fetters.

And could Quebec, or for that matter any other province, have ever hoped to achieve compensated opting-out via a judicial route? No constitutional doctrine that I can think of would have permitted a court to fashion compensated opting-out. This practice, which has encompassed payments to institutions as well as shared-cost programs, could only have been invented by federal-provincial negotiation. The multiple uncertainties and limitations which in the past have made governments loath to resort to litigated solutions are in the main untouched by s. 106A. What is new is the added legitimacy of federal conditions and the enhanced certainty of federal compensation to an opted-out province when this becomes a constitutional obligation.

I consider that the added legitimacy which s. 106A accords to federal conditions actually *reduces* the possibility that federal-provincial fiscal relations might become judicialized because it is a deterrent to *private* litigation, not only over future programs, but past programs as well. It seems to me that a constitutional challenge such as the one envisaged to the Canada Health Act by the Ontario Medical Association in the heat of the extra-billing issue is a far more risky undertaking with s. 106A than without it.

As for head-to-head litigation between governments, potential judicialization of fiscal relations must be posited on the hypothesis that the equilibrated balance of terror which has deterred recourse to the courts in the past has been disturbed. But why should governments seek to test whether day care, let us say, is "early childhood education", and therefore an area of exclusive provincial jurisdiction subject to compensated opting-out, or is instead "labour market adjustment", and therefore beyond the reach of s. 106A as an area of concurrent jurisdiction? I can discern the possibility of judicialization if I posit that a national (multilateral) shared-cost program which governments mutually agree deals with an exclusively provincial matter has been pursued to the point where it has been authorized by Parliament, and the federal finance minister has been unable to negotiate a level of compensation that is acceptable to his counterpart from an opting-out province. It is only in the face of such a conjuncture of events that I consider judicialization a reasonable possibility, and even here, the prospect of a court-imposed settlement that attempted to juggle tax points, equalization and cash is likely a strong deterrent to intergovernmental litigation.

In sum, the prospect that s. 106A may have the net effect of judicializing federal-provincial fiscal relations appears trivial.

SECTION 106A AND THE CONDUCT OF FEDERAL-PROVINCIAL FISCAL RELATIONS

In this setting, I find it reasonable to anticipate that s. 106A will have minimal consequences for the conduct of federal-provincial fiscal relations. If anything, it will simply reinforce a pattern of conduct that is in line with trends whose outline has emerged with growing clarity in recent years. I refer to (1) the tendency for federal-provincial initiatives to encompass matters that occupy the gray areas of the division of jurisdiction; (2) the growing prominence of bilateral federal-provincial shared-cost arrangements tailor-made to the particular economic and social circumstances of individual provinces; and (3) enhanced recourse to tax expenditures as a means of pursuing national and provincial objectives.

The modern Canadian welfare state was erected in large part through the application of the federal spending power to shared-cost programs, including the very specific categorical conditional grants that waxed and waned between 1945 and 1965. Once in place, the welfare state does not require reconstruction from scratch. The new avenues of government intervention have shifted from the educational, health and social matters most likely to impinge upon objects of exclusive provincial jurisdiction to matters in which the elements of economic and social policy are intertwined. These lie precisely in the gray areas of the division of jurisdiction where education shades into research, municipal affairs into development and housing, and social infrastructure into economic adjustment. In all of these areas there is ample room for federal-provincial acrimony and indeed for what

Alan Cairns calls "competing unilateralisms".[11] But one would be hard pressed to conjure an initiative that would constitute a federal intervention in a matter of exclusive provincial jurisdiction and hence trigger s. 106A. A federal initiative that so intervened would have had to be transparently designed with this end in mind. If so, s. 106A might come into play, but the resulting asymmetry that arose from compensated opting-out will have been intended by politicians rather than being an outcome to which they have been fated by the Constitution.

Where there is good reason for intentional asymmetry in federal-provincial fiscal relations, bilateral undertakings of the DREE-DRIE-ERDA variety are the logical instrument for marrying federal and provincial objectives, not national shared-cost programs encompassed by s. 106A. Involving as they do a mixture of economic and social objectives and constitutionally underpinned as they are by s. 36 of the Constitution Act, 1982, bilateral arrangements permit just about any kind of government intervention in which national objectives are sensitive to provincial peculiarities. I suggest that such sensitivity is precisely what is suited to the age that lies beyond the welfare state, that of economic and social adjustment in a global environment.

Finally, it is important to bear in mind that tax expenditures have been displacing spending programs as enormously potent instruments for the achievement of economic and social objectives by federal and provincial governments. Where desired, these instruments, particularly in the form of income tax credits, can be designed to produce their intended effects whether or not a federal-provincial tax collection agreement is in place. In any event, they are untouched by s. 106A.

In sum, I consider that s. 106A will have minimal consequences for the conduct of federal-provincial fiscal relations precisely because it does not encompass the realm where the action lies. These relations will remain the preserve of our eleven first ministers and ministers of finance. Like the country that produces them, they will be conflictual as well as consensual, competitive as well as co-operative, asymmetrical as well as symmetrical. And they will remain insulated from the dead hand of any particular generation of constitution writers and from the opinions of a judiciary with no particular claim to fiscal expertise or sensitivity.

---

11 A. Cairns, "The Embedded State: State-Society Relations in Canada" in K. Banting, ed., *State and Society: Canada in Comparative Perspective*, Macdonald Commission Studies, vol. 31 (Toronto: University of Toronto Press, 1986) at 82.

The Meech Lake Accord And The Federal Spending Power: A Good Maximin Solution

Pierre Fortin

The basic concerns expressed in the two parliamentary debates following the Meech Lake Accord, first in Quebec City and then in Ottawa, were diametrically opposed. In Quebec the central question was: do we ask and obtain enough, or are we selling out? In Ottawa, it was instead: do we yield too much? The two debates about the distinct society were vivid testimony that Quebec and the rest of Canada were as far apart as ever about the nature of the country. Whether one likes it or not, the two solitudes remain a fundamental fact of Canadian life. It is a sad commentary on the state of French-English relations in our country that not only are we not *back* to square one, but we may have never left it.

THE TWO SOLITUDES: HERE WE GO AGAIN

Quite clearly, Quebec still cares mostly about its own distinctiveness, while many in English Canada are still reluctant to recognize the French fact as anything more than just another charming fragment of the celebrated mosaic. They find Quebec's defensive attitude surprising, if not reprehensible. After all, the separatist forces were defeated 3 to 2 just seven years ago, and the current ruling party in Quebec is clearly federalist. A widespread sentiment is thus: be they separatists or federalists, don't trust these guys!

It should be remembered, however, that Quebec's nervousness

has been shaped by more than 200 years of struggle for survival. This feeling was exacerbated by the postwar attack on provincial finances, the rocambolesque university grants episode, the invasion of provincial jurisdiction through a string of shared-cost programs, the unilateral 1983 modification of the medical and health care program, the attack on the caisse de dépôt, and the recent wave of civil disobedience to Quebec's Bill 101.

Most important, Quebec's apprehensions were reinforced five years ago by the isolation of the province from a constitutional revision that restricted its powers unilaterally and was imposed in spite of unanimous rejection of its terms by the provincial legislature. After two decades of painful introspection, we had just said yes to Canada, and Canada answered with a flat no. The counterargument that no constitutional deal of any sort would have been acceptable to the Parti Québécois government is simply wrong. Premier Lévesque had signed the April 1981 agreement of the eight provinces.

As a partial reparation for the 1982 Act, the 1987 Accord is received with relief in Quebec, but fireworks are nowhere to be seen in the sky of Montreal, as pollsters have dutifully reported. The lack of enthusiasm is quite understandable. We are now allowed to promote our own distinctive identity, but only under a new rule of interpretation that will have to be balanced against similar rules concerning bilingualism and multiculturalism. We are all for bilingualism and multiculturalism, but if they happen to be enforced without circumspection on the only island of French in this sea of 250 million North American anglophones, God knows what the end result may be. I ask the question: without a distinct Quebec, what is left of a distinct Canada?

Nevertheless, most of us trust the future of the constitutional process. "Ce n'est qu'un début," as Premier Bourassa keeps repeating. We trust the wisdom of the courts, the political determination of our people, our new economic strength, and the good faith of our English Canadian partners. We believe that a fair social contract will finally emerge in Quebec that will protect and promote our identity, and yet remain generous for our English minority. But until then, we are holding our breath.

While the signature of the Accord has not raised much enthusiasm in Quebec, its eventual *rejection* by provincial governments would be certain to spark a fire in Quebec, as Ivan Bernier emphasizes.[1] Few

---

1 See I. Bernier, "Meech Lake and Constitutional Visions" in this volume at 239.

outside the province realize that throughout the last quarter century the overwhelming majority of Québécois, on average 75 per cent, have supported an increase of provincial over federal powers, and that over 40 per cent (50 per cent among Francophones) still back sovereignty-association.

Viewed in this light, the Meech Lake Accord is a good deal for Canada. Through it, Quebec not only says yes to the Canadian Charter of Rights, as opposed to its own, but it *de facto* puts on the back burner its traditional demands for increased power in the areas of manpower, income security, regional development, communications, marriage and divorce, and international relations.

There have been groups on the two sides of the fence that have torn their shirts in public and are ready to descend from heaven to save Quebec from a sell-out, to shield Canada from so-called balkanization, or, believe it or not, to provide Quebec women — who have otherwise said they do not feel threatened one bit — with solicitous protection against the distinct society. I first thought that these interventions were a disgrace in an otherwise very elevated debate. I just couldn't understand how more power for Quebec compared to the 1982 Act could be viewed as less power by one side, how recognizing and protecting the glaring fact of Quebec's distinctiveness could be felt by the other side as a threat to a country that, again, is frantically looking for means of distinguishing itself from its southern neighbour, or how arresting the federal government from invading exclusive provincial jurisdiction at will and without prior consultation or agreement, could be considered so wicked. But after awhile I realized that these offsetting extremisms have rendered the country the great service of identifying exactly where the moderate centre lies. May we stay there. My contribution to this book precisely amounts to characterizing the two extreme positions on the spending power amendment, and to explaining why I believe they are flawed and won't fly.

THE PROCESS IS THE MESSAGE

What is the meaning of Meech Lake for the exercise of power in the federation? In my view, no answer to this question can be complete without considering process as well as substance.

There is no doubt that the process of Meech Lake and of its Ottawa extension is just as important as the substance of the Accord itself. The federal-provincial consensus reached after so many hours of difficult, but honest, negotiations marks the end of 20 years of conflict and confrontation between Ottawa and the provinces. It is quite arguable that the display of rediscovered unity at Meech Lake is *the* major factor behind the public support for the Accord and behind the general disapproval of former Prime Minister Trudeau's flashy intervention in May. Given the enormous tensions that existed in federal-provincial relations until he left only three years ago, the spirit of the Accord is an incredible achievement.

It may also hold the promise of a much brighter future. The very experience of consensus reached in full mutual respect, and in a way that was consistent with the superior national interest, may breed more similar experiences in years to come, if only the old guards of the last two decades can be kept where they now belong — out. National interest will be better served if eleven governments work for it than if only one pretends it does. Here, institutional support for co-operative federalism is wisely entrenched by the amendments requiring annual first ministers conferences on the economy and on the Constitution.

Likewise, the nomination of senators through a double-veto federal-provincial procedure (until an agreement on the reform of the Senate is reached) introduces a welcome element of checks and balances between the two levels of government and of increased legitimacy of regional representation in federal institutions. In addition, this is a victory for democracy over the end-of-mandate rush to nominate political friends that was so common in the past, and particularly conspicuous in June 1984.

Some have argued that the new rule of unanimity in constitutional matters of cardinal importance, and the compensated opting-out provision for provinces that do not agreed to be stripped of their constitutional jurisdiction, would make the process of constitutional amendment much more laborious in the future. This is fallacious mathematics. Even if the unanimity rule was not entrenched until now, it was solidly rooted in constitutional tradition. You simply cannot run a federation in matters of fundamental importance in the same way as you decide about housing regulations in Antigonish — that is, by scores of 8 to 3 or even 10 to 1 — as in 1982. The ultimate criterion for legitimate constitutional action is whether good faith and mutual trust are present, or not. If they are, unanimity is not a constraint. If they are not, we are in a deadlock whatever the decision rules.

Of course, this raises the question of why the unanimity rule and the compensated opting-out provision for important constitutional amendments were entrenched, if they are naturally enforced by tradition. The answer is that the history of the 1982 constitutional revision has clearly demonstrated, at least to Québécois of every political persuasion and to many others throughout the country, that "natural enforcement" is not enough. If the Constitution cannot legislate good faith, it can, in some instances at least, protect us against the consequences of future abuses of power.

It may be that the democratic process was not given sufficient time to bear on the Meech Lake consensus. It is an obvious line of defence for Québécois who believe the Accord was a sell-out, and for Canadians who think too much was yielded to Quebec and other provinces. But I should nevertheless point out that open discussion on the final content of the Accord began at least *one year* before it was finally signed. One should not confuse public indifference to constitutional matters with a breach of the democratic process. By comparison, the November 1981 agreement between the federal government and the nine provinces was reached in *one night* only. It is hard to understand why laments about the democratic process were much less heard of then, than now, outside Quebec.

BALKANIZATION? NO, SWISSIFICATION

In substance, the constitutional amendment limiting the federal spending power has stirred a lot of controversy. At one extreme, concern was expressed that the new s. 106A would have Canada "end up with a patchwork quilt of programs with little or no room for co-ordination between them" (Donald Johnston),[2] that it would "allow the provinces to complete the balkanization of languages and cultures with the balkanization of social services" (Pierre Elliott-Trudeau),[3] that it would "destroy the sense of Canadians that they were entitled to the same kind of services wherever they went in Canada", and that it would, to that extent, impede the development of a "common consciousness" across the nation (Al Johnson).[4]

The foregoing statements grossly exaggerate the significance of the proposed amendment. To labour the obvious, let us recall that s. 106A states that Ottawa shall provide reasonable compensation to a province that chooses not to participate in a program only if five

---

2 *The [Montreal] Gazette* (May 15, 1987).

3 *La Presse* [de Montréal] (May 27, 1987).

4 A.W. Johnson, "The Meech Lake Accord and the Bonds of Nationhood" in this volume at p. 145.

very stringent conditions are met simultaneously: (1) a *national* program must be involved; (2) it must be a *new* program; (3) it must be a *shared-cost* program; (4) it must be in an area of *exclusive* provincial jurisdiction; and (5) it must be replaced in that province by a program or initiative that is *compatible with the national objectives*.

As Reed Scowen said, the amendment is intended only "to stop the central government from acting, without prior consultation, in areas where it has *no jurisdiction at all*" (his italics) and "from doing indirectly what it has no right to do directly"![5] Bilateral agreements are unaffected; tax expenditures are still allowed; past programs are untouched, federal programs in areas of mixed jurisdiction are permitted; programs that are fully federally-funded are allowed; and the non-participating province is forced to replace the national program by a compatible initiative. To reject even this extremely mild limitation to the federal spending power comes close to negating the very concept of exclusive authority of the provinces in *any* area and the central importance of the regional dimension to the very existence of the federation. There is one constitutional alternative that would at least have the merit of clarity: transform the provinces into big city governments and Canada into a unitary state.

It is quite obvious that the doom and gloom predictions of the opponents of s. 106A hide a very stark view of what Canada is about or where it should go. That view is that the struggle for nation-building must rely on a stronger central government (like Germany). They tend to view provincial power as a lesser evil that is acceptable only because it is also temporary. Those who support the amendment believe, on the contrary, that a strong central government is neither necessary (consider Switzerland, not the Balkans), nor sufficient (consider Belgium) for national unity and consciousness.

The two groups have been fighting over their conflicting views and for the hearts and minds of their fellow countrymen for at least 200 years. They are not about to stop fighting. What the Meech Lake Accord does at this particular time of history is to strike just about the right political balance between the maximalists and the minimalists after 20 years of exhausting federal-provincial confrontation.

My own perception of the political realities of Canada is that those who genuinely seek to maintain an equilibrium between unity and diversity, as the Greek philosophers advised, and view Canada as a "community of communities" defend a position that is in closer conformity with our history and traditions. They certainly have the

---

5 *The [Montreal] Gazette* (May 22, 1987).

overwhelming support of the Quebec population, which had consistently sent the same unequivocal message for 120 years: "Un Québec fort dans un Canada uni." There was no contradiction in their equal respect for Lévesque and Trudeau.

WHY DECENTRALIZE: COST MINIMIZATION AND WELFARE MAXIMIZATION

There are sound economic arguments for decentralization as well. Global economic efficiency requires that the provision of public goods and services should pass two tests: minimum unit cost and maximum satisfaction of preferences (or "welfare").

In many instances, and most evidently in areas of exclusive provincial jurisdiction, cost minimization is better achieved at the delivery level in the provinces than in Ottawa. The provincial level is where the information on technology, products, and financing alternatives essentially resides, and where innovation and experimentation naturally takes place. It would be foolish for the central government not to recognize that program cost minimization requires, first, that careful attention be paid to the varied experiences of the ten provinces in these areas. This is especially true in a period of slow economic growth and tight budgets. Think of the current efforts in many provinces to contain health care costs, of the ongoing discussions about new avenues for the financing of post-secondary education, of the innovations in the new area of "workfare", or of potential new shared-cost candidates like child care, home services for the elderly, and municipal infrastructures.

Part of the incentive for cost minimization comes from inter-provincial emulation and competition. Surely, if competition is so good for the private marketplace, it must also have something going for it in the public marketplace. From my experience in giving economic advice to the Quebec government, I have learned that competition with Ontario is an extremely powerful argument for cost minimization in the provision of public goods and services in my province. To some extent, then, centralization establishes a monopoly, and, with it, higher costs and higher taxes, while decentralization brings more competition, lower costs and lower taxes. As Tom Courchene keeps reminding us, the national interest is often best served by decentralization of initiative.[6]

---

6 See, for example, T. Courchene, *Economic Management and The Division of Powers* (Toronto: University of Toronto Press, 1986), MacDonald Commission Studies, vol. 67.

Differences in preferences for the quantity and quality of public goods and services exist across provinces. For example, the resistance to extra billing of medical services is probably much stronger in some provinces than in others. More generally, views on the appropriate shares of the public and private sectors in the delivery and financing systems are far from uniform from east to west. Differences in the nature of community networks across regions may call for important variations in the design of provincial welfare regulations. Differences in institutions and practices may require very different vehicles for manpower policy (think of the Canadian Jobs Strategy) from one province to another. There is also no doubt that the emerging debates on possible future child care or municipal infrastructure programs will reflect wide differences in provincial needs and preferences.

Maximum satisfaction of wants (with a given amount of money) obviously requires that national programs accommodate the existing variations in individual preferences to some extent. Provincial differentiation of the programs often helps to meet this objective. This is not new, and fortunately many existing shared-cost programs do recognize this need. But we may not have gone far enough. The proposed s. 106A simply entrenches this practice in areas of exclusive provincial authority, while requiring that national objectives be met everywhere. It clearly does seek to maintain a fair balance between national principles and the flexible regional implementation of these principles. Where's the trap?

DO WE REALLY NEED TO LIMIT THE FEDERAL SPENDING POWER?

It may be argued that the practice of regional flexibility within national shared-cost programs is so obviously beneficial to all that it need not be entrenched. But the point of the proposed amendment is precisely that too many federal politicians and public servants in the past did not seem to see the benefit. In that sense s. 106A is the direct consequence of perceived past abuses of the federal spending power. Without them we might never have heard about such an amendment.

Fortunately, one consequence of entrenchment may actually be that we will never need it in the future. The threat of provincial non-participation in new shared-cost programs and of the associated court litigation will create a greater incentive for the federal government to negotiate the terms of future shared-cost programs with the provinces so as to arrive at a national consensus tailored to special regional needs. This will not be a true constraint on any federal authority that already understands the key potential contribution of the provinces to the economics of the programs and the power of national consensus. In sum, there is a reduction in "flexibility" only for those who show no respect at all for the exclusive constitutional authority of the provinces in the relevant areas. Unfortunately, again, past abuses have shown that we do need this sort of "rigidity."

All provinces will also be induced to contribute to the definition of the national objectives, because they will be bound by those objectives whether or not they participate in the national program, and because public opinion will be merciless for provincial governments that take too lightly their participation in programs perceived as highly desirable. As many have observed, a likely consequence is that new shared-cost programs would either be supported by federal-provincial consensus (*if*, in addition, there is money around!) or they would not come into existence at all. In this context, the feared judicialization of the process will simply not materialize.

QUEBEC WORRIES: WAS TOO HIGH A PRICE PAID FOR OPTING-OUT?

It is important to realize that the proposed s. 106A was widely criticized in French Quebec for reasons that are entirely different from those heard in the rest of Canada. While the debate over the federal spending power in English Canada essentially focused on whether it would be a threat to the process of strengthening Canadian unity, the whole debate in French Quebec centred on the diametrically opposed concern that too much federal power was being acknowledged or conceded in s. 106A. The pressure on Premier Bourassa was so strong that at the Ottawa meeting he demanded and obtained the safeguard that nothing in the proposed section on the federal spending power "extends the legislative powers of the Parliament of Canada or the legislatures of the provinces."

A few participants in the Quebec debate questioned the very existence of the federal spending power, but legal opinion everywhere was that it existed and permitted the federal government to *spend money* in federal or provincial areas, but not to *legislate* in respect of matters falling under exclusive provincial jurisdiction. As Guy Tremblay pointed out, Quebec should not be fearful that the principle of the spending power be recognized explicitly by the proposed s. 106A. The reason is simply that the principle does apply to provincial as well as to federal spending. In particular, it allows the provinces to spend money in matters of international relations.[7]

Another concern was that the opting-out condition requiring an alternative provincial program or initiative compatible with the national objectives would amount to an implicit recognition that the federal government could legislate these objectives without consultation or agreement with the provinces even if the area was one of exclusive provincial jurisdiction. The safeguard clause introduced in the final wording of the Accord in Ottawa deals with that concern. While it may not be perfectly clear yet whether federal conditional grants to provinces are constitutional (that is, whether they amount to legislating in exclusive provincial areas), the Accord will, at least, not make matters worse for the provinces.

Assuming that the national objectives of a new shared-cost program are acceptable to a province, or otherwise constitutional, the next question is whether any condition *at all* should be imposed on a province in order to receive compensation if it chooses not to participate in the national program, given that its exclusive jurisdiction is being "invaded". I think it is fair to say that most public interventions in Quebec, including those of several constitutional experts, tended to answer the question negatively and recommended unconditional compensation as a matter of principle.

It is hard to see how any new shared-cost program would be created if unconditional compensation were granted by s. 106A. As Peter Leslie recently said, we have yet to hear from a provincial treasurer who preferred a dollar with strings on it to a dollar with none. *That* would have justified Al Johnson's worst fears. Moreover, requiring unconditionality would have made compensated opting-out politically impossible to entrench. Provincial rights would not have been necessarily served better.

It is also important to recall that the condition of "a program or initiative compatible with national objectives" is sufficiently general to meet most differences in regional preferences. It is difficult to imagine that a program considered vital by everyone outside Quebec would not also be viewed as such in Quebec. In addition, the constraint of national *objectives* should be much less effective on provincial priorities than the more specific *norms and standards* would have been.

---

7 *Le Québec et Le Lac Meech* (Montreal: Guérin littérature, 1987) at 111.

CONCLUSION

If anybody still doubts that Quebec is a distinct society, he has only to review the proceedings of the parliamentary debates in Quebec City and in Ottawa following the Meech Lake Accord. The concerns in the two capitals were diametrically opposed. The Accord was seen as a minimum gain in French Quebec and a maximum concession in English Canada. All in all, my feeling is that the proposed s. 106A constitutes a fair deal for all sides — a good maximin solution.

Economic Policy Implications Of The Meech Lake Accord

Robin W. Boadway, Jack M. Mintz and Douglas D. Purvis

The Meech Lake Accord contains provisions that will undoubtedly have far-reaching effects on many issues of concern to Canadians; in this paper we discuss some of those that will have important and direct implications for economic policy. In assessing the implications for economic policy of the Accord, we consider how the Constitution limits the powers of the federal and provincial governments and ask what economic policy obligations it imposes on them. In the first section we outline the basic economic analysis of policy-making in a federal system of government and identify two key problems inherent in a federal system, which then become the focus for our analysis of the effects of the Meech Lake Accord. The Accord, however, cannot be evaluated in isolation, but rather it should be viewed as a continuation of the process of Constitutional revision begun in 1982, and in the second section we summarize how the 1982 amendments changed the balance of economic power. We then turn to an assessment of the Meech Lake Accord itself. In the third section we discuss the federal spending power; joint consideration of the Meech Lake Accord and the 1982 amendments allows an evaluation of how the post-Accord balance of economic powers in the Canadian federation differs from that of the pre-1982 era. In the fourth section we discuss federal-provincial co-operation and the proposed national economic conferences.

POLICY MAKING IN A FEDERAL SYSTEM OF GOVERNMENT

Federal systems of government by definition involve some degree of decentralization of powers to lower levels of government. The degree to which powers are decentralized differs across federations, and there is no uniquely ideal degree of decentralization. The choice involves a trade-off between the benefits of decentralization and those of centralization, and different circumstances dictate different degrees of decentralization.

Broadly speaking, decentralization allows local variations in policies to account for local preferences and conditions, possibly allowing for more accountability and responsiveness of government to citizen preferences, and possibly allowing for more innovative policy responses in the face of competition with other localities. On the other hand, centralization enables governments to take national concerns fully into account in situations where the effects of policies cross the boundaries of provincial jurisdictions, and also allows economies of scale at the national scale to be exploited.

However, a perfect matching of policy responsibilities with jurisdictions is not generally possible. Issues which are primarily of a regional nature and which are decentralized to the provincial level may nonetheless have some national effects. In such circumstances it would be beneficial to institute policies which retain the benefits of a decentralized system and at the same time induce provinces to take account of the broader national interest. The literature on fiscal federalism is largely devoted to devising such policy mechanisms.

A related issue is that, by their very nature, some policy objectives cannot be assigned exclusively to one level of government. For example, such pervasive objectives as distributive equity and full employment cannot be assigned exclusively to the federal government. Since there are many policy instruments which have consequences for these goals, it is impossible to think of either goal as being the assigned responsibility of only one level of government. As a result, these objectives are jointly pursued by both levels of government; in the absence of co-operative behaviour, the independent actions of each level of government may be at least partly self-defeating.

The above discussion suggests that there are two sorts of policy problems inherent in federal economies. The first is the need to ensure that decentralized policies take account of any national interests that exist in areas of policy assigned exclusively to the provinces. The second is the need to ensure that federal and provincial policies are consistent in areas of overlapping jurisdiction. Two broad sorts of policy initiatives have evolved to deal with these co-ordination problems. The first is a system of federal-provincial grants. The second is federal-provincial co-operation in particular policy areas.

The extensive literature on grants has led to a considerable consensus among economists on their design. Grants either to redistribute among provinces or to transfer tax resources from the federal to the provincial level of government should be unconditional. In the Canadian context, equalization payments provide an important example of unconditional grants. The appropriate size of such grants is a matter of dispute, but the principle of the grants is not a matter of economic or constitutional controversy.

Grants are also useful as a means of providing both the resources and the incentive to provinces to take the national interest into account when making their expenditure decisions. To provide the appropriate incentive, such grants need to be conditional. Thus, from an economic point of view, the spending power is a necessary adjunct to a federal system of government. The difficulty in providing for the use of the spending power in the Constitution is to proscribe the limits of its use.

Canada has had a great deal of experience with conditional grants, as have other federations. However, with some exceptions, there has been far less experience with federal-provincial co-operation in areas of concurrent jurisdiction. One of the most successful Canadian examples of co-operative policy formation is the implementation of Tax Collection Agreements; others might include immigration policy, agricultural policy, and some areas of resource policy. But, by and large, unilateral federal or provincial action is the rule.

THE CONSTITUTION ACT, 1982 AND THE BALANCE OF POWER

The provisions of the Constitution Act, 1982[1] that are relevant to economic policy include the amendment to the Constitution Act, 1867[2] involving natural resources, explicit recognition of the commitment to equalization in the Constitution, and introduction of the Canadian Charter of Rights and Freedoms.[3]

---

1 Being Schedule B of The Canada Act 1982 (U.K.), c. 11.

2 (U.K.), c. 3.

3 Being Part I of the Constitution Act, 1982.

Natural Resources

The natural resources amendment which added s. 92A to the Constitution Act, 1867 gives provinces exclusive rights to make laws in relation to exploration, development, conservation and management of natural resources. It allows provinces to make laws governing the export of resources from one province to the others, but prohibits the exporting provinces from discriminating amongst the recipient provinces in terms of prices or supplies. Under the provisions of s. 92A, Parliament can also make laws governing interprovincial trade in resources, and in the case of conflict the federal laws prevail. Provinces are also given the right to levy any type of tax on resources they like, provided they do not discriminate between that consumed domestically and that exported to other provinces.

Equalization and regional disparities

Section 36 of the Constitution Act, 1982 commits Parliament and the legislatures to promoting equal opportunities, furthering economic development to reduce disparities in opportunities, and to providing essential public services of reasonable quality to all Canadians. It also explicitly commits the federal government to the principle of making equalization payments to ensure that provinces have sufficient revenues to provide reasonably comparable levels of public services at reasonably comparable levels of taxation. These stipulations have potentially far-ranging implications. They could be used to justify almost any nationally-funded social program, since most have an equity dimension. In fact, this new commitment to equality and equalization explicitly defines equity as a national objective and could therefore affect the interpretation of the spending power clause in the Meech Lake Accord.

It has perhaps been insufficently recognized that this provision represents an explicit recognition of the federal role in equity objectives, and is inherently centralizing. The provision also imposes an obligation on the federal government which could be argued to go well beyond the formal equalization scheme.

The Charter of Rights and Freedoms

The Charter contains a number of clauses with economic dimensions. For example s. 6, the mobility rights provision, guarantees the right to enter and leave Canada, and the right to take up residence and work in any province. Mobility rights do not preclude the use of affirmative actions programs that economically assist residents in provinces with high unemployment relative to the national average. While the 1982 amendments ensure mobility rights for labour, they do not guarantee the free flow of goods and services across Canada nor the mobility of capital. Another relevant provision is s. 15 which deals with equality rights. It guarantees equality before the law, but does not preclude affirmative action programs. Section 15 could be interpreted as applying to economic equality. These provisions of the Charter clearly could be used to justify federal economic policies. Again, the inherently centralizing effect of these provisions has not been widely recognized.

THE MEECH LAKE ACCORD AND THE SPENDING POWER

The Meech Lake Accord provides for a new section, s. 106A, to be added to the Constitution Act, 1867. The primary purpose of s. 106A is to grant the provinces the right to opt-out with compensation from any national shared-cost program. However, s. 106A appears to recognize explicitly that the federal government may establish shared-cost programs in areas of exclusive provincial jurisdiction. Prior to the Meech Lake Accord, this role for the federal government had been, at best, only implicitly recognized; there had been no court decision clarifying the constitutional right of the federal government to engage in shared-cost programs with the provinces. While the Accord takes care to stress that it does not involve an extension of federal spending powers, it does resolve any uncertainty about the extent of such powers in favour of the federal government.

Enshrining in the Constitution the ability of the provinces to opt-out at will from future shared-cost programs essentially regularizes a procedure which had been allowed on a once-and-for-all basis in the past. The federal government had allowed Quebec to opt-out of the federal post-secondary grant system in 1960 in return for a corporate income tax abatement and cash transfers. In 1965 it offered all provinces an opportunity to opt-out of the various shared-cost programs that existed at the time (essentially hospital insurance and welfare); only Quebec accepted the offer.

It is important to recognize one aspect of the 1965 opting-out arrangement which is relevant for evaluating the possible impact of s. 106A. Under the terms of the 1965 arrangement, opting-out only changed the form in which the financial support was received from the federal government. Instead of giving a cash grant, the federal government transferred income tax points, thus giving the province more tax room; an adjustment was made to ensure the province received the same funding it would have had if it received a cash grant. A province was eligible to receive full compensation from the federal government only if its programs met various conditions defined by the federal government. The effect of this was to leave unaltered the set of incentives for provinces to participate in the shared-cost programs. In the case of health care, for example, the conditions that Quebec was required to meet were identical to those imposed on the participating provinces, and the funding it received was based on the same criteria as for other provinces.

Interpreting s. 106A

Section 106A is potentially a many-edged sword. Its wording gives rise to many possible interpretations, and accordingly to different possible consequences for future federal shared-cost programs. The most important ambiguities arise in the provision that a province which opts-out of a federal "shared-cost" program is entitled to "reasonable compensation . . . if the province carries on a program or initiative that is compatible with the national objectives."

If "compatibility" is interpreted as it was in the opting-out arrangements of the 1960s, the force of the provision will be to require the provinces to comply fully with the conditions of the federal program in question in order to qualify for full compensation. In this case the entitlement to compensation will in no way detract from the coercive nature of the federal grant; it will only change the form in which the money is transferred. However, the courts may instead give a looser interpretation to what is required of a provincial program to be compatible, so that provinces may opt-out rather freely and the federal spending power will be diminished.

The meaning of the term "national objectives" is also obviously open to interpretation. It could certainly be argued that the scope of national objectives has been explicitly broadened by the provisions of the Charter and the equalization provisions contained in the 1982 amendment. In particular, anything which contributes to reducing inequities can be seen to have a national objective. This would seem to expand the set of legitimate types of federal grants.

The restriction of the provision to shared-cost programs introduces a further element of ambiguity to the Accord. Shared-cost could be interpreted quite narrowly, in which case it would be possible for the federal government to circumvent any restrictions on its spending power by providing conditional grants in a manner that will be interpreted as other than cost-sharing with the provinces. For example, federal grants could have conditions attached to them which have nothing to do with provincial expenditure levels, as with the Canada Health Act.[4] However, the courts could instead interpret shared-cost very broadly, so that provinces would have the right to opt-out with compensation from virtually any federal policy initiative.

Consequences of s. 106A

Will these changes be centralizing or decentralizing? This is an important issue that goes to the heart of federal-provincial relations. On the face of it, since the changes guarantee the right of the provinces to opt-out, they would seem to restrict the power of the federal government to introduce national social programs. This seems to be a widely held view of the Accord, and has given rise to some rather extreme statements condemning the Accord on the grounds that the federal government has surrendered too many powers and abrogated its responsibilities.

However, as we have argued above, it is quite possible that the provisions of the Accord will be interpreted so as to extend the federal spending power compared to the pre-1982 situation. For one thing, the perceived right of the federal government to engage in new shared-cost programs in areas of exclusive provincial jurisdiction seems to be enhanced by the recognition that this is justified when a national interest is served. This is especially so when one takes into account the new provisions on equalization in the Constitution Act, 1982 in determining what is in the national interest. This provision imposes on the federal government the commitment to promote equal opportunities for the well-being of Canadians. It would now seem to be enough to show that a national equity objective is being served to justify federal action on the social policy front. For example, the Canada Assistance Plan could easily be argued to have a national equity objective, as could conditional grants in the area of health, education and day care.

Further, the requirement to allow opting-out with compensation

4 S.C. 1983-84, c. 6.

may not detract from this enhanced federal power in any perceptible way. The provision for compensation requires that the province carry on a program that is compatible with the national objective in order to receive reasonable compensation, even though the program is in an area of exclusive provincial jurisdiction. If that is interpreted as a particularly restrictive requirement for the provinces, akin to the opting-out conditions of the 1960s as discussed above, then the section does not appear to restrict the coercive force of the federal spending power even in areas of exclusive provincial jurisdiction, provided a national objective is served. The section also implies that the spending power has always been in place by the statement that "nothing in this section extends the legislative powers of the Parliament of Canada . . .".

Even if the opting-out provisions are not innocuous, it could still be argued that the effect of s. 106A will be centralizing. Guaranteeing the ability of provinces to opt-out with compensation from federal grant schemes may remove some existing inhibitions to introducing controversial federal programs in areas of provincial jurisdiction. The increased possibility for dissenters to opt-out may thus reduce the consensus required for a new federal program to be introduced.

Our reading of the Accord, therefore, does not lead us to support the extreme view that the federal government has paid too high a price by turning too much power over to the provinces; by and large the provisions serve mainly to enshrine existing practice. Hence, taking into account both the 1982 and 1987 constitutional amendments, the spending power provisions of the Accord will likely turn out to be centralizing.

THE MEECH LAKE ACCORD AND FEDERAL-PROVINCIAL CO-OPERATION

In addition to the spending power, the other important area in which economic policy might be influenced by the provisions of the Meech Lake Accord is federal-provincial co-operation. The Accord adds a new s. 148 to the Constitution Act, 1867, which enshrines the institution of an annual national economic conference. While the mandate of the conference as cited in the Accord is simply to "discuss the state of the Canadian economy and such other matters as may be appropriate", it seems reasonable to infer that its purpose is to promote better co-ordination of policies by the two levels of government. The question we pose is whether federal-provincial co-operation will be improved by the Meech Lake Accord and we consider the role that an annual national economic conference might play.

The National Economic Conference

Despite the obvious desirability of federal-provincial policy co-operation, one can question the usefulness of an annual national economic conference enshrined in the Constitution in promoting such co-operation. The need for co-operation is widely acknowledged, and indeed a considerable amount of co-operation already occurs under existing arrangements. Most takes place at the bureaucratic level, and involves both policy development and "trouble shooting." In addition, federal and provincial finance ministers meet regularly, and irregular first ministers' conferences have also been called to address economic issues.

Thus, while a good deal of the existing activity is formalized in federal-provincial committees, they largely receive their direction from the working level and thus respond to real operating problems of existing programs. National economic conferences, particularly ones with a regular schedule enshrined in the Constitution, may mean that some of this working level co-operation is replaced by a much more political process. The history of such political processes in Canada has produced two sorts of outcomes, neither of which is necessarily good for policy co-ordination.

The first outcome is that the national platform provided by first ministers' conferences has often led to a very confrontational style of interaction, with little or no policy content. It is difficult to say how regularizing the national economic conference would affect this, but one might look for clues from the international summits that have been held annually for the last decade and a half. This evidence shows a good deal of confrontation (with the little guys seizing the opportunity to "gang up" on the big guy), very little policy development, and enormous bureaucratic effort in preparing in advance an innocuous joint statement to be issued by the politicians. Crises tend to get handled in a manner largely external to the summitry process. Witness the famous "Plaza Agreement" to lower the external value of the U.S. dollar made by the Group of Five in September of 1985; the regular summit process and two summit participants, Canada and Italy, were ignored completely in reaching that agreement.

The second experience with first ministers' conferences, of which the Meech Lake Accord itself is an example, is that the Parliament of Canada and the provincial legislatures are presented with what is essentially a *fait accompli* hammered out by leaders behind closed doors. Such an elitist process often circumvents the careful study and analysis that accompanies policy development at the bureaucratic level, as well as the close scrutiny that policies receive when debated at the caucus and committee levels. While there may be occasions that call for dramatic action of this kind, it seems clear that an annual conference is difficult to justify on these grounds.

One major positive aspect of international summits is that they keep the lines of communication open, and allow ongoing relationships to be established which often help in reaching agreement on key issues. For example, it seems clear that the close relationship between Finance Minister Michael Wilson and U.S. Secretary of the Treasury James Baker played an important role in reaching the dramatic eleventh-hour free trade agreement in October 1987.

Given that the annual national economic conference is enshrined, there is a need to depoliticize it as much as possible. Further efforts should be directed to using the conference as a vehicle for improving communication between the economic policy branches of the two levels of government, allowing for a shared approach to assessing issues and developing policy responses. Considerable benefits could arise from co-ordinating policies on a number of particular policy fronts, including deficits and debt management, tax harmonization, social policy, financial regulation and immigration policy. Except for the latter, these issues were not explicitly addressed in the Accord; nevertheless, since they are areas where co-operation is called for, they will be influenced by the Accord insofar as the Accord influences the environment in which the two levels of government interact.

CONCLUSIONS

Rather than attempt to summarize our arguments, we conclude by raising the basic question of the role of the Constitution in guiding economic policy. Constitutions are by design intended to change only slowly, responding to perceptible and permanent changes in the society's circumstances. Enshrining details of economic policy in a Constitution constrains the ability of governments to respond to changing economic conditions — it reduces their ability both to introduce new policy initiatives and to forsake old policies which are no longer appropriate.

In this context, one could question the wisdom of embedding

in the Constitution such specific mandates as the commitment of the federal government to make equalization payments to poorer provinces, the immigration provisions of the Accord, or such specific requirements as that of "shared-cost" programs for the opting-out provision. One could also question the wisdom of creating enormous ambiguities about the division of powers, and hence impairing policy development in areas such as social policy and financial regulation where events occur rapidly. To be effective, policy response in such areas must be equally rapid. The courts, and the Constitution, may provide wise guidance for longer-term policy evolution, but they are inappropriate vehicles for providing policy responses quickly when they are needed.

Part III

Competing Visions
of
Constitutionalism

Meech Lake and
Constitutional Visions

Ivan Bernier

The argument in the following pages rests on two basic propositions. First, the dire predictions as to the impact of the Meech Lake
Accord, derived from the wording of the proposed amendments, have
probably more to do with the political preferences of those who make
them than with reality. Constitutional texts, once adopted, can be
interpreted in various ways; they can develop in new and unexpected
directions, be circumvented or even become totally obsolete. From
that point of view, the discourse on Meech Lake is definitely more
revealing than the proposed amendments themselves. The second
proposition is that the Meech Lake agreement, whether one likes it
or not, has already assumed the position of a constitutional symbol,
and is perceived as such, both in Quebec and in the rest of Canada,
irrespective of whether it becomes law or not. The chances are that
Meech Lake will stand as a watershed in Canadian constitutional history
and will have a lasting impact.

Canadian constitutional history is replete with examples of
apparently straightforward constitutional provisions that have given
rise to unexpected developments. Thus the widely held belief, in the
early years of Confederation, that Canada was a quasi-federal state
dominated and led by the central government — a view based on
a literal reading of the Constitution Act, 1867[1] — has had to yield
to the Privy Council vision of a truly federal state. This has prompted

---

1 (U.K.), c. 3.

such a learned author as Eugene Forsey to speak of the Privy Council
members as the "wicked stepfathers of confederation".[2] But this value
judgment has been challenged by other authors, the best study of the
question being that of Alan Cairns.[3] Is it necessary to add that if the
decisions of the Privy Council were much criticized in English Canada,
they were, on the contrary, well received in French Canada where
they were seen as very much in line with the true spirit of the political
agreement leading up to the Constitution Act, 1867?

Much more disappointing, from a French-Canadian perspective,
was the fate of s. 23 of the Manitoba Act, 1870,[4] which was intended
to introduce into the new province of Manitoba the linguistic
obligations imposed on Canada and Quebec by s. 133 of the Constitution
Act, 1867. At that time, it will be remembered, the population of
Manitoba was equally divided between anglophones and francophones.
Twenty years later, the situation having substantially changed in favour
of the English speaking group, a provincial Act made English the only
official language of Manitoba, while another one abolished the system
of denominational schools, thereby depriving the linguistic minority
of its school system. It is only 90 years later, in the *Forest*[5] case, that
the constitutional paramountcy of s. 23 of the Manitoba Act, 1870,
as confirmed by the Constitution Act, 1871,[6] was finally recognized.

In the same vein, if the French speaking minority of Ontario had
thought, since Confederation, that their separate school system was
protected by s. 93 of the Constitution Act, 1867, they learned with
dismay, in 1917, that the abolition of French teaching by the Ontario
government was perfectly constitutional, s. 93 being concerned
exclusively with denominational schools. A decade later, in the *Tiny*[7]
case, they were further told that the denominational schools guaranteed
by s. 93 essentially referred to primary schools, a decision that was
reviewed in the *Separate High Schools Funding*[8] case. It is not devoid
of interest, on the other hand, to recall that as recently as 1985, the
Quebec Association of Protestant School Boards was able to challenge

---

2 Eugene Forsey, in P.W. Hogg, *Constitutional Law of Canada*, 2nd ed. (Toronto: Carswell, 1985)
   at 89.
3 A. Cairns, "The judicial committee and its critics" (1971), 4 C.J.P.S. 301.
4 S.C. 1870, c. 3.
5 *Forest v. A.G. Man.* (1979), 101 D.L.R. (3d) 385 (S.C.C.).
6 (U.K.), c. 28.
7 *Tiny Separate School Trustees v. R.*, [1928] 3 D.L.R. 753 (P.C.). See also Donald D. Lange,
   "Constitutional Jurisprudence, Politics and Minority Language Rights" (1980), 11 Man. L.J.
   33.
8 *Reference Re An Act to Amend the Education Act (Ontario)* (1987), 40 D.L.R. (4th) 18 (S.C.C.).

successfully, on the basis of s. 93, a Quebec Government plan to reorganize the school system along linguistic lines.[9] The irony of this development is that it has worked to preserve the integrity of the Protestant School Board of Greater Montreal which, as pointed out by one of its commissioners, functions essentially as an English political structure, notwithstanding the fact that one-third of its students are taught in French.[10] Constitutional texts sometimes yield curious results.

Not only is their content substantially affected by judicial interpretation; sometimes these texts are purely and simply circumvented through political arrangements between governments. A first example of this is the development of the practice of conditional grants through the use of a federal spending power whose limits have never been defined, because neither the federal government nor the provincial governments had much to gain in clarifying the situation. At another level, and over a longer period of time, constitutional conventions are sometimes used "to bring outdated legal powers into conformity with current notions of government."[11] This is how the federal power of disallowance, for instance, has become for all intents and purposes extinct.

Through judicial interpretation or otherwise, constitutional texts develop in directions that are not easily predictable. This is why it is difficult to concur with those who affirm with assurance that Meech Lake is a legal and political aberration and will yield catastrophic results. Let us deal briefly with three such viewpoints that project a bleak future for Canada on the basis of the wording of the agreement.

The first and best known of these views is the one that considers the Meech Lake agreement as "an agenda for the dismemberment of our country,"[12] or a sure way to turn Canada into "a loose collection of ten independant duchies with a central clearing house in Ottawa for tax collection, foreign relations and our fitful gestures in the direction of defence."[13] The strongest proponent of that view, of course, is former Prime Minister Pierre Trudeau who, in a devastating article, published at the end of May 1987,[14] predicted that the agreement concocted between the Prime Minister of Canada and the ten provincial premiers would make Canada impotent, divide Canadian society in

---

9 *Quebec Association of Protestant School Boards v. A.G. Que.*, [1985] C.S. 873.

10 *Le Devoir* [de Montréal] (September 26, 1987) 7; (November 10, 1987) 4.

11 Hogg, above, note 1 at 20.

12 M. Bliss, *The [Toronto] Globe and Mail* (23 May 1987) D2.

13 R. Fulford, August 1987 *Saturday Night Magazine*.

14 P.E. Trudeau, *La Presse* [de Montréal] (27 May 1987).

two and put an abrupt end to the dream of those who had viewed the Constitution Act, 1982[15] as the point of departure for a new millenium in Canadian constitutional history. It is impossible to discuss, here, each of the arguments supporting such gloomy conclusions; suffice it to say that the basic theme of this paper — that a nearly perfect constitutional scheme such as the Constitution Act, 1982 can be sterilized by weak and devilish politicians — perfectly illustrates the point that predictions regarding the political future of a state, euphoric as well as gloomy, generally have a short life.

A second pessimistic view regarding the future of Canada after Meech Lake portrays a situation where women's rights could end up being gradually abolished, retreating before the distinct society concept. This view, supported by various Canadian women's groups (but rejected by the Quebec Federation of Women) and strongly supported also by Professor Ramsay Cook in a letter sent to various newspapers, including *Le Devoir*, applies presumably only to Quebec women.[16] Not surprisingly, the argument has been seen as paternalistic ("Le paternalisme n'a plus de sexe," wrote a Quebec woman in a letter published in *Le Devoir*),[17] and somewhat degrading for Quebec women who are made to appear as if they would not protect their own interests. The argument also assumes that Quebec politicians are only too ready to abolish those rights, or at least to halt the march towards full equality for women. Only an enlightened judiciary, presumably with a majority of non-Québécois, could therefore save women's rights. There are a lot of assumptions behind this gloomy prediction. And to make matters worse, it is not clear why judges, who are trusted in their balancing of women's interests against other interests, could not do the same when the time comes to consider the distinct society concept.

A third pessimistic view regarding the impact of Meech Lake originates from Quebec, where it finds support among nationalist movements, the Parti Québécois and individuals advocating the independence of Quebec. This view suggests that the distinct society concept, as formulated in the agreement, offers no guarantee whatsoever that there will subsist a francophone space in Canada and North America; quite to the contrary, by formally recognizing a federal spending power, it opens the doors to a new invasion of provincial

---

15 Being Schedule B of The Canada Act 1982 (U.K.), c. 11.

16 Ramsay Cook, Letter to the Editor of *Le Devoir* [de Montréal] (8 September 1987) 7.

17 Letter to Editor of *Le Devoir* (8 September 1987) 7.

powers, thus leaving Quebec even weaker than before. The picture painted is black, and the possibility of a new, more positive dynamic developing between Quebec and Canada is simply not envisaged. Here, as in the preceding instances, the best solution is manifestly no agreement at all.

Indeed, it is a common characteristic of the three worst scenarios briefly described that they straddle the fence between legal logic and political preferences with a surprising degree of ease. What they really tell us about the Meech Lake agreement is that it is important, not so much because of what it says, literally, but because of what it represents, symbolically. It is generally agreed that as a matter of law, the Meech Lake exercise was not required to bring Quebec back into the constitutional fold: even if Quebec had never assented to the Constitution Act, 1982, it was legally bound by it. The significance of Meech Lake, therefore, must be found elsewhere, and that can only be at the symbolic level. As a symbol, however, it is far from univocal, being perceived differently by different groups of people. For the Quebec government, and probably also for a majority of the Quebec people, it represents the formal acceptance by the rest of Canada of the fact that a francophone presence and space exists within Canada that is here to stay, is essentially part of the Canadian fabric and contributes to defining the Canadian identity. For the federal government, and for the provincial governments who have found themselves in agreement with the Meech Lake compromise, it represents a new vision of the federal-provincial relationship, and hopefully the end of the constitutional debate about the place of Quebec in Confederation. Among those opposed to the Meech Lake Accord, there is, in the first place, the Parti Québécois and various other Quebec independentist movements, with their followers, who see Meech Lake not only as a dangerous attack on the autonomy of the province, but also as the symbol of definitive acceptance by the Quebec government of the constitutional changes that were imposed by force on Quebec in 1982. Secondly, there are those, gathered around former Prime Minister Trudeau, the old guard of the Liberal party of Canada, and Toronto intellectuals of the Canadian nationalist school, who consider Meech Lake a betrayal of the ideal of a Canada that is one, bilingual and multicultural, with a strong centre, and individuals all treated equally under the Canadian Charter of Rights and Freedoms.[18]

This last vision is generally presented and defended in a language

18 Being Part I of the Constitution Act, 1982.

that carries with it a strong moral overtone, its opponents being characterized simultaneously as intellectually wrong and morally devious. Consider the kind words of historian Michael Bliss about "eleven power-hungry politicians,"[19] or study that model of moral rectitude and intellectual arrogance, the Trudeau letter;[20] ponder the sincerity of those, like Robert Fulford, who argue that, with the distinct society concept, the Quebec government will be able to explain that unilingual signs, imposed by law, are constitutional, as if the existence of unilingual signs in the rest of Canada did not matter at all.[21]

Not surprisingly, this truly Canadian vision has been contrasted with the sell-out of Canada to the provincial governments and to Quebec that represents the Meech Lake Accord. But for those, again, who support the Accord, the problem with this virtuous Canadian vision lies not so much in the values that it promotes — after all, many Canadians would agree that the central government must have the power to exercise its constitutional responsibilities, or that individual rights and freedoms must be protected — but rather in its refusal to admit the validity of other views stressing regional concerns or affirming the existence of collective rights. For them, Meech Lake represents, on the contrary, a rejection of that cosy certitude that what is good for central Canada (Ontario) is also good for Canada, and that the Quebec issue has definitely been solved with the Official Languages Act[22] and the Charter provisions on the language of education.[23] It stands, as a gesture of reconciliation between the regions and the centre, between Canada and Quebec.

Whether Meech Lake becomes law or not, chances are that it will be seen as a watershed in the constitutional evolution of Canada. If the proposed amendments become law, the Accord will serve, first, as an indication that not all was said with the 1982 constitutional package, and that further amendments are indeed possible. The provinces, through the power to nominate future Supreme Court judges and senators, and their participation in an annual first ministers' conference, will be made to feel that national affairs are also their affairs, and will be offered the possibility of measuring up to the challenge of assuming collective responsibilities where collective action is required. Quebec will be made to feel that as the only province

---

19 Bliss, above, note 12.
20 Trudeau, above, note 14.
21 Fulford, above, note 13 at p. 6.
22 Official Languages Act, R.S.C. 1970, c. 0-2 (as amended).
23 Section 23 of the Canadian Charter of Rights and Freedoms.

with a French majority and an English minority, which constitutes its specificity, it has the obligation to preserve and promote the distinct society so composed, thus contributing, together with the Parliament of Canada and the other provincial legislatures, to the preservation of a Canadian identity characterized by its bilingualism and its multiculturalism. And the question "What does Quebec want?" will have finally found an answer, not to the taste of every Québécois, but probably acceptable to the majority.

This new constitutional package can also be seen, in a sense, as a leap of faith — faith in the capacity of the provinces and Quebec to respond to the challenges described above. But no guarantee as to the result is offered, and no such guarantee can be offered, even if improvements to the proposed amendments can be imagined. The provinces could use the new opportunities offered to them to promote their own petty interests and indulge in more "fed bashing." Quebec could use its new responsibilities as a pretext to present a new set of constitutional demands. But ideal solutions in constitutional law are rare. Meech Lake has the merit of being there and the capacity to generate a new dynamic.

If rejected, Meech Lake could signal, first, the gradual disappearance of constitutional amendments as a method of adapting the Canadian Constitution. If an agreement between the Prime Minister of Canada and the premiers of all provinces is not enough to lead to constitutional change under the existing formula, it is difficult to see how new constitutional amendments can be adopted in the future, particularly in a situation where Quebec's collaboration in constitutional law-making runs the risk of being very limited. Second, the defeat of the proposed constitutional amendments will likely stand as a confirmation that the recognition of Quebec's specificity by the rest of Canada is a forlorn hope, something to forget *definitively*. That this could lead to renewed unrest in Quebec appears doubtful. More plausibly, Québécois could develop, with time, a greater interest in the United States than in Canada, the sense of preserving a distinct Canadian identity, after being denied their home, having been somewhat eroded.[24] The same tendency to look south could also become more obvious in those provinces that would feel betrayed in their attempt to gain a greater say in the development of national policies. Thus, the rejection of Meech Lake and the ultimate triumph of the

---

24 For an interesting development on this theme, see M. Lubin, "Quebec-U.S. Relations: An Overview" (1986), XVI Am. Rev. of Can. Stud. 25 at 35-37.

1982 constitutional vision could ironically pave the way to a movement of greater political and economic intergration with the United States, something that is already suggested in the way our courts interpret the Canadian Charter in light of the American experience. But then so many things can happen meanwhile that such a prediction, as many others, could easily turn out to be erroneous.

The Limited Constitutional Vision
of Meech Lake

Alan C. Cairns

The difficulties of the Meech Lake Accord begin at the beginning. The very label is inaccurate, for the agreement struck at Meech Lake was significantly modified at the Langevin meetings. It is an additional minor irritant that an inappropriate dualism extends to the spelling of Meech Lake which, in the Joint Committee proceedings, is frequently spelled Meach Lake. Regrettably, or perhaps fortunately, given my task of writing a short critique of the Accord, there is bigger game in the woods surrounding Meech Lake than such small fry of interest to locational purists and grammarians.

The Meech Lake process, as well as its substance, expresses a powerful constitutional vision, specifically of the proper role of leaders and citizens in constitutional change, which will be discussed below. In order to reduce suspense as to my own position, I hereby express my hope that future first ministers will see themselves as guardians, not owners of the Constitution, and that they will view the Meech Lake procedures as a regrettable aberration, justified, if at all, only by extraordinary circumstances, but in no way to constitute a model for future constitutional change. To be "Meech-Laked" twice would surely be considered "cruel and unusual treatment or punishment," a provision of the Charter which, unfortunately, is subject to the override.

The second part of this paper argues that our constitutional theory is in disarray. The federal government Joint Committee hearings, following on the intergovernmental accord, graphically reveal a basic contradiction between those who view the Constitution and its modification as an affair of governments, and those who have caught a glimpse of what I call the "citizens' constitution". These two perspectives, one of which goes back to Confederation, while the other is a new arrival stimulated by an emerging rights consciousness given constitutional sustenance by the Charter, will not be easily reconciled. Their advocates inhabit divergent moral and political universes. They disagree on the nature of the Constitution and, therefore, on the procedures appropriate to changing it.

The relative influence of citizens and governments in constitutional change has varied from the marked impact of civil rights constituencies on the evolution of the Charter in 1980-81[1] to the demobilization of citizens to the status of spectators by the government elites which dominated the fashioning of the 1987 Accord. The competitive coexistence of contradictory views by citizens and governments of the same Constitution suggests that Canadians now have a two-party system in constitutional matters which is not Tweedledum and Tweedledee.

The two main parts of this paper, respectively labelled "Some Obstacles to Democracy in English Canada" and "Whose Constitution is It?" are closely related. Disagreement on the answer to the latter lies behind the acrimony over procedures between those who seek to erect and those who seek to erode obstacles to a more participant version of constitutional change. Both parts of this paper suggest that Meech Lake is discordant with powerful strands in contemporary Canadian constitutional culture.

SOME OBSTACLES TO DEMOCRACY IN ENGLISH CANADA

The generational imperialism called constitutional change deserves the closest scrutiny. All long term politics, as Popper reminds us,[2] is institutional. Thus the elaboration of constitutional machinery to mold the behaviour of unborn generations is the supreme act of a free people. Accordingly, as working Constitutions are responsive to emerging needs as well as anchored in tradition, the visions which motivate the agents of constitutional change are crucial data for

---

1 Canadian Charter of Rights and Freedoms, being Part I of the Constitution Act, 1982 [enacted by the Canada Act 1982 (U.K.), c. 11, s. 1].
2 K.R. Popper, *The Open Society and Its Enemies*, vol. 1 (London: Rutledge, 1945) at 110.

students of the Constitution. Such visions are not confined to the substance of proposed changes, but also inhere in the methods employed to achieve them. For example, the referendum instrument employed by the Parti Québécois survives as an honourable part of its constitutional legacy, even if its use derailed the drive to sovereignty-association. Equally, the Meech Lake/Langevin constitutional process is inescapably part of the constitutional vision and legacy of those who engineered it. It is a precedent available to inform future acts of constitutional transformation by succeeding generations, and it informs us of the attitudes of our elected servants to their responsibilities as constitutional guardians. Does the process educate and elevate the citizenry? Are citizens encouraged to participate meaningfully in the unfolding of their constitutional fate? Should women, aboriginals, social policy activists, northerners, and those Canadians who are not founding peoples be encouraged to sleep soundly and securely when future first ministers reshuffle, in private, the constitutional relationships among the governments and peoples of Canada yet one more time?

Regrettably, the answer to these questions is "No!" At the federal level, the nature of the hearings process has hampered public understanding and input in a host of ways identified by group after group which appeared before the Joint Committee — the timing of the hearings in mid-summer, the short time given to prepare briefs, the seeming *fait accompli* which witnesses confronted, and the unworthy suggestion that some of the critics were really anti-Quebec.

The public need for understanding has also been ill-served by the unity of leadership of the government and of both national opposition parties behind the Accord. There was no such unanimity over Bill C-60 in 1978, or over the patriation exercise which followed the 1980 referendum. In both cases, the clash of views was highly educational. Further, of course, the disagreements among governments and parties gave public opinion and group concerns an influence discouraged by the more monolithic Meech Lake process.

The muting of the adversarial process in Parliament greatly restricts the flow of information to the public. When it is combined with the executive solidarity of first ministers behind the Accord, major competing visions of Canada are deprived of official spokespersons. It is left to politicians who courageously break party ranks, and pay a price, to a former Prime Minister, to the Senate, and to academics, various interest groups and the media to remind the leaders of eleven governments and of the three national parties that neither their Meech Lake view of Canada nor their elitist secretive processes are unquestioned orthodoxies.

Public understanding and discriminating judgment are hampered by a paucity of information on the jockeying among governments in the Meech Lake/Langevin process. Those who seek to play the role of citizen or informed analyst are reduced to a Canadian version of Kremlinology in which journalistic tidbits are supplemented by selective disclosures of who did what to whom. Is it true that Bourassa was surprised to get more than he had asked for with respect to immigration and the Supreme Court?[3] that Mulroney acted more like a mediator/arbitrator between provincial contestants than the leader/defender of the federal government, but was "not unhappy" when Pawley or Peterson attempted to speak for national interests?[4] and that the extension of unanimity to the admission of new provinces was, as Spector said, necessary to avoid a breakdown of the deal?[5]

In the Meech Lake process an intergovernmental version of cabinet solidarity applies to the participants in federal-provincial accords which precede formal constitutional amendment, with unfortunate consequences. A "cabinet-like" solidarity of first ministers from eleven governments is without the redeeming features of its practice within jurisdictions. In the latter, collective solidarity derives from the system of responsible government, and the fact that ministers and their party will share a common fate before a future electorate. The former, however, share no common fate, and do not confront partisan adversaries who can unseat them. Neither electorates nor legislatures can reward or punish a united intergovernmental elite of first ministers. Further, first ministers' solidarity across jurisdictions also inhibits citizens' control of governments within jurisdictions. Take the case of British Columbia: little is known of what the B.C. government was seeking in advance of the meetings, of the Premier's behaviour at the meetings, or of the government's subsequent evaluation of the Accord. In the circumstances, it is virtually impossible to hold the government accountable for its behaviour. The conflict between executive federalism and eleven systems of responsible government

---

3 Pierre Elliott Trudeau, *Minutes of Proceedings and Evidence of the Special Joint Committee of the Senate and of the House of Commons on the 1987 Constitutional Accord Issue*, No. 14 (Ottawa: Queen's Printer, August 27, 1987) at 137 (hereafter cited as *Special Joint Committee*).

4 Attributed to Premier Pawley by Frances Russell in the *Winnipeg Free Press* (June 9, 1987), as cited in *Submission of the Honourable Donald J. Johnston to the Special Joint Committee on the 1987 Constitutional Accord* (July 22, 1987) mimeo, at 7.

5 Norman Spector, *Special Joint Committee*, No. 16 (Sept. 1, 1987) at 13.

is serious under the most favourable conditions. It is compounded when the private meetings from which agreements emerge are preceded by intensive intergovernmental contact and lobbying to pave the way.

The difficulty in keeping governments accountable for their actions is further aggravated by the smokescreen that Meech Lake was to be the Quebec round, and hence other provinces were to hold back on their constitutional demands. Theoretically, therefore, what the other provinces got, if anything, could not be assessed against any prior understanding of what they sought. This alleged self-control of the other nine provinces was never more than a half-truth, for they gained much on the coat-tails of Quebec under the principle of the equality of the provinces. Politically, the image of altruistic provincial governments has the effect of shielding nine premiers from informed criticism, and deflecting attention from the rewards they received for an abstinence they did not practise.

The overall result of the Meech Lake syndrome is a unilateralism of eleven governments which leaves legislators and citizens gasping on the sidelines with an unpalatable choice between an uninformed deferential gratitude for bringing Quebec back into the constitutional family, and an important frustration that any flaws they find will be defined away as less than egregious.

The strictures in the preceding paragraphs have a greatly diminished application to the government of Quebec. Both the Parti Québécois and the Quebec Liberal Party developed constitutional proposals, the meeting of which would produce the willing adhesion of the government of Quebec to the Constitution. The election victory of the Quebec Liberal Party in December 1985 was followed by the speech of Gil Rémillard, Minister for Canadian Intergovernmental Affairs, to a conference in Mont Gabriel in May 1986, at which he laid down the five requirements of the Quebec government. The Quebec proposals, modified by the process they have gone through, and now clothed in legal language, have found their way into the Constitution, or will, if the Meech Lake amendments are passed by the legislatures of all eleven governments.

So, from a Quebec perspective, the Meech Lake process has been relatively open; the objectives of the government and the constitutional instruments to achieve them were laid out in advance, and the proposed Meech Lake amendments can thus be assessed as adequate or inadequate in the light of known means and ends. The Quebec National Assembly held a reasonably thorough debate on the initial version of the Accord between the Meech Lake and Langevin meetings, and after the

Langevin changes the National Assembly debated and passed an appropriate resolution. In such circumstances, the constitutional constituency of journalists, scholars, intellectuals, and engaged citizens in Quebec could have an intelligent debate on Meech Lake. Their counterparts outside of Quebec have not had equivalent possibilities, nor have Québécois in their capacity as Canadian citizens.

The public process of examination and approval by legislatures is fragmented into eleven jurisdictions. As a result, the eleven actors who in secret conclave redefined Canada are never available as a group for collective questioning and challenging. No provincial government participated in the Joint Committee hearings either as defendant or interlocutor. Joint Committee members were deprived of the opportunity of hearing from Quebec representatives the expansive interpretations of what they hoped would flow from the distinct society clause and the limitations on the spending power. Those who appeared before the Joint Committee and were told that their proposed amendments would unravel an interdependent agreement designed to bring the Quebec government back into the constitutional family could not question the representatives of Quebec or other provinces on this point, for there were none. In general, Quebec participation before the Joint Committee was very limited, which was unfortunate, given the shaping effect of Quebec's demands on the outcome.

The women's groups from English Canada, concerned that the distinct society clause might weaken s. 28 and equality rights in Quebec, or even the Charter's more general application in Quebec, have lacked an arena in which they can confront the government of Quebec. Citizens and government elites from Yukon and the Northwest Territories, outraged that their aspirations for provincehood have been stifled by the unanimity requirements for the creation of new provinces, are not only denied the opportunity to confront the provincial governments responsible, but are reduced to gossip and speculation as to the identity and objectives of the "culprits."[6] It is difficult to disagree with their assessment of the process as dishonourable.

The combination of discussions and decision-making in secret, followed by a fragmented process in eleven discrete arenas where separate governments seek approval from their legislatures, makes it

---

6 "No explanation has ever been given to us by the federal government or anybody else as to why this [veto] power was sought." Tony Penikett, Government Leader and President of the Executive Council, Government of Yukon, *Special Joint Committee*, No. 15 (August 31, 1987) at 100.

difficult to grasp the total package of constitutional change that is Meech Lake/Langevin. Meech Lake/Langevin is a special Canadian version of divide and rule, where the governing elites decide, then divide and explain themselves before separate audiences. In a number of cases, of course, the approval process in provincial legislatures will be perfunctory and formal, with no hearings, and limited debate between government and opposition parties. So far (mid-October 1987) in British Columbia, a constitutional reform package which will significantly enhance the B.C. government's role in the Canadian federal system is a non-event.

An additional weakness in the process, which has attracted little comment,[7] is the absence of serious justificatory position papers issued by the federal government. This deficiency aggravates the problem of assessing the relationship of the provisions of Meech Lake to any explicit constitutional philosophy. For the long-time constitutional observer, whose files are bulging with federal government documents on the Constitution from the late sixties, with the detailed federal position papers which accompanied Bill C-60, with the competing presentations by the "Yes" and "No" forces — including the federal government — in the pre-referendum period in Quebec, and with the provincial position papers from Alberta, British Columbia, Saskatchewan and Newfoundland leading up to the 1982 Constitution Act, the pickings from Meech Lake/Langevin are slim indeed.

We have extensive official rationales for a host of causes that failed — sovereignty-association, fifth region status for British Columbia, the 1980 proposals for the economic union, and many others. However, for the second most comprehensive package of constitutional changes since Confederation, we have remarkably little to go on beyond the public knowledge of Quebec's demands. One example may illustrate the point. Under the guise of a transitional measure, Canadians have embarked on the most extensive Senate reform in our history. Several observers have described the transformed Senate which will result from the composite provincial-federal government nomination and appointment process as one of the most consequential institutional changes brought about by Meech Lake.[8] Also, with some exceptions, the prevailing opinion is that the temporary will become

---

7 See, however, Ramsay Cook, *Special Joint Committee*, No. 5 (August 11, 1987) pp. 47-49.
8 Thomas J. Courchene, "Meech Lake and Federalism: Accord or Discord?" (August 1987), mimeo, revised version reproduced in this volume at 121; Eugene Forsey, *Debates of the Senate* (June 26, 1987) at 1443.

the permanent. This transitional Senate reform, slipped in almost without public explanation, will have a major impact on parliamentary government and probably on federalism.

The inference to be drawn from the proposed nomination-appointment process is that this transitional Senate reform is a response to the intrastate analysis which attributes the weakness of the federal government to its lack of provincial sensitivities. However, as the British Columbia government discovered in its Senate reform proposals of the late seventies to strengthen the regions at the centre, the bulk of the Senate's workload concerns matters for which provincial cleavages are of minimal relevance — that the Senate is, in fact, however poorly it performs, a reviewing chamber for Canada-wide concerns.[9] How the engineers of transitional Senate reform view its historic primary role in the light of the new nomination/appointment process is unknown.

For some time, the Senate has been a useful safety valve in providing governments with cabinet ministers from provinces with minimal representation in the government caucus. Will this be feasible in future Senates composed entirely of appointees from provincial government lists? Occasionally an imbalance in regional representation has been rectified by appointing an intended minister to the Senate from a province weakly represented in the government caucus. If the availability of this practice is to disappear, as seems inevitable, does that mean that the price of a stronger, more provincially-oriented Senate is a less representative cabinet?

To say the least, the almost complete absence of written or spoken explanation of what is intended for this reformed Senate in these and other matters is extraordinary. We have government by oracle rather than government by reason, a circumstance likely to induce either an ineffectual flailing or an exasperated silence from constitutional commentators. The outside analyst/critic is disarmed by the denial of material necessary to an effective dialogue with those elected servants who govern us.

An additional aspect of Senate reform is constitutionally anomalous. The political accord states that "Until the proposed amendment relating to appointments to the Senate comes into force, any person summoned to fill a vacancy in the Senate shall be chosen from among persons whose names have been submitted by the government of the

---

9 Province of British Columbia, *British Columbia's Constitutional Proposals, Paper No. 3, Reform of the Canadian Senate* (Victoria: Queen's Printer, 1978).

province to which the vacancy relates and must be acceptable to the Queen's Privy Council for Canada." This is a repudiation of the role of legislatures in the amendment process, which is constitutionally required for Senate reform by ss. 38(1) and 42(1) of the 1982 Constitution Act. The combination of executive federalism and party discipline may mean that the presumptous use of the word "until" will not be belied by future developments. Nevertheless, legislatures and the citizens they represent have been constitutionally humiliated by the implication that the approval of the legislatures of eleven governments can be assumed. Further, this prejudgment leaves open the possible constitutional embarrassment of a situation in which an anticipatory practice has been implemented and the amendment which it anticipates does not pass. In such circumstances, what is the status of the eleven government agreement in the political accord? Do we revert to the *status quo ante*? Or do we just carry on with our anticipations, ignoring the repudiation by one or more governments? Does a future federal government try to apply the Meech Lake/Langevin nomination/appointment process for the Senate in a province whose government has "scuttled" the package of amendments the process anticipates? This premature anticipation of what is described as a transitional practice may add excitement to undergraduate lectures on the Senate, but it is a novel way to change a Constitution.

WHOSE CONSTITUTION IS IT?

Both the process and substance of the Meech Lake/Langevin Accord reflect the concerns of governments, with the exception, of course, of Yukon and the Northwest Territories, whose absence from the bargaining table led to the placing of more hurdles in the way of their future advance to provincehood. Governments controlled the process. They met in secret conclaves. They consulted their own interests, albeit in the context of the "Quebec round." When they emerged, they announced, as a pact of honour, that they would not break ranks, that, in the words of the Prime Minister, only "egregious errors," as defined by the participants, would justify the reopening of the Accord. Consequently, the indirect democratization of the amending process implied by the 1982 Constitution Act requirement of legislative approval was to be rendered as nugatory as possible.

In a narrow, technical sense, this effort may succeed; the Constitution may be amended along Meech Lake lines. The reconciliation of the government of Quebec may be achieved. Conceivably the amendments will usher in a period of intergovernmental harmony and co-operative policy-making which will make today's critics and doubters hope that their words were not recorded. While I am happy to be classified as one of the doubters, my doubts are less significant than what the process revealed about the contradictions at the centre of our constitutional life.

Alongside the relative aggrandizement of state power at both levels in recent decades, and the concomitant enhanced capacity of governments to shape their societies, an enlarged conception of citizenship has evolved. This new citizenship changes the relation of the Canadian Constitution to Canadian society. Even the most obtuse readers of the briefs presented to the Joint Committee must detect the implicit and explicit assumption of groups and interests defined by gender, by ethnicity, by aboriginal background, by social policy concerns, and by basic conceptions of a national community of rights bearers that the Canadian Constitution of the late 1980s with its Charter of Rights is a citizens' Constitution.

Much of the anger which ran through many of these groups' presentations derived from a sense of outrage at the illegitimacy of governments perceived as playing fast and loose with a Constitution which they had forgotten was no longer theirs alone. That anger and frustration was also fed by many witnesses' distrust of what they apprehensively viewed as the provincializing tendency of the package. On the whole, these groups which, at the cost of some ambiguity, may be called "Charter Canadians," see themselves as citizens of a national community. They tend to be more sympathetic to the national than to provincial governments, at least in English Canada. They view the national government as a more plausible ally and supporter than the provincial governments whose majoritarianism and sporadic populism they somewhat fear. Without always realizing it, they are adherents of Frank Scott's dictum that provincial rights are not the same as minority rights.[10]

Their frustrations with the Meech Lake process are additionally fed by their belief that they should be involved in constitutional change. They have their separate histories of triumphs — memories of when biculturalism was replaced by multiculturalism, when they won s. 28, when their aboriginal rights received constitutional recognition, when Métis were brought under the rubric "aboriginal peoples" in the Constitution, and so on. They also have their memories of defeats,

---

10 F.R. Scott, "The Privy Council and Minority Rights" (1930), 37 *Queen's Quarterly* 668.

exclusions, and failures — usually the removal of some right or recognition they thought they had won, or were on the verge of winning. Such defeats normally occurred when governments met in secret, and on occasion they were subsequently reversed by vigorous public campaigns. In essence, then, to generalize outrageously, these groups — or at least their elites — look back on a history of hard-won gains which gives them a somewhat precarious niche in the constitutional order. They do not hold their constitutional recognition and their rights as self-confident possessions. They are, accordingly, would-be constitutional actors, ever fearful that if their participatory "rights" are ignored, their previous constitutional gains may be eroded. In simple terms, they do not trust governments meeting in secret to represent them.

This new variegated constituency is a product of the constitutional process of recent years, which has politicized and constitutionalized a broad range of interests. The intergovernmental competition for constitutional advantage of the last quarter of a century produced mobilizations of the citizenry as governments sought the justifications appropriate to a democratic political culture. The high-water mark of this tendency was the Quebec referendum, which sought popular backing for the pursuit of sovereignty-association. The rhetoric of the federal government from the late 1960s onwards stressed that the recognition of citizen rights should be the first item on the constitutional agenda, before the division of powers. In the summer of 1980 Ottawa brilliantly contrasted the rights of the people with the selfish pursuit of governmental advantage, and identified itself with the former through its "Peoples' package," and its provincial government opponents with the latter. The same federal government also proposed the use of the referendum device for future constitutional amendments when governments could not agree.

Thus the discourse leading up to the 1982 Constitution Act suggested that governments alone did not always have the authority or legitimacy to implement major constitutional change. In a halting way a variety of cues intimated that citizens might have a real voice in the drama of constitutional change. Some of them were listening.

The constitutional process induced a variety of interests organized around non-territorial cleavages to see the Constitution as a potentially useful instrument for their future advantage. The story has been frequently told of how the alliance between various components of the growing civil rights constituency and the federal government strengthened the Charter and gave credibility to Trudeau's threatened unilateralism. The subsequent success of women's and aboriginal groups in gaining the reinstatement of constitutional protections which had been removed at the behest of several provincial premiers appeared to confirm both the necessity and the utility of political pressure in constitutional politics. Later, aboriginal elites were involved in separate constitutional discussions which focused on self-government.

Cynthia Williams has discussed the rapid diffusion of a popular language of rights in Canada.[11] Other observers have noted the international sources of rights consciousness,[12] which make Charters of Rights increasingly necessary attributes of statehood in the contemporary era. While the expected divergences in the evaluation of the Canadian Charter are beginning to appear, the fact is that the Charter has taken root. For many groups the Charter is the Constitution. The Charter has acquired many defenders, who often focus on particular clauses as the source of their rights and as confirmation of their status in the Canadian community. For the groups involved, these Charter recognitions are both status-enhancing and a promise of future benefits and protection.

An unanticipated consequence of the Charter and the Constitution Act, 1982 is that different parts of the Constitution seem, psychologically, to belong to different groups, a phenomenon which gives new meaning to the Innisian aphorism "Divided we stand!" Women's groups identify with the Charter through s. 28; for traditional third force Canadians, s. 27 is their lodestar; visible minority women appeal to both s. 28 (for gender equality) and s. 15 (for racial equality);[13] for aboriginals it is a combination of s. 25 of the Charter, s. 91(24) of the division of powers, and ss. 35 and 37 (now obsolete) of the Constitution Act. Section 35, by defining aboriginals to include the "Indian, Inuit and Métis peoples of Canada," has expanded the aboriginal community, strengthened its constitutional identity, and exacerbated the cleavages within it. Should the Meech Lake Accord become law, aboriginals and multicultural groups will also look to its s. 16, which asserts that the interpretation clause of the proposed constitutional change — with the words "distinct society" — does

---

11 C. Williams, "The Changing Nature of Citizen Rights" in A. Cairns and C. Williams, eds., *Constitutionalism, Citizenship and Society in Canada*, MacDonald Commission Studies, vol. 33 (Toronto: University of Toronto Press, 1985) at 99.

12 John Boli, "Human Rights or State Expansion? Cross-National Definitions of Constitutional Rights, 1870-1970" in G.M. Thomas *et al.*, eds., *Institutional Structure: Constituting State, Society, and the Individual* (Beverly Hills: Sage Publications, 1987).

13 See the evidence of Ms. Akua Benjamin, *Special Joint Committee*, No. 15 (31 August 1987) at 155-56.

not affect sections of the Charter, the Constitution Act, 1982 and the Constitution Act, 1867 which they identify as theirs.

The conjunction of a growing rights consciousness, the linking to the Constitution of groups who previously had little or no constitutional recognition, and the symbolic power of the Charter have modified the Canadian constitutional order in ways that will take decades to work out. This change goes beyond the conventional assertion that the Supreme Court has acquired an enhanced role as a national policy-maker. An even more profound change is taking place at the citizen base of the constitutional order. Yesterday's deference to governing elites in constitutional matters has been replaced by a resentment when citizens who think of themselves as constitutional actors are defined as spectators by governments.

In the eyes of many of the group elites, for whom this psychological change is most pronounced, and who see their fate as affected by constitutional change, the Constitution is no longer an affair of governments. In addition to the governments' Constitution, which tends to focus on federalism, there is a citizens' Constitution which the Charter symbolizes. A central task for the constitutional theory and practice of future decades is to find ways in which these two visions, warring in the bosom of the Canadian Constitution, can be reconciled. The major site for that reconciliation must be the amendment process where, as Meech Lake exemplifies, their incompatibility is most pronounced.

A constitutional reform agenda which theoretically addressed Quebec concerns, but which in fact became a vehicle for strengthening the provincial role in Canadian federalism, was almost bound to alienate or bypass the concerns of the new citizen constitutional activists. For example, the reform of the process of selecting judges for the Supreme Court by giving nominating responsibilities to provincial governments is a response to the concerns of the 1970s which indeed go back to the 1949 abolition of appeals to the Judicial Committee of the Privy Council — about the impartiality of the Supreme Court as an umpire of federalism. Such a reform, however, does not address the issue of a nomination procedure appropriate to the new jurisprudential concerns which the Court faces in the era of the Charter.[14] Indeed, the proposed reform may make its attainment

---

14 See the presentation of the Canadian Bar Association, *Special Joint Committee*, No. 8 (August 18, 1987) at pp. 116-117, and of the Canadian Association of Law Teachers, *Special Joint Committee*, No. 15 (August 31, 1987) at 8.

more difficult because of the operational fragmentation of responsibilities which the proposed nominating/appointing procedures involve, and the unanimity requirement for their amendment.

The 1982 Constitution Act gave initial constitutional recognition to social categories based on gender and ethnicity, and extended the constitutional recognition of aboriginals beyond the limited 1867 division of powers reference in s. 91(24) to "Indians, and Lands reserved for the Indians." The interpretation clause of the proposed constitutional change, which defines linguistic duality as "a fundamental characteristic of Canada", describes Quebec as a "distinct society," and affirms the "role of the legislature and government of Quebec to preserve and promote the distinct identity of Quebec," was viewed as a threat by the groups advantaged by the earlier 1982 recognition. The inclusion of s. 16 on the road from Meech Lake to Langevin went only part way to calm the concerns of aboriginals and other ethnic leaders. They pointed out that their groups also constituted fundamental characteristics of Canada, that the interpretation clause with its linguistic duality and distinct society applied to the entire Constitution, while the multiculturalism clause of the Charter, s. 27, was an interpretive principle for the Charter only. Women's groups who protested the absence of s. 28 of the Charter (the gender equality section) from the s. 16 Meech Lake exemptions were not reassured by the assertions that the potency of s. 28 in the Charter — compared to the weakness of the multiculturalism clause (s. 27) — meant that gender equality rights did not require similar protective treatment.

The complexities of the multiple interpretive criteria which the Meech Lake amended Constitution will contain, and what hierarchy if any exists among them, have been discussed by Professor Wayne MacKay of Dalhousie University with a dexterity to which a non-lawyer is happy to defer.[15] For our purposes, the significant issue is the difference between those cleavages which are linked to governments, and which therefore have powerful sponsors, and the others which are more free floating. Not surprisingly, in a constitutional process dominated by governments, the social cleavages invested with special governmental salience received priority attention — hence the distinct society and linguistic duality provisions. It may be, however, that the historic dualist characteristics of Canada singled out by Meech Lake are losing ground to cleavages derived from ethnicity and race.

Finally, of course, a basic assumption of federalism that the

---

15 *Special Joint Committee*, Issue No. 3 (August 5, 1987) at 49-51.

territorial particularisms which provincial governments reflect and foster are the primary divisions in Canadian society — an assumption which pervades Meech Lake — is challenged by those who represent the new societal cleavages which the 1982 Constitution Act both reflects and fosters.

CONCLUSION

Meech Lake underlines a basic contradiction at the very heart of the Canadian constitutional system. The constitutional division of powers from which strong interventionist governments have emerged lends continuing credence to the thesis that federalism in Canada is about governments. That thesis is reinforced by the executive supremacy which party discipline and the theory of responsible government sustain. In the intergovernmental arena of constitutional politics the practice of federal-provincial diplomacy, as Meech Lake almost exaggeratedly confirms, is the very perfection of governmental hegemony when unanimity of governments can be achieved in private.

However, while federalism may still be largely about governments, federalism itself has lost relative status in the Constitution as an organizing principle. The Constitution is now also about women, aboriginals, multicultural groups, equality, affirmative action, the disabled, a variety of rights, and so on. Since it is not possible to separate clearly the concerns of the governments which dominate federalism from the concerns of these newly constitutionalized social categories, it logically follows that the Constitution with its many non-federal concerns can no longer be entrusted exclusively to governments in the process of constitutional change. Government domination of the constitutional process structures outcomes in terms of one set of cleavages; the public hearings process responds in terms of different cleavages. The latter delegitimates the former.

Those who ran the Meech Lake constitutional show falsely assumed that the Meech Lake agenda could be confined to federalism, and thus could be dominated by governments with little opposition. Meech Lake may succeed and the Constitution may be changed accordingly. However, the constitutional contradiction laid bare by the Meech Lake process will not go away. In that sense, both parts of this paper are linked — perhaps even by a seamless web, as the federal government describes the Accord — because the dispute about constitutional process derives directly from a lack of agreement about whose Constitution it is anyway. In the circumstances, it is not surprising that the limited constitutional vision of Meech Lake seems to have a higher degree of support from political scientists who study federalism, and who specialize in territorial particularisms, than it receives from other academic disciplines and from group leaders who respond to an emerging agenda of non-federal cleavages.

The 1987 Constitutional Accord and Ethnic Accommodation

*John D. Whyte**

The summer of 1987 was frustrating for advocates of women's rights. The text of the Meech Lake Accord in its clause requiring the Constitution to be interpreted in recognition of English-speaking Canada and French-speaking Canada did not seem to trigger alarm about the impact of language concerns on constitutional claims for gender equality; however, after the refinements produced at the Langevin meeting in early June, women's rights groups began to see a diminution of gender equality in what the first ministers had produced. The Langevin text altered the social fact that was to act as an influence in constitutional interpretation to the existence in Canada of English-speaking Canadians and French-speaking Canadians. The special fact that was to operate in discerning the meaning of our Constitution was not the geographical placement of two distinct Canadas, but the distribution of two sorts of Canadians — two language sorts of Canadians — within Canada. In the changed text, the characteristic of language was heightened beyond all other personal characteristics. What became of greatest significance in understanding the purposes of our statecraft was the English-speaking capacity or French-speaking capacity of Canadians and not their gender — or race, or religion, or wealth.

More worrisome from the perspective of women's rights groups

᠎ deeply indebted to Professor Phil Goldman of the Department of Political Studies, Queen's University, whose insights into the meaning of the Meech Lake Accord have formed a significant part of this paper.

was the final clause of the Langevin text. It said that the influence of the French and English language characteristics of Canadians in constitutional interpretation should not defeat the impact of the meaning of Charter rights of two other formerly recognized social facts: the multicultural make-up of the Canadian population and the existence of aboriginal peoples who hold special aboriginal rights. This explicit presentation of the constitutional importance of these personal and social conditions seemed, by contrast, to leave all other saliences, including gender, with a defeasible constitutional quality.

To the response that it was inconceivable that the interpretation of the Constitution in recognition of language duality would bear on the position of women, women's rights groups immediately produced legal opinions in which legislative scenarios were developed to show that respect for language could sometimes be gained at the expense of women. Furthermore, they did this while striving mightily to avoid the political trap of saying that either Quebec nationalism or French-language protectionism were likely to be practised at the expense of equality for women.

For all their considerable political and analytical efforts, women's rights groups were blandly assured by the Prime Minister and some premiers, and by apologists for the Accord that it could not possibly lead to constitutional interpretations that diminished women's rights as established in the 1982 Charter of Rights.

It is clear that women's rights advocates did not and do not accept these reassurances. It is also clear that provincial premiers are loath to do anything that would give explicit textual representation to what they claim to be the clear case, that is, that gender equality is untouched. It is, I think, illuminating to examine what lies behind the frustration expressed by women's rights groups and the resolute stand by political leaders not to accept the legitimacy of this frustration.

First, the frustration of advocates for gender equality is not just that they see a whole series of legal claims being compromised by the Accord. They see the resurrection of a political process that they faced down in November 1981, and vanquished. Political leaders shaping the terms of our fundamental national arrangement can, and do, forget interests that are not represented in federal-provincial conflict. They can forget women and aboriginal peoples and the poor. They do not forget the owners and producers of resources or the major language groups. (Quebec may have been excluded in 1981; it was not forgotten.) The mobilization of women's rights groups, following the November 1981 accord, demonstrated that social interest groups can interfere in the accommodations that are reached between political elites. This message was heard and lessons were learned. Two years later, pensioners engaged successfully in a parallel form of mobilization.

In 1987, the old politics returned. This was shown not only by the fact of there being two meetings of first ministers — after all, such meetings are a constant of Canadian politics. Rather it was the genre of bargaining and deal-making — long hours spent in seclusion, the systematic prevention of access to advisors and constituencies (the features that Norman Spector, Secretary of the Federal-Provincial Relations Office proudly hailed as the innovations that brought success to constitutional politics) — that most graphically showed women, ethnic groups and other social groupings that they simply have no right of access to those decisions that can turn their public worlds upside down. If the Italian community in Toronto had not been mobilized in the week before the Langevin meeting and if it had not gained an audience with Premier Peterson on June 1, the day before that meeting, the place of multicultural interests would also have been ignored and seriously diminished by the new interpretation clause.

Not only did the process tell women's rights advocates that the lessons of 1981 had been forgotten, but also that the conditions enabling a politics of transcendent social interests had come to an end. When the Charter of Rights came into force in 1982 and the equality provisions in 1985, incentives for political mobilization along new lines and according to new divisions were created. For instance, the political agenda on behalf of women's rights, insofar as it can be pursued in the courts under the Charter of Rights, leads to two positive effects. First, since the Charter is national, the political force behind a claim can be national and in numbers there is strength — and comfort and hope. Second, it eradicates the need to acquire electoral dominance. Those whose social goals can be pursued through the Charter need not capitulate on the recognition of the unpopularity of their claims.

After Meech Lake, and in particular the undertaking in the agreement to repeat forever the same process of first ministers constitutional conferences, the only possible conclusion was that federal-provincial politics, the politics of the electorally successful, was the major politics for Canada's future. Not only was the old way of living as a nation back, its specific agenda seemed to be to undo the precise constitutional protections that had made the new politics possible. Witness the undercutting, so it seemed, of gender equality. Witness also the provincialization of the Supreme Court of Canada, the chief forum in which the new politics was to be played out.

In the same vein, the politics of social interests was undercut by other features of the Accord. Witness the provincialization of the Senate, which only recently has presented itself as available to take stands against the policies of the government and as willing to stand on the side of the dispossessed — the sick and the refugees from political oppression. Witness also the provincialization of the nation's capacity to generate national responses to social pathologies through changes to the spending power. This is not to suggest that provinces have not been important agents for social reform. In fact, they have in our history a better record of social innovation than Parliament. However, in trying to understand the frustration of women's rights groups, we must recognize the diffusing effect of these changes on the efforts of those who seek to improve the social conditions of women and other groups.

Perhaps it ought also to be recognized that understanding last summer's political impasse between women's rights groups and political leaders requires us to accept that the Prime Minister and premiers understand exactly what Meech Lake represents and what all those future constitutional conferences will mean to the new politics of social interests. The habit of constitutional alteration among eleven first ministers for their mutual benefit will erode more surely than even the frequent use of the Charter's notwithstanding clause, Canadian constitutionalism; the high inconvenience of constitutionalism to those who govern will become controllable. Hence, when women's rights groups rage against being ignored by Meech Lake, they rage on behalf of a side in which all of us have an interest.

These comments are, however, only a prelude to the deeper ironies of the Meech Lake Accord. The story of the treatment of women's rights groups allows us to see that the Accord has the effect and the design of stopping short a form of political organization. It restores to importance our traditional political saliences of founding languages and provincial interests. Ironically, in constitutionalizing ethnic duality in a more dramatic way than at any time since 1840 when Upper Canada and Lower Canada were united, the Meech Lake Accord produces a shift away from ethnic accommodation more profoundly understood. Likewise it is an irony in the Accord that in vesting a stronger form of political community for Quebec and, of course, the other provinces, it hampers the development of what might be a richer and more suitable political form.

Let me elaborate on these points. This country has for two centuries been deeply engaged in the politics of ethnic accommodation.

We have been fortunate in being forced to practise this politics in the past, since it has now become the one constant of politics everywhere in the world. As Professor Lustgarten has written, "one of the most pressing issues of liberty in these times [is] how, within the over-arching political unity, conflicts engendered by the existence of diverse and at times opposed cultural values and ways of life [are] to be resolved?"[1] The question is whether our historical practices, and political virtues, can be adapted to meet the current nature of ethnic diversity and conflict.

In Canada, constitution-making and refinement has been directed to, more than to any other object, achieving a workable co-existence between French-speaking Canada and anglophone Canada. The mechanism adopted in 1867, after the failure of the United Canadas experiment, was the creation of distinct political communities through the creation of a federal state. The conferral of autonomous legislative and governmental powers through federalism did not serve only Quebec, the seat of French Canada, but its most fundamental purpose was the protection of the French minority in Canada.

The fragility of this mechanism of limited self-determination was exposed in November 1981 when important parts of the constitutional framework were altered without the participation or consent of the people or government of Quebec. The ethnic accommodation represented by the 1867 Constitution was seen to be seriously dislocated and the likely consequences of this traumatizing — from the francophone perspective, at least — event was the renewal of Quebec nationalism. Certainly, it has been assumed, notwithstanding the change in direction of social energies from political nationalism to economic activity in the years following 1981, that when Quebec nationalism once again becomes the political preoccupation, the exclusion of Quebec from the 1981 constitutional compromise will serve as a powerful symbol of political isolation and vulnerability. Not only was Quebec excluded in the process, but also the substantive terms of the federal-provincial compromise eroded Quebec's powers to represent the cultural interests of its population and did so in a more pronounced way than for any other Canadian community.

These facts and anxieties provided the political imperative for

---

1 L. S. Lustgarten, "Liberty in a Culturally Plural Society" in A. P. Griffiths, ed., *Of Liberty* (Royal Institute of Philosophy Lecture Series 15) (Cambridge: Cambridge University Press, 1983) 91, quoted in M. McDonald, "Collective Rights and Tyranny" in G. LaFrance, ed., *Pouvoir et tyrannie* (Philosophica 31) (Ottawa: Editions de l'Université d'Ottawa, 1986) 115 at 117.

the opening of constitutional discussions in 1986 and, more than any other factor, drove the parties toward the agreement reached at Meech Lake. The terms of the agreement were Quebec's terms, adjustments that were made were in response to Quebec's gnawing doubts about its ability to protect its own distinctive community within Canada. For example, it was hoped that the erosion of autonomy over language policy produced by the Charter would be off-set by the distinct society clause. The changes to the spending power met concerns that traditionally have been expressed most forcefully by Quebec's leaders over the federal spending power's potential to undermine federalism. The compensation clause in the amendment provisions was Quebec's *quid pro quo* for the loss of a Quebec veto over amendment. The increased range of matters requiring unanimous consent from the provinces represents Quebec's conception (a conception, however, to which other provinces may also be committed) of how the Constitution should be altered. Provincial participation in appointments to the Supreme Court of Canada meets an anxiety over the Court's centralizing bias that has been expressed most frequently and most forcefully in Quebec. Changes to immigration jurisdiction touch on concerns over demographic shifts that Quebec alone has expressed.

All of this is not to express resentment over Quebec's gains in the Meech Lake process. Rather it is to underscore the claim that Meech Lake is a reflection of the traditional Canadian ethnic tension; it provides an accommodation that is distinctively traditional — the accommodation between French Canada situated in Quebec and the balance of Canada.

The question is whether this tension and this accommodation is appropriate for Canada at the end of the twentieth century. In considering this question, the first point to be observed is that the Meech Lake agreement does not embrace ethnic pluralism. If, as has been suggested earlier, the real ethnic tensions to be faced in Canada are no longer the tensions between French and English but, rather, the tensions of multiculturalism and multiracialism, then the special regard for Quebec as the protector of French is at best non-responsive and, at worst, illiberal. The political values of tolerance, adaptation, accommodation, celebration of diversity and promotion of the worth of difference are not represented in the Meech Lake agreement. The fundamental restructuring of the state that has taken place in the Meech Lake process seems to be sadly anomalous and out-of-date. In fact, constitutional changes in our present age that do not strive to express the worth of cultural diversity fail to perform one of the chief roles of a Constitution — the expression of a social vision, even a utopian social vision. In Meech Lake we have let this opportunity for visioning our future fall prey to the frantic process of recapturing our past.

Furthermore, the Meech Lake Accord provides a decidedly federalist accommodation. It controls central institutions and central powers that have the potential to erode provincial interests. It confers new powers on provinces to determine not only the terms of adjustment in our constitutional order, but also the terms of new national policies. These changes do not produce an unworkable state and they do not violate any externally-driven conception of an appropriate federal balance, but they most decidedly do address and alter the terms of the federal arrangement; they build for Canada a future in which political accommodation will be the accommodation between federal and provincial interests. By enhancing the role of this relationship in Canadian politics and by weakening the role of other relationships — between legislatures and courts, between producers and consumers, between labour and capital, between industry and the environmentally concerned, between the powerful and the marginalized, between aboriginal peoples and those who have inherited the benefits of European settlement — we have to a large extent determined both the form and substance of future political accommodation.

It is possible that the current features of modern political conflict, whatever they may be, are bound to be more transient and more subject to alteration than the basic Canadian tension between the interests of Canadians defined by their place — their regional and provincial interests — and their language. If this is so, then Meech Lake, although a reversion to an older Canadian politic, is not a sadly obsolete document. On the other hand, if the better political future for Canada is to be found in the sharpening of other saliences and in the mobilization of the political forces concerned with gender, age, environment, destitution, ethnicity and employment, then we must ask whether Meech Lake will produce the conditions that will encourage this new politics. Women's rights groups have proceeded on the assumption that the conditions in which social groups and interests will flourish politically are conditions which encourage national mobilization.

Perhaps women's rights groups are wrong. Perhaps the best possible political environment for all Canadians — the powerful *and* the dispossessed — is an environment in which reform politics is channelled to a large extent through provinces. Perhaps Canada's best future is to allow social and other interests to persuade provincial Legislatures to regulate and intervene, in which case Canada will not have been damaged. Perhaps the attack on national politics and national self-determination that the Meech Lake Accord mounts will not hamper the development of a mature and effective political community. But Canadians owe to women's rights groups gratitude for causing us to stop and wonder whether the strengthening of the federal structure represents the best possible innovation to our national structure.

Political Vision and the 1987 Constitutional Accord

Jennifer Smith

The Meech Lake Accord is the most recent in a long line of venerable attempts to establish political and institutional arrangments acceptable to French-speaking and English-speaking Canadians or, to use the terms of the nineteenth century, the two nationalities. It is also the latest in a shorter line of statements on the constitutional relationship between the federal government and the provincial governments. Although the Accord's proposals fall within the mainstream of political discourse on these matters, they appear to favour one side in the debate. I wish to evaluate the proposals on the nationality question and on the federal principle. The two matters are related, of course, but for analytical purposes I treat them separately.

THE NATIONALITY QUESTION

Constitutional Background

If the 1987 Accord is accepted, it will not be the first constitutional document to show particular regard for Quebec, or to single out and address the province's two major language communities. However, the authors of the Accord will be the first to have used the phrase "distinct society" and the first to have supposed it important and essential to declare the point.

The habit of identifying communities and treating them differently began with the Quebec Act, 1774[1] which named, and provided for the continuation of, two institutions of the majority population — the Roman Catholic religion and the French civil law — that distinguished it from the newly-arrived minority. In the Constitutional Act, 1791,[2] the British Parliament continued the process of distinguishing and separating the anglophone and francophone communities by severing the largely English-speaking population in the western section of the colony from the remainder, thereby establishing two colonies that proceeded to develop on their own.[3] By the time Lord Durham came to write his Report on the societies of the Canadas, less than fifty years later, he found the French-speaking majority and the British minority, as he termed it, in Lower Canada to be different from each other in most important respects — indeed, in effect to be isolated from one another.[4] At the same time he observed that Upper Canada, being largely English-speaking and therefore not beset by the nationality question, followed the customary pattern of political conflict in liberal politics, that is, the conflict between reformers and conservatives, or sometimes simply between the ins and the outs.[5]

The Union Act, 1840,[6] which followed the Report, departed from its constitutional predecessors in appearing to ignore political claims based on nationality and in uniting the two Canadas under one government in the Province of Canada. Certainly it ignored some claims of the French-speaking community, for example, in the provision establishing English only as the language of record for the Legislative Council and Legislative Assembly of the new province.[7] However, colonial politicians confounded the assimilationist intent of the union, in part by developing informal practices or conventions that recognized and reaffirmed the very community divisions that Durham hoped the new institutional framework would suppress. In time these practices produced a political impasse in the government of the province and the fourth constitutional document, the Confederation agreement embodied in the Constitution Act, 1867,[8] returned to the remedy of

---

1 (14 George 3, U.K.), c. 83.
2 (31 George 3, U.K.), c. 31.
3 W.P.M. Kennedy, *Statutes, Treaties and Documents of the Canadian Constitution, 1713-1929*, 2nd ed. (Toronto: Oxford University Press, 1930) at 138-139 and 194.
4 Sir C.P. Lucas, ed., *Lord Durham's Report on the Affairs of British North America*, vol. 11 (Oxford: Clarendon Press, 1912) at 27-45.
5 *Ibid.*, at pp. 145, 151.
6 (3-4 Victoria, U.K.), c. 35.
7 Kennedy, above, note 3, at 439-440.
8 (U.K.), c. 3.

separation. The Act divided the Province of Canada into two provinces, Ontario and Quebec, and entrusted local government to the majorities in each. And it paid particular attention to the French-speaking community in Quebec in, for example, the assignment of property and civil rights in the province to local jurisdiction, and in the exclusion of Quebec from the uniformity-of-laws clause in s. 94. It also recognized the claims of the English-speaking minority in the province in s. 93(2) which extended to its dissentient schools the same protections in law that were enjoyed by Roman Catholic separate schools in Upper Canada at the time of the union.

From the point of view of Quebec, the Constitution Act, 1982,[9] arguably the most important constitutional document since 1867, marked a resolutely liberal and individualistic addition to the Confederation agreements. With the exception of the provision on aboriginal rights and freedoms, and possibly that on multicultural heritage, the guarantees of rights and freedoms specified in the Charter of Rights and Freedoms[10] are expressed in the language of individual rights. Even the minority language educational rights section refers to the rights of individuals rather than to the claims of a community, a point in no way altered by the prudent deference shown to Quebec in the application of one of the provisions of the section.[11] As a result, I am inclined to view the proposed 1987 Accord as a corrective to the 1982 amendment, that is, a return to the practice of giving constitutional recognition to the claims of Quebec, claims that other provinces do not generally make. These singular claims, and the response to them, together constitute the reality of the province's special status.

The 1987 Accord

The Accord reaffirms Quebec's special status in three ways, each different from the others, while at the same time proclaiming the principle of the equality of the provinces. How is this possible? The Accord's authors do not state the ground of the provinces' equality although it is obviously not political equality, as is evident from the remarkable words of the motion for resolution preceding the text of the Accord, words that give contemporary expression to the special

---

9 Enacted by the Canada Act 1982 (U.K.), c. 11, s. 1

10 Being Part I of the Constitution Act, 1982.

11 See s. 59 of the Constitution Act, 1982.

place of Quebec in Confederation.

The resolution begins by reiterating the political failure of the Constitution Act, 1982 — the fact that Quebec refused to sign the agreement that formed the basis of the Act. It then offers a remedy, which is Quebec's remedy, that is, the Quebec government's five proposals for constitutional change, the acceptance of which is the condition of the province's political and public consent to the 1982 amendments. These five proposals, the resolution continues, are met in the terms of the Accord. No one else's proposals are mentioned.

The distinct society clause in the text of the Accord is another statement of Quebec's special position. The Accord makes two observations about Canadian society. One identifies as a "fundamental characteristic" the existing distribution in the country of communities defined in terms of the two official languages. The other asserts that Quebec constitutes a "distinct society." The courts are enjoined to interpret the Constitution in a manner consistent with these observations. The distinction drawn between Canada and Quebec is emphasized in the provisions that follow on the roles assigned to political institutions. Parliament and the provincial Legislatures are assigned the role of preserving the fundamental characteristic of Canada as that is described. To the government and Legislature of Quebec is assigned the role of preserving and promoting Quebec's distinct identity. The political institutions of Quebec, on the one hand, and Canada and the provinces, on the other, are linked to different societal objectives.

Finally, there is the immigration question. The Accord includes a set of provisions on immigration and aliens that elaborate upon s. 95 of the Constitution Act, 1867. It indicates the scope of an agreement on the subject into which Canada and any province can enter, and the procedures under which such an agreement acquires constitutional status. However, the political accord outlines the terms of an agreement on immigration that Canada and Quebec have worked out already. From the standpoint of the principle of the equality of the provinces, this agreement is an illustration of the kinds of agreements into which Canada and the other provinces might enter. Viewed from the perspective of Quebec's special status, on the other hand, the opportunity that is extended to the other provinces appears to be their condition for accommodating Quebec's intense interest in the subject. In conclusion, in these instances the Accord, in my view, speaks primarily to Quebec, and this helps account for the puzzling lack of interest in it on the part of many Canadians outside the province.

THE FEDERAL PRINCIPLE

In addition to reaffirming Quebec's special position within Confederation, the Accord addresses some long-standing provincial grievances. For example, the provinces have complained often that the exercise of the federal spending power in relation to matters assigned exclusively to them constitutes an unwarranted interference in their public policy agendas. The Accord's solution is not to limit the spending power, but to require the federal government to provide financial compensation to provinces choosing to pursue on their own the objectives of new national shared-cost programs that fall within the sphere of provincial jurisdiction. This would appear to give the provinces more flexible political and administrative options than exist now.

Similarly, the Accord seeks to redress another and even older bone of contention — provincial sensitivity on appointments to the Senate and the Supreme Court of Canada — by defining a role for the provinces in the appointment process. The role is limited to the submission of names of candidates. On the other hand, the federal government is required to make its selection from among the names thus submitted. Whatever one thinks of this proposal, its significance cannot be disputed. It gives the provinces a role in the make-up of national institutions that they have never had before. Critics have raised the obvious practical question, that is, whether over time the process of selecting candidates from provincial nomination lists will alter subtly the character of these institutions in a manner favourable to the provinces. For students of federalism, some theoretical considerations arise as well. In the past, theories of Canadian federalism have taken account of the fact that our federal and provincial governmental bodies are institutionally separate. The provinces, for example, are not formally represented in federal governmental institutions. The development of executive federalism in the post-war period, requiring as it has the establishment of new and extra-constitutional institutions, reinforces the point. Viewed in this light, the Accord's proposal on provincial participation in appointments to two national institutions represents a departure from past practice. It is a step in the direction of what is termed intrastate federalism, which in the past has been viewed as a feature distinguishing American national political institutions from our own. The provisions on appointment, then, do not affect simply the balance of power in federal-provincial relations. They mark a shift in the theory and practice of Canadian federalism.

The same can be said, with some qualifications, for the provisions on first ministers' conferences. The Accord requires the Prime Minister to convene two first ministers' conferences annually, one on the economy and one on the Constitution, thus institutionalizing the most visible event in the practice of executive federalism. Because these conferences have become a fixture of Canadian politics in recent years, it is easy to overlook the significance of making them constitutionally required. As a constitutional institution, the first ministers' conference becomes a reliable component of the political landscape around which political actors, especially provincial premiers, can plan strategies.

Finally, the proposed changes to the amending formula strengthen the hand of the provinces in a procedure that is not unfavourable to them now. Financial compensation now available to provinces opting-out of an amendment transferring matters relating to education and culture from provincial jurisdiction to Parliament will be extended to provinces opting-out of amendments dealing with all provincial matters. This would have the effect of making opting-out a more attractive alternative to dissenting provinces. It also proposes to extend the reach of the unanimity formula to some items now subject to the less onerous consent requirements of the general amending formula. Since the requirement of unanimous consent is tantamount to a veto protection, the extension places all governments, and especially provincial governments, in a strong defensive position when it comes to constitutional change.

CONCLUSION

The 1987 Accord pursues two themes: special status for Quebec and an enhanced role for the provinces in the federal system. It addresses positively the claims of Quebec in particular and the provinces in general. Following the tradition of earlier constitutional documents, it deals with governments and their powers. In this respect, it differs very much from the Charter, which for the most part speaks to individual Canadians rather than to governments, and indeed, sets out guarantees of rights and freedoms that Canadians can assert against governmental powers.

Critics of the Accord who are worried about its effects on the Charter have resorted to arguments based on fears of what provincial governments, armed with powers they did not possess before, might do. In particular, they have expressed apprehension about the use that Quebec governments might make of the distinct society clause. What is the basis of their apprehension? It appears to flow from a conception of politics as a process constituted by an opposition between individual rights and governmental powers. Individuals are understood to assert rights against governments under the protective fold of the judicial sphere, rather than to participate fully in the political sphere and its public policy process. Implicit in this conception is a distrust of politics in general, and a lack of confidence in the Canadian political system in particular. Naturally, then, proposals that have the effect of strengthening the powers of provincial governments are alarming simply because they multiply the arenas in which political battles have to be fought. This is an incapacitating conception precisely because of the vitality and strength of Canada's decentralized federal system, displayed once again in the dynamics underlying the Meech Lake negotiations. On the other hand, the lack of confidence in the political process that these critics manifest points to the need for a different constitutional agenda, one that is devoted to the reform of our governmental institutions.

Competing Visions of Constitutionalism: Of Federalism and Rights

Katherine Swinton[*]

Much of the debate about the significance of the Meech Lake Accord involves competing visions of federalism and differing views about the proper roles of the federal and provincial Governments in Canada. Whether or not the Accord will reduce the amount or acerbity of federal-provincial conflict, and whether it will dangerously hobble the nation-building capacity and role of the federal Government have been the subject of much discussion in political and academic circles — and rightly so, for the Accord will have an important impact on the conduct of federal-provincial relations and the powers of our governmental institutions in the future.

I leave to others the discussion of the Accord's impact on relationships between federal and provincial Governments in Canada. In this paper, I plan to deal with another important aspect of the Meech Lake Accord. Competing visions of Canadian constitutionalism rooted in individual rights and federalism have emerged in the debate about the proposed amendments to the Constitution Acts and will necessarily arise in the future interpretation of the Constitution. In the debate about the Meech Lake Accord, not only federal and provincial government interests are at stake; therefore, a discussion of its significance must not be framed solely in terms of competing views of national and regional communities. There is, in the debate about

[*] I am grateful to Carol Rogerson and Ken Swan for their comments on an earlier draft of this paper.

the impact of the Accord on the Canadian Charter of Rights and Freedoms,[1] another vision of Canadian constitutionalism, which focuses on the importance of the rights of the citizen against government, and sees community not in terms of regional identity, but in terms of individual characteristics such as sex, ethnic origin or religion. Community thus connotes membership in groups that share such characteristics. In this paper I shall explore the interaction between federalism and rights that emerge, in particular, from the distinct society clause of the Accord. I shall also explore issues of interpretation of the Charter in light of federalism concerns. This, I believe, will assist in evaluating the new provincial role in appointments to the Supreme Court of Canada.

COMPETING VISIONS OF CONSTITUTIONALISM

From Confederation, federalism has been the dominant theme in Canadian political life. While there are many reasons to extol federalism as a system of government,[2] debates about the shape of the Canadian federal system and the respective jurisdiction of federal and provincial governments have revolved around competing conceptions of community.[3] The communities relevant to this constitutional debate have traditionally been limited to the federal and provincial governments, with Quebec laying claim to a special status as the homeland of a distinct society or nation. The debate about national and provincial communities shaped the original distribution of powers in 1867; it has influenced constitutional reform debates and negotiations; and it has emerged in judicial decisions about the interpretation of the distribution of powers provisions in the Constitution. Indeed, for most of our history, federalism has been the "stuff" of Canadian constitutional law and discourse, and our preoccupation has been the proper allocation of powers between competing territorial communities.[4]

---

1 Being Part I of the Constitution Act, 1982 [enacted by the Canada Act 1982 (U.K.), c. 11, s. 1].

2 See R. Simeon, "Criteria for Choice in Federal Systems" (1982-83) 8 Queen's L.J. 131, which sets out three competing, although overlapping, perspectives of federalism — community, democratic, and functional. This is further developed in K. Norrie, R. Simeon and M. Krasnick, *Federalism and the Economic Union in Canada*, MacDonald Commission Studies, vol. 59 (Toronto: University of Toronto Press, 1986).

3 Simeon, *ibid.* at p. 137. See also Norrie *et al.*, *ibid.* at 26.

4 There are, of course, other themes in the literature and debates about the distribution of

After the Second World War, however, a competing vision of Canadian constitutionalism, not territorially based, emerged with vigour. Rights consciousness led to pressure from interest groups and citizens for constitutional guarantees of individual rights against government, and statutory safeguards against discrimination both public and private. Political actors increasingly recognized the legitimacy of such claims through the enactment of protective human rights legislation and adherence to international instruments pertaining to individual rights.[5] The entrenchment of the Canadian Charter of Rights and Freedoms in 1982 was a further significant recognition and approbation of rights consciousness, altering the nature of the Canadian Constitution in a fundamental way. No longer is the Constitution's primary focus the allocation of powers to competing levels of government, for the Constitution Act, 1982 also limits the powers of those governments in the interests of individual and group rights and freedoms.

This is not to say that there is a sharp distinction between federalism and rights in Canadian constitutional discourse. Indeed, the debate about the entrenchment of the Charter was very much influenced by federalism. One of the major objectives of the Trudeau government in seeking entrenchment of the Charter was to strengthen the ties of individual Canadians to national institutions, both through the Charter, with its guarantee of rights to all Canadians, regardless of region, and through the oversight role assigned to the Supreme Court of Canada, a national institution with the responsibility for determining the scope of those rights.[6] Thus, an important objective underlying the constitutional protection for individual and group rights was the strengthening of the national community.

During the negotiations over the constitutional amendments, provincial governments were understandably concerned about the

---

powers, and considerations of efficiency and individual rights emerge in the debate and also influence visions of community.

5 Historical background is found in I. Hunter, "The Origin, Development and Interpretation of Human Rights Legislation" in R. St. J. Macdonald and J.P. Humphrey, eds. *The Practice of Freedom* (Toronto: Butterworths, 1979), 77; W. Tarnopolsky and W. Pentney, *Discrimination and the Law* (Toronto: Carswell, 1985) at ch. 2.

6 A. Cairns and C. Williams, "Constitutionalism, Citizenship and Society in Canada: An Overview" in A. Cairns and C. Williams, eds. *Constitutionalism, Citizenship and Society in Canada*, MacDonald Commission Studies, vol. 33, (Toronto: University of Toronto Press, 1985) 1 at 3; R. Knopff and F.L. Morton, "Nation-Building and the Canadian Charter of Rights and Freedoms" in Cairns and Williams, *op. cit.*, 133 at 144-150; P. Russell, "The Political Purposes of the Canadian Charter of Rights and Freedoms" (1983), 61 Can. Bar Rev. 30 at 36-42.

Charter, since it would set limits on certain types of legislative action that would diminish both federal and provincial powers.[7] Often, this provincial concern was expressed as a belief in parliamentary supremacy and democratic decision-making, which, it was feared, would be undercut by judicial review of legislation by appointed judges. But there was a harmony between the protection of parliamentary supremacy and province-building, since pursuit of the first objective would result in safeguards for provincial legislative autonomy.[8] When the Charter was entrenched in the Constitution, its ultimate shape reflected these concerns about parliamentary supremacy and federalism by including the legislative override in s. 33 and the limitation on mobility rights in s. 6(4).[9]

The entrenchment of rights in the Constitution has had an important impact on Canadian politics and the constitutional order. Cairns and Williams have stated that "recognition of a right is accompanied by an altered conception of community."[10] I would rephrase that statement, when looking at the impact of the Charter, to say that the recognition of rights in that document reinforced existing conceptions of community that were not territorially based and gave them new impetus. The Charter did not lead women, the handicapped, or multicultural and religious groups to coalesce for the first time and to recognize themselves as groups with shared interests and rights.[11] What it did, rather, was to give them an important and

---

7 As Russell notes, *ibid.* at p. 42, while the federal government asserted that there was no diminution of powers of the provinces vis-à-vis the federal government, the Charter does put restrictions on provincial legislative action.

8 A. Cairns, "The Politics of Conservatism" in K. Banting and R. Simeon, eds., *And No One Cheered: Federalism, Democracy and the Constitution* (Toronto: Methuen, 1983) 28; Knopff and Morton, above, note 6 at 137.

9 The override permits governments to shelter laws from certain guarantees under the Charter (s. 2, the fundamental freedoms section; ss. 7 through 15, the legal and equality rights). Section 6(4) is a limitation on the mobility rights guarantee, permitting a province to initiate programs for the socially and economically disadvantaged if the rate of employment in the province is less than the national average.

    Other provisions of the Charter also reflect provincial diversity — see, for example, the language rights provisions (ss. 16 through 21, dealing with institutional bilingualism, which apply to the federal and New Brunswick governments; s. 23(1)(a), dealing with language of instruction, which comes into effect in Quebec only on the consent of that province).

10 Cairns and Williams, above, note 6 at 3.

11 Indeed, these groups played an important role in the political process leading up to the entrenchment of the Charter, whether through appearances before the Joint Senate and House of Commons Committee studying the constitutional amendment bill or through lobbying

potentially powerful tool for pursuing their visions of Canadian society, whether through legislative lobbying or litigation.[12] Often such groups have, in past, lacked sufficient political power to assert their policy views successfully before government. With the Charter, they have a new way to attack existing government action and to influence the debate on new initiatives, and they have been active in using that tool, often with government financial support.[13]

It is too early to say whether the entrenchment of rights in the Constitution will have the effect of strengthening the national community and citizens' identification with the nation as a whole, as desired by the Trudeau government. What it has done, in the short run, is to reinforce concepts of community based on shared characteristics such as race, sex or handicap, that transcend provincial boundaries. However, much of the Charter litigation to date and many of the lobbying efforts based on the Charter have continued at the provincial level among coalitions centred in the province.[14]

And then came the Meech Lake Accord. When the federal and provincial premiers signed the agreements at Meech Lake and at the Langevin Block, they acted within the traditional mode of Canadian Constitution-making: they drafted an agreement reflecting their concerns about the future balance of federal and provincial powers in Canada. Thus, the Accord deals with the spending power, provincial input into Senate and Supreme Court appointments, and the amending formula. It also states, as a new s. 2 of the Constitution Act, 1867,[15] that the Constitution shall be interpreted in a manner consistent with the recognition of the existence of French-speaking Canadians centred in Quebec and English-speaking Canadians concentrated outside

---

about its terms and limitations. See, for example, Cairns, above, note 8; Knopff and Morton, above, note 6 at pp. 152-155; C. Hosek, "Women and the Constitutional Process" in Banting and Simeon, above, note 8 at p. 280; D. Sanders, "The Indian Lobby" in Banting and Simeon, above, note 8 at 301.

12 Often litigation is a lobbying tool — for example, the action of Intercede, an organization representing domestic workers in Ontario, prodded the Ontario government to change the regulations governing overtime and working conditions for domestics under the Employment Standards Act, R.S.O. 1980, c. 137.

13 Groups like LEAF (the Women's Legal Education and Action Fund) and COPOH (Coalition of Provincial Organizations of the Handicapped) have received government funding for Charter litigation, while the federal government has a special fund to support Charter litigation. Other groups, such as the Canadian Civil Liberties Association, are funded through private contributions.

14 Many of these groups have ties across the nation. For example, women's groups engaged in lobbying and litigation in the provinces often work through LEAF.

15 (U.K.), c. 3.

Quebec as a fundamental characteristic of Canada, and with the recognition of Quebec as a distinct society.

That the Accord is imbued with concerns about federal and provincial powers is not surprising. After all, the impetus for an agreement was to gain Quebec's support for the 1982 constitutional amendment, while Quebec's negotiating agenda was shaped by long-standing concerns about its autonomy. Not surprisingly, the other provincial premiers did not miss an opportunity to bargain for matters that were consistent with their visions of provincial autonomy as well. But the preoccupation with federalism and federal-provincial government concerns in the Meech Lake Accord comes into conflict with the competing rights consciousness that received new vitality with the 1982 Constitution Act and the early Supreme Court decisions interpreting the Charter. Those decisions made it clear that the Court would give effect to the provisions of the Charter and would not relegate it to the toothless status of the Canadian Bill of Rights.[16] The distinct society clause of the Accord has been particularly problematic to some interest groups, especially representatives of the women's community, because it seems to subordinate the rights in the Charter to federalism concerns. Moreover, the inclusion, by virtue of the Langevin agreement, of s. 16 of the Accord, which provides that nothing in s. 2 (the distinct society clause) affects ss. 25 and 27 of the Charter (the aboriginal rights guarantee and the multicultural heritage provision) suggests to these groups that other parts of the Charter, especially equality rights, are generally of a lesser status and, in particular, are subject to the new s. 2.

There is, in their protest, a fear as to the way in which this provision will be interpreted by the courts, which I shall discuss in the next section of this paper. But there is, as well, a sense of outrage, both because of the closed process used in reaching the agreement, without public input and open consideration of the implications of the language, and because of the apparent subordination of rights to federalism concerns.[17] Although the Constitution Act, 1982 added a

---

16 S.C. 1960, c. 44. In several early decisions under the Charter, the Supreme Court of Canada found legislation or administrative action unconstitutional. See, for example, *A.G. Que. v. Quebec Assn. of Protestant School Bds.* (1984), 10 D.L.R. (4th) 321; *R.v. Big M Drug Mart Ltd.* (1985), 18 D.L.R. (4th) 321; *R. v. Therens* (1985), 18 D.L.R. (4th) 655.

17 The following quote from Marilou McPhedran, an active lobbyist for women's rights, catches the concerns about Meech Lake, even though it was addressed to the 6 November 1981 Accord — "What went in as a Charter of Rights, came out as a Charter of federal-provincial relations." (Quoted in Knopff and Morton, above, note 6 at 155.)

new pillar to Canadian constitutionalism, that of individual rights against government, the 1987 Accord seemed to affirm federalism as the primary pillar of Canadian constitutionalism, a proposition that many groups would not accept.

Whether or not their concerns are overstated depends on how one interprets the Charter and the new amendments, an issue that suggests the importance of the identity of those who do the interpretation, subjects explored in the next two sections of this paper.

FEDERALISM AND CHARTER INTERPRETATION

Those concerned with the impact of the Meech Lake Accord on the Charter of Rights, particularly women's groups, are fearful that it will permit Quebec, and perhaps the federal government, to pass laws infringing rights, especially women's equality rights, which will be upheld on the basis that they promote the distinctiveness of Quebec's society or its linguistic concerns.[18] Often the examples used to illustrate the point are drawn from the Duplessis era, with arguments made that Quebec's padlock law or its suppression of Jehovah's Witnesses would, in the future, be defensible under the distinct society clause.[19] More modern concerns are expressed as well; women's groups have speculated that laws restricting access to abortion might be upheld in the interests of expanding Quebec's population base.

It seems likely that these fears are overblown, although there is room for debate about the interpretation of the amendments, and a final determination of the meaning of the provisions can only be given by the Supreme Court of Canada. On a practical level, the parties making up the present Quebec National Assembly are not likely to pass such laws. But, of course, Constitutions speak not only to present governors and societies, but to the future as well. They also deal not only with wild excesses, but with minor transgressions as well. How, then, is the new language likely to affect the interpretation of the Charter?

One of the first things to note is that s. 2 is said to be an interpretive clause. Indeed, its language is similar to s. 27 of the Charter, which

---

18 While the Accord recognizes Quebec's role in preserving and promoting the distinct society, the proposed s. 2(2) affirms the role of the federal and provincial governments to preserve the linguistic duality of Canada. There has been some suggestion that women's equality rights could be jeopardized by such a power.

19 The references are to the laws and practices under consideration in *Switzman v. Elbling*, [1957] S.C.R. 285, and *Saumur v. City of Quebec*, [1953] 2 S.C.R. 299.

states that the Charter shall be interpreted in a manner consistent with the preservation and enhancement of the multicultural heritage of Canadians. The section does not expressly confer on Quebec the power to do anything it wishes in order to safeguard or promote its distinctiveness.[20] As a result, when a Charter right is said to be infringed by Quebec government action, s. 2 will be considered, but as part of the interpretation process. It is most likely to emerge in the application of the reasonable limits provision in s. 1 of the Charter, with Quebec arguing that limits on a right such as freedom of expression are necessary to promote Quebec's distinct society. Clearly, one of Quebec's main concerns is to use this provision to protect its language laws from attacks under s. 2(b) of the Charter, the freedom of expression guarantee, and s. 23, the language rights provision. At times, the distinct society clause may also enter into the delineation of the scope of rights, particularly in s. 15, the equality guarantee, if there is, within that section, some consideration of the reasonableness of classifications used by Legislatures.[21]

The best interpretation of the distinct society clause is that it does not, in its language, "trump" s. 1, but works with it — that is, Quebec's limitations on rights must be demonstrably justified in a free and democratic society, albeit one that is distinct culturally and linguistically. Undoubtedly, there will be circumstances where the courts will find that Quebec cannot impose certain limits on the

---

20 There is, admittedly, room for debate about the meaning of the term "affirmed" in the new ss. 2(2) and 2(3) proposed by the Accord. Does it recognize a power that has always existed, or does it indicate a new source of power for Quebec and the other governments? I do not believe that the section gives the province of Quebec expanded legislative jurisdiction under s. 92 of the Constitution Act, 1867, since s. 2(4) states that nothing in the Accord "derogates" from the powers, rights or privileges of the federal or provincial governments. Any attempted expansion of Quebec's legislative powers under ss. 2(1) and 2(3) would be a derogation from federal power and would indirectly derogate from the powers of the other provinces, since they would not share a co-ordinate status with Quebec, which they have always had. Moreover, the resolution accompanying the Accord refers to the equality of all the provinces (captured in the revised amending formula with the increased number of amendments requiring unanimity), and this, too, suggests, that s. 2 is a recognition of the existing distribution of powers and a guide to interpretation only.

21 There are different approaches emerging in appellate courts in the interpretation of s. 15. Some have held that governments do not violate s. 15 if they make distinctions between groups that are reasonable and fair, having regard to a principle of equal treatment (e.g. Re Andrews and Law Society of British Columbia (1986), 27 D.L.R. (4th) 600 (B.C. C.A.); R. v. Century 21 Ramos Realty Inc. (1987), 58 O.R. (2d) 737 (C.A.)). Others feel that distinctions which disadvantage groups shift the consideration of justification for the treatment to s. 1 (e.g. Smith, Kline, & French Laboratories Ltd. v. A.G. Can. (1986), 3 D.L.R. (4th) 584 (Fed. C.A.)).

rights in the Charter because there is a floor of rights (what Mr. Justice Beetz once called a *jus gentium*)[22] which cannot be violated, even in the interests of a distinct society, because the limitations are inconsistent with the principle of a free and democratic society. The degree to which the Courts will impose uniform standards on provinces and the federal government under the Charter will be explored shortly. First, it is necessary to consider s. 16 of the Accord and other views concerning the significance of inserting the new s. 2 in the Constitution Act, 1867.

Section 16 creates a hierarchy of rights under the Charter, a proposition understandably disturbing to many. It provides that multiculturalism and aboriginal rights are not to be subordinated to Quebec's interest in a distinct society when rights are defined or limited under the Charter. Equality between the sexes and religious groups, or freedom of expression, are not given such priority and, apparently, may be limited in the interests of a distinct society, if s. 1 criteria are also satisfied. Thus, on the interpretation of the distinct society clause I have set out above, Quebec's interest in protecting or promoting its distinct society enters into the calculus of reasonable limits in s. 1 when gender or religious equality or freedom of expression is at stake, but it does not do so if equality is denied on the basis of ethnic origin or aboriginal status. By making some equality rights more protected than others — indeed, some would say, by limiting rights generally in the interests of a distinct society — the Accord has taken away important protections for individual rights.[23]

From this technical, albeit brief, consideration of the interaction of the distinct society clause and the Charter, I shall now move to a more general point. The debate about interpretation involves the important interpretive issue of the role of federalism in Charter interpretation. To what degree will provinces and the federal government be able to impose different limits on rights; to what extent is the distinctiveness of Quebec (but of other regions as well) a factor that should enter Charter interpretation, even in the absence of a

---

22 *A.G. Can. v. Canard* (1975), 52 D.L.R. (3d) 548 at 579 (S.C.C.).

23 Many women's groups are also particularly fearful of s. 2 because of its place in the Constitution Act, 1867 in light of Wilson J.'s words in *Reference re An Act to Amend the Education Act (Ontario)* (1987), 40 D.L.R. (4th) 18 at 60-61 (S.C.C.). Like Wayne MacKay, who writes earlier in this volume in "Linguistic Duality and the Distinct Society in Quebec: Declarations of Sociological Fact or Legal Limits on Constitutional Interpretation?" at 65, I do not believe the 1867 Constitution is immune from Charter scrutiny nor superior to it. Rather, the provisions of the 1867 document enter into the interpretation of the Charter.

distinct society clause? Obviously, the Charter will impose some degree
of uniformity in laws across the country. That has been the experience
in the United States, and there seems to be some indication that it
will have some standardizing influence in Canada as well.[24] The
Charter will necessarily have some nationalizing influence in the sense
that if a law is struck down in one province, it is often unlikely that
the identical law would survive in another jurisdiction. Thus, if
citizenship is impermissible as a criterion for membership in one
provincial law society, it is hard to see how a similar criterion would
survive in another.

But in every Charter case, when the courts find a violation of
rights, they must determine whether the government's limitation is
reasonable and demonstrably justified in a free and democratic society.
There is room, here, for the courts to consider claims for diversity
among jurisdictions to meet different needs or policy preferences
among regions. Recognition of such diversity may be explained by
courts as deference to the Legislatures and a recognition of the
limitations of judicial review. At the same time, a deferential approach
would reinforce values of federalism and diversity among provincial
communities and weaken the nationalizing tendencies of the Charter.[25]

There is some indication both in decisions of the Supreme Court
of Canada and in lower courts to date that federalism or diversity
is a consideration, explicit or implicit, in the interpretation of the
Charter; while the Charter will impose some degree of uniformity
in legislation across the country, there will still be some leeway for
provinces and the federal government in the kinds of statutory regimes
they can establish in areas affecting rights. In the Supreme Court's
early jurisprudence there was some indication that this might not be

24 Knopff and Morton, above, note 6 at 148, concluded that there is a strong unifying influence
to date because of the number of successful challenges to provincial laws and actions. For
another view on success rates, see P. Monahan, "A Critic's Guide to the Charter" in R.J.
Sharpe, ed. *Charter Litigation* (Toronto: Butterworths, 1987) 383, especially at 396.
   One must be careful in looking at success rates in cases alone to predict the impact
on provincial autonomy, for many of the cases to date which have found against governments
do not strike down legislation, but deal with administrative practice and the administration
of justice.
25 Knopff and Morton, above, note 6 at pp. 170-171 argue that the courts should not recognize
a value of diversity in the interpretation of s. 1 of the Charter. Such an approach would,
in their view, "render the Charter a practical nullity." They go on to say, "Under it, the
Charter would apply only to policies that transgressed virtually unquestioned norms and
would not apply to policies about which reasonable differences exist — that is, to the kind
of policy most likely to be challenged under the Charter." As the text indicates, I do not
agree.

the case. In *Oakes*,[26] Chief Justice Dickson set up a stringent test under s. 1 of the Charter which seemed to indicate that a government could only limit rights to achieve a substantial and important government objective provided that the objective was pursued by the least restrictive means available — that is, by means which impaired the right "as little as possible." If this test were followed strictly, the flexibility of governments would be limited.[27]

The Court appears to have relaxed that test somewhat in *Edwards Books and Art*,[28] where Chief Justice Dickson asked whether the restriction on religious freedom abridged the right "as little as is reasonably possible." This leaves more room for variation among jurisdictions, a fact that Mr. Justice La Forest remarked upon in a concurring judgment, where he indicated that there should be flexibility for provinces to set up different regimes for Sunday closing of retail establishments.[29] While his concern is expressed, in part, in the language of federalism, it also reflects a view of the proper role of the judiciary in interpreting the Charter, one which defers to the Legislature on many controversial questions of social policy which seem to impinge on rights.[30] As in the initial debate about Charter entrenchment, in the application of the Charter, questions of democratic theory intertwine with federalism in Canada.

Lower courts have also dealt with federalism issues in their

---

26 *R. v. Oakes* (1986), 26 D.L.R. (4th) 200 at 227 (S.C.C.).

27 For example, if the purpose behind a mandatory retirement law was to use age as a proxy for capacity to work, one could argue that the objective could be achieved by less restrictive means, such as individual testing for capacity. These arguments have been made in challenges to mandatory retirement laws and limitations on the protection against age discrimination in human rights legislation (*Re McKinney and Board of Governors of University of Guelph* (1986), 32 D.L.R. (4th) 65 (Ont. H.C.), affirmed (1987), 24 O.A.C. 241 (C.A.), *Harrison v. University of British Columbia* (1986), 30 D.L.R. (4th) 206 (B.C. S.C.), reversed [1988] 2 W.W.R. 688 (C.A.)).

28 *Edwards Books and Art Ltd. v. R.* (1986), 35 D.L.R. (4th) 1 at 44 (S.C.C.).

29 He stated, "The simple fact is that what may work effectively in one province (or in a part of it) may simply not work in another without unduly interfering with the legislative scheme. And a compromise adopted at a particular time may not be possible at another; one cannot be bound constitutionally to facts found to exist when the studies preparatory to legislation were made." (*Ibid.* at 72)

30 La Forest J. went on to say (*Ibid.* at 75) that choices about Sunday closings are essentially legislative decisions. His language is reminiscent of the majority judgments in the trilogy of cases dealing with the right to strike and the guarantee of freedom of association, where Le Dain J. also expressed the view that decisions about limitations on strikes should be left to the Legislatures (*Reference re Public Service Employee Relations Act (Alta.)* (1987), 38 D.L.R. (4th) 161 at 240; *Public Service Alliance of Canada v. The Queen in Right of Canada* (1987), 38 D.L.R. (4th) 249; *Gov't of Sask. v. Retail, Wholesale, and Department Store Union* (1987), 38 D.L.R. (4th) 277).

Charter decisions, and all courts will have to do so even more with the increasing number of equality cases. Often a litigant attacking the reasonableness of limits under s. 1 invokes the legislation of other provinces and jurisdictions outside the country. While this comparative material is considered in decisions, legislative choices in other juris-dictions have not been accepted as determinative of the reasonableness of limits.[31]

Courts are recognizing that uniformity in legislation across the country is not required, but they have not yet had to articulate the circumstances in which diversity is impermissible because of the impact on individual rights. In *Hamilton*,[32] the Ontario Court of Appeal found a violation of the Charter's equality guarantee because a sentencing provision of the federal Criminal Code was proclaimed in some provinces, but not in Ontario. The Code had provided that the provision would only come into effect on the consent of the provinces. While the Court acknowledged that provinces could pass different penal and regulatory laws without running afoul of the Charter, it refused to uphold federal criminal legislation which resulted in different penalties for impaired driving from province to province.

The extent to which diversity is permitted in laws applicable either across the country or within a particular jurisdiction will be a difficult problem under the equality rights guarantee. Governments make different choices and have different priorities in their regulatory policies, and some jurisdictions have more funds to extend their programs and benefits than do others. For example, one of the smaller provinces may choose to send handicapped children to another province for their education because of lack of funds and facilities within the province. While one member of the Supreme Court has said, in the *Singh*[33] case, that arguments of administrative convenience are not acceptable in a s. 1 calculus, the Court will have to consider such arguments when discussing the concepts of equality and obligations of governments to accommodate differences or to accord equal treatment.

---

31 In the *Reference re Public Service Employee Relations Act, ibid.* at 184–85, Dickson C.J.C., in a dissenting judgment, discussed comparative materials and indicated that they were persuasive, but not conclusive.

32 *R. v. Hamilton* (1986), 57 O.R. (2d) 412 (C.A.).

33 *Re Singh and Minister of Employment and Immigration* (1985), 17 D.L.R. (4th) 422 (S.C.C.), per Wilson J. at 469. Wilson J. spoke for herself and two others in a case in which three judges held the refugee determination procedures under the *Immigration Act*, S.C. 1976-77, c. 52, violated s. 7 of the Charter and three judges found a violation of the Canadian Bill of Rights.

The problem of differences among, or even within, regions is not new to the interpretation of human rights documents. Federalism enters into the consideration of the American Bill of Rights,[34] and a parallel to federalism concerns permeates the interpretation of international human rights legislation.[35] In Canada, the concerns about permissible limits on rights and the scope of the equality guarantee will inevitably raise questions about diversity among and within communities in Canada and the degree to which governments can respond to that diversity without violating the Charter.

With this in mind, the distinct society clause need not introduce a dramatic new factor into Charter interpretation. It has always been possible for Quebec to try to justify its laws under s. 1 of the Charter by arguing that the purpose was to preserve Quebec's distinct culture and language. Indeed, such an argument was advanced in *Quebec Association of Protestant School Boards*.[36] The addition of the distinct society clause makes explicit the relevance and legitimacy of such an argument, but it does not ensure that the claim for diversity will outweigh the individual's claim to protection of his or her rights. The distinct society clause states explicitly that federalism concerns should enter into Charter interpretation when Quebec laws are challenged. Even without it, decisions of the courts indicate that diversity among and within communities is relevant to the determination of rights, including equality rights, and reasonable limits on rights under the Charter. Federalism, it seems, will enter into the interpretation of guaranteed rights under the Charter, either explicitly or intertwined with concerns about deference to the Legislature.

SELECTING THE ADJUDICATOR

From one perspective, the Meech Lake procedures for provincial input into Supreme Court appointments reflect traditional federalism concerns. There has been longstanding provincial criticism that the Supreme Court, the final umpire of federal-provincial disputes, is appointed by one side to the dispute, and thus its neutrality is open

---

34 See, for example, M. Durschlag, "Federalism and Constitutional Liberties: Varying the Remedy to Save the Right" (1979), 54 N.Y.U.L. Rev. 723; R. B. Stewart, "Federalism and Rights" (1985), 19 Geo. L. Rev. 917.

35 A.D. Renteln, "The Unanswered Challenge of Relativism and the Consequences for Human Rights" (1985), 7 Human Rights Quarterly 514.

36 Above, note 16.

to question.[37] The new appointment procedure seems to respond to these criticisms by providing a provincial voice in appointments, although without provincial control of the outcome.[38] Indeed, the federal government's document on the Accord suggests that the underlying purpose was to give the provinces a say in the selection of the "referee in constitutional disputes."[39] One can understand why Quebec would have a special interest here, since there is room for debate about the meaning of the new s. 2(1)(b) added by the Accord and whether it adds to provincial legislative powers under the Constitution Act, 1867.

But the new appointment procedure is of interest to the provinces not only because of concerns about distribution of powers disputes. Once again, federalism and rights adjudication intersect, for the provinces have reason to be interested in the selection of judges to the Supreme Court because of the Charter of Rights. Judges who conceive of a limited role for the courts in the application of the Charter will leave greater room for legislative diversity in public policy, with the result that provincial governments will be less constrained by the standardizing impact of the Charter. Thus, the provincial claim to input into Supreme Court appointments rests on federalism concerns broader than the distribution of powers.[40]

Many of the critics of the Accord's appointment procedure suggest that this new provincial role overemphasizes regional interests, politicizes the Court, and may interfere with the appointment of individuals who bring experience relevant to the interpretation of the Charter, such as women, minorities, and those from ethnic and religious backgrounds inadequately reflected in the Supreme Court's past makeup. On a practical level, there is no greater certainty that the federal government will pursue diversity in the Court's composition

---

37 There have been charges of bias in favour of the federal government — for example, from Premier Blakeney of Saskatchewan after two unfavourable decisions in the 1970s. See, also, P. Hogg, "Is the Supreme Court of Canada Biased in Constitutional Cases?" (1979), 57 Can. Bar. Rev. 721; G. L'Écuyer, *La Cour suprême du Canada et la partage des compétences 1949-1978*, Québec, Gouvernement du Québec, Ministère des Affaires Intergovernmentales, 1978.

38 Quebec has the greatest voice in appointments, since the three Quebec judges must be from a list put forth by the government of that province. With judges from outside Quebec, the federal government has the choice (or bargaining lever) to seek appointees from the list of any province, even though there is a convention of regional representation on the Court.

39 Canada, *Strengthening the Canadian Federation* (Ottawa, 1987) at 7.

40 Peter Russell, above, note 6 at p. 43, recognized this interest several years ago, stating: "To be able to maintain that a transfer of power from politicians to judges entails 'no transfer of power from the provinces to the federal government' it may become necessary to give provincial governments a share of the action in the judicial appointment process."

than will the provinces in making up their lists. Moreover, the federal government can exert leverage in finding candidates acceptable to it by, for example, threatening to seek a person from another province's list or, in the case of Quebec, refusing to make an appointment.

More important, the charge that the provincial role will politicize the Court ignores the fact that the Court's role has already been politicized. The high profile federalism decisions of the Court in the 1970s and early 1980s, such as *Anti-Inflation*, *CIGOL*, and the *Patriation Reference*,[41] involved the Court in important and controversial political disputes. Every case involving the distribution of powers requires the Court to exercise discretion and, thus, inevitably generates criticism. While judges like Justices Laskin, Beetz and Martland shared a common interpretive framework in such cases, it was clear that they had distinct views about the role of the Court and the proper allocation of powers under the Constitution, and this affected the outcome in any given case.

The entrenchment of the Charter expanded significantly the political role of the courts, especially the Supreme Court of Canada, and decisions to date demonstrate the variety of views among the judges about their role on judicial review and the content of the rights under the Charter. Politicizing of the Court will not come with provincial input into appointment; it started long before this, and the Court's political or policy role is increasingly clear in Charter cases. Indeed, the Court's policy role has become even more significant with this Accord, for the Accord's language is so problematic and open to so many interpretations that it essentially confers on the judges of the Supreme Court of Canada the responsibility to define precisely the powers of the federal and provincial governments under the revised Constitution and to determine the interaction of the Charter and the new s. 2.

Thus, the nature of the Court's task in constitutional adjudication is political, in the sense that it is imbued with important and complex policy considerations. Provincial input into appointment comes too late to politicize the Court. The Accord recognizes that the identity of the decision-maker is important in constitutional adjudication and involves provincial governments as well as the federal government in the selection of the men and women who will shape both the

---

41 *Reference re Anti-Inflation Act* (1976), 68 D.L.R. (3d) 452 (S.C.C.); *Canadian Industrial Gas & Oil Ltd. v. Gov't of Sask.* (1977), 80 D.L.R. (3d) 449 (S.C.C.); *Reference re Amendment of the Constitution of Canada (Nos. 1,2,3)* (1981), 125 D.L.R. (3d) 1 (S.C.C.).

distribution of powers between levels of government and the limitations on all governments.

CONCLUSION

While the Meech Lake Accord reflects a new approach to federal-provincial relations, it also reinforces the importance of federalism in Canadian constitutionalism by making clear that, in Canada, federalism remains an important influence in the delineation of rights.[42] Regional diversity, and particularly Quebec's distinct character, are elements that would likely have been considered in the adjudication of rights in any event, although the degree to which federalism will influence the content of the Charter of Rights ultimately depends on the interpretation of the constitutional document by the Supreme Court of Canada. The Accord, with the distinct society clause and the provincial role in Supreme Court appointment, emphasizes that federalism — visions of diverse regional communities — should enter into the adjudication of rights. Many in Canada do not share this vision, and much of the opposition to the Accord rests on a different view of the Canadian community than provincialism or dualism, one that sees the Charter as a tool to guarantee rights across the nation and avoid provincial variations. Their vision may yet emerge as the dominant one; we shall only know after many more years of Supreme Court interpretation of the Charter of Rights.

---

42 Norrie, Simeon and Krasnick, above, note 2 at 28, suggest that a model of community based on rights does not engage federalism directly. In fact, in Canada, there seems to be an important interaction between concepts of community based on region and concepts based on individual and group rights.

Meech Lake and Visions of Canada

Richard Simeon

To an extent which would have amazed most of the pragmatic framers of the British North America Act,[1] constitutional discourse in Canada has come increasingly to be framed in terms of "visions of Canada." The Constitution is not seen merely as a framework for governing, nor as a solution to a set of problems which must be solved. Rather, it must somehow capture and encapsulate the "essence of Canada." It must be a symbolic representation of what we are as a people; it is to be a marker of one's place in the Canadian political order. If one's group, or conception, is written into the Constitution, one is a legitimate part of the Canadian community; if not, one is marginalized, and somehow excluded from the political world. A Constitution, or sets of amendments to it, is therefore to be judged in terms of whether one sees oneself, one's own conception of what Canada is in some abstract sense, mirrored in the text. If not, it must be rejected.

To view matters in this way places an enormous burden on constitutionalism, one which carries with it a great many dangers. As an empirical matter, it is almost certainly impossible to design a Constitution which embodies or reflects any single vision of Canada or any "essence" of Canadianness. But even if it were possible, it would be undersirable. Both the claims made on the Constitution, and our expectations of it, should be much more modest.

I begin my own view of Meech Lake with two basic propositions. First, there is no single vision of Canada; rather there are multiple,

---

1 1867 (U.K.), c. 3 [now the Constitution Act, 1867].

often competing, visions which interact with each other in complex ways. The task, therefore, is not to enshrine one to the exclusion of others, but to provide the framework for a continuous dialetic among them, both by balancing and compromising existing ideas, and by accommodating shifts in perceptions and values which occur over time. Second, as a normative proposition, I do not believe that the Constitution, any Constitution, should be seen as a secular version of the 35 Articles of Faith. I do not want a government, much less a Constitution, to prescribe or define my identity for me. I want it to be open to many identities, including my own.

Hence, the relevant question with respect to the "visions of Canada" found in a constitutional document is not whether it defines and embodies "my Canada," but whether it permits all citizens to express their sense of Canada, in their own lives, in their relations with others, and in their political activities. One should reject it only if it closes off the possibilities which some might seek. The test lies not so much in what the Constitution says, but in what it permits (or, conversely, does not permit). The Constitution should not be one which defines, determines, preempts or closes; rather it should be open, permissive, flexible, accommodating, responsible, capacious. It should leave the greatest possible room for the operation of the political process to shape and reshape the substantive meaning of community and citizenship over time. Hence I am uncomfortable with the tendency to cast the debate as one between exponents of various defined visions, each rating the Accord according to how closely it matches particular models.

THE CHARACTER OF THE DEBATE

The political imperative behind Meech Lake, of course, was to find a way to secure Quebec's voluntary adherence to the constitutional innovations enacted in 1982.[2] Despite the obvious point that these changes applied to Quebec with or without its agreement and that therefore Quebec's adherence was technically unnecessary, the importance of such an achievement surely cannot be denied. It was equally part of the political imperative that this reconciliation be achieved while not undermining some other primary concerns: in particular, without stripping power from the federal government, denying the validity of minority language rights, repudiating the juridical equality

---

2 Constitution Act, 1982 [enacted by The Canada Act 1982 (U.K.), c. 11, s. 1].

of the provinces, or subverting the Canadian Charter of Rights and Freedoms,[3] all of which have become central to our political culture. The political accomplishment was to find a way to do virtually all these things. This was no mean thing, and cannot simply be dismissed as something desperately cobbled together in a single all-night session or two. It was indeed a political process, a product of executive federalism, with all its flaws. But it was a process in which the participants saw a practical problem and sought practical ways of dealing with it. The outcome bears all the resulting marks of political compromise.

The Meech Lake debate — especially on the side of its most articulate opponents — has been framed in very different terms; it has been cast in the language of competing visions, with each of the many sides tending to argue something close to an absolutist position. There is a remarkable contrast between the careful, compromised terms in the agreement and the rhetorical excess of much of the criticism. This has had two interesting consequences. One is that much of the debate quickly abandoned any direct connection to the text and the plain words in it. It is the presumed implicit thrust of the Accord — or, indeed, the presumed motives behind it — which are identified as malignant, and then often taken to some logical extreme. Or conversely, the text is scrutinized minutely in the search for any hint that it might eventually be used, in some circumstances, at some time in the future, to undermine someone's central values.

In many ways, the tendency to see Meech Lake in these terms is understandable. Constitutions do indeed have important symbolic consequences, even though I suspect that they tend often to be much exaggerated. How they are achieved may also act as a template for the future, although probably for a limited period. The more detailed the provisions of the Constitution, and the more difficult they are to change, then the more important it is to ensure that one's primary values are reflected in it. And we have, indeed, in recent years added greatly to the Constitution, while equipping ourselves with an amending formula which in many respects does call for an extraordinary degree of consensus before change can be achieved. One might note, however, that between the 1950s and 1982, all political actors in Canada operated on the assumption that the unanimity rule was absolute, not only for changes in the division of powers, but for most institutional changes touching federalism as well. Similarly, the more

---

3 Being Part I of the Constitution Act, 1982.

central the role of the courts in interpreting the Constitution, the more care must be taken to ensure that their future scope for doing so in ways unfavourable to one's interest is circumscribed. It is also true that the more one feels oneself to be a disadvantaged minority, the more crucial it is to be recognized in the text, and thus to be protected against the vagaries of majority rule.

The Meech Lake debate also reflects the extent to which, since Quebec raised the constitutional issue in the 1960s, constitutional discourse had become a central arena through which claims to recognition have been made and political conflicts carried out. One may regret this tendency, but it has now become an established element in our political process. The stakes of constitutional politics are high, and high stakes politics are likely to be ideological politics.

Another characteristic of much of the debate has been its historical character. It is as if Meech Lake were a clean slate on which we were inscribing our constitutional values for the first time. But of course that is not the case. First, Meech Lake must be considered alongside the constitutional changes achieved in 1982. Each of these two constitutional developments "tilts" in different directions, although in neither case is the tilt unambiguous. Thus 1982 strengthened a nation-centred and rights-oriented conception of Canada, notably through the Charter of Rights, with a national institution, the Supreme Court, as its arbiter. It made virtually no concession to a conception of Quebec as a distinct society, but did assert a more bilingual view of the country, in very limited ways. The 1987 Accord, while not setting aside 1982, tilts the other way, both towards a view of Quebec as a distinct society, and towards a somewhat more provincialist conception of national institutions and their amendment. Taken together, each acts as a counterbalance to the other. But, at the same time, each is a compromise in itself. The nationalism of 1982 was countered by the highly provincialist amending formula adopted at the time. In the same way, 1987 embodies compromises both with respect to federal and provincial powers (best expressed in the spending power provision) and between the competing views of how best to represent the presence of French and English-speaking Canadians in Canada, recognizing both dualism and the distinct society.

In addition, the provisions of 1982 helped shape the results of 1987. For example, critics of the opting-out provisions in Meech Lake forget that the groundwork for that was laid in 1982. In 1982 the principle of the equality of all provinces was firmly established; that, in turn, limited the ways in which Quebec's distinct society could be accommodated in 1987 — and, in particular, explains the extension of unanimity to national institutions. The only way to ensure Quebec a veto was to ensure one for all provinces.

In the longer view, there are precedents, both in formal constitutional proposals, and even more in political practice, for virtually all the elements in Meech Lake. There was no sudden constitutional *coup d'état*. Proposals for limitations on the spending power, for a provincial role in Senate and Supreme Court appointments and so on, have all been widely discussed previously and widely accepted. As mentioned above, unanimity was the accepted principle for constitutional amendments for many years. Opting-out, and even the variation of purely federal programs such as Youth Allowances to accommodate provincial preferences, have been part of political practice for a very long time. Most important, the recognition of Quebec as a distinct society, not only in a sociological or linguistic sense, but in law and in political practice, has been a central characteristic of Canadian governance throughout our history. The whole history of the use of the spending power, from university grants in the 1950s, to pensions and a host of other programs in the 1960s, to established programs in the 1970s, has been shaped by the political reality of Quebec as a distinct society, and by recognition of the limited ability of the federal government to use its spending power to regulate provincial activity in a detailed way, except in extraordinary circumstances. Thus, Meech Lake represents not so much the breaking of new constitutional ground, but rather the incorporation into the Constitution of what we have already been doing. Some of the critics seem not to recognize this: their objection is less to Meech Lake itself than to a larger evolution of Canadian federalism which they reject. Thus in no sense can Meech Lake, much less Meech Lake when read alongside the Constitution Act, 1982, be seen as a radical innovation, which repudiates past practices and sets us on a new course.

THE POLITICS OF VISIONS

The first and most fundamental problem with constitutional politics as the politics of visions is that there are so many of them in contention. To ask of a Constitution that it enshrine one is to require it to reject many others. It is therefore to do violence to the genuine diversity and fluidity of Canadian society and opinion. We may wish that there were a consensus about the essential character of the country, and that the Constitution would therefore be able to embody it. But there is no holy grail of consensus which a perfectly democratic process would reveal. In the absence of such a consensus, then to enshrine one view is to impose it on others, and that is a recipe for fundamental conflict. It is also to polarize the debate in a way which I believe to be wholly at odds with the underlying views of most Canadians.

The competing visions today can be divided into two broad categories. First are those which relate to the traditional, historic divisions or cleavages which have shaped Canadian political life. These include relations between French and English-speaking Canadians, between provincial and national communities and between federal and provincial governments. Meech Lake is really about these themes — a resolution of a traditional and continuing agenda. It is about the pattern of Canadian federalism. Second, are "visions" which represent a quite different set of axes, those which are based on a desire to reorient Canadian politics around alternative conceptions of the most important defining characteristics of Canadian society and identity, much as writers like Porter and Horowitz once sought to shift the poles of Canadian political debate from what they saw as the stultifying, reactionary preoccupation with regionalism, federalism and unity to the more "creative" politics of class.[4] Each set of axes has generated quite different assessments of Meech Lake.

Let us examine briefly what Meech Lake (and the 1982 amendments) say about each of these dimensions. Recent Canadian debate has polarized around two views of how best to represent the presence of French and English Canadians in Canadian political institutions. One has focused on the image of Quebec as a distinct society, the one territory and government in which French Canadians constitute a majority and possess the political, as well as social, educational and economic institutions through which that majority can express itself and pursue its purposes; the other suggests that linguistic equality must be expressed through guarantees of minority rights across the country and through equal partnership in national institutions. We have tended to see each as mutually exclusive.

Meech Lake and 1982, taken together, refuse to make this choice between the two models; they incorporate both. They recognize bilingualism at the national level, provide some guarantees, especially in educational rights, across the country, and affirm a responsibility

---

4 G. Horowitz, "Conservatism, Liberalism and Socialism in Canada: An Interpretation" (1966), 32 Can. J. of Ec. and Pol. Sci. 141; J. Porter, *The Vertical Mosaic* (Toronto: University of Toronto Press, 1965).

on all governments (for the first time) to protect these rights. At the same time, Quebec's distinctiveness, along with a recognition that the Quebec provincial government is the primary instrument for expressing it, are affirmed. Advocates of a bilingual Canada find a limited, perhaps grudging, reflection of their model. But equally the distinct society provisions are a minimal embodiment of this principle. It is a matter of a rule of interpretation, with no shift in the division of powers. What we have then is a delicate balance — between Quebec's distinctiveness and the equality of all provinces, and between the two views of French and English in Canada. It is not neat or clean, but it is a reasonable balance. It recognizes both fundamental dimensions of linguistic dualism in Canada, while excluding neither. Thus while it tempers both polar visions, it is surely consistent with both the historical reality of Canada and the mix of attitudes within the country.

The same can be said of the balance between a conception of Canada focused on the primacy of the national community and one focused on the primacy of provincial communities. The image of federalism communicated by our two recent rounds of Constitution-making is one in which the strength of the national political community is predicated in large part on the diversity and strength of its constituent parts and, equally, in which the strength of the parts is dependent on the existence of the whole. Again, this seems to me to be entirely consistent with the whole sweep of Canadian history, and with the lessons we derive from all the recent survey research on Canadian identities. That research shows virtually equal identification with national and provincial communities, and the widespread sense that these loyalties are mutually reinforcing and complementary, not opposed to one another — in other words, that Canadians are good federalists.

With respect to the roles of federal and provincial governments, there is again balance. There is no substantial transfer of jurisdiction among the governments. The spending power provision is at least as likely to strengthen and legitimate the federal ability to influence provincial priorities through shared-cost programs as it is to weaken it. It is clear that several provisions do strengthen the federal character of national institutions. The provisions with respect to the Senate and Supreme Court appointments underline that in a federal system these are institutions of the federation, distinct from either level of government, and that to see them as the creature of one or the other order of government is inconsistent with federalism. Their membership is now a joint, shared responsibility. The spending power underlines the shared responsibility of the two orders of governments in meeting the needs of Canadians. The annual meetings of first ministers on the Constitution and economy similarly symbolize the reality that policy-making has become a question of partnership between two orders of government. Thus, Meech Lake is neither confederal, nor unitary in approach, but federal. In this, too, it simply reflects — rather than changes — the Canadian reality.

Recent debate about intergovernmental relations has revolved around two dimensions: centralization and decentralization, and whether the appropriate mode of federal-provincial interaction should be a consensual, collaborative pattern or a competitive one. Meech Lake does not predetermine which way we go with respect to either of these dimensions. The institutions of shared responsibility are equally adapted to competition or harmony. And while transfer of authority through constitutional amendment is indeed very difficult — as it always has been — the relative weight of the two orders of government will depend a great deal more on the issues that face the country, the goals of each level of government, and their ability to mobilize and speak for public opinion than it will on the new constitutional provisions.

Thus with respect to the historic divisions of Canadian politics, Meech Lake does not select any of the competing conceptions. Instead, it embodies elements of all of them. It reaffirms the existing pattern of Canadian federalism, rather than changing it. And perhaps more important, it signals the end of the polarized debate between mutually exclusive images of the country which so poisoned constitutional debate over the last 20 years. It suggests that we are now prepared to move beyond them — that we will be better off by accepting the validity of each of the elements, and building a model which allows for a dialectic between them, over time, rather than by making a once and for all choice.

The second set of criticisms of Meech Lake focuses not on its image of federalism and the related cleavages of language and territory, but on the fact that, in addressing itself to the resolution of some outstanding conflicts about federalism, it pays too little attention to other, evolving, elements which define the Canadian community. And, it is argued, in so responding to federalist problems, the Accord may actually undermine these other dimensions, erecting further hurdles to their effective political expression. These are indeed the most difficult issues to deal with.

At one level, the issue is whether the very basis of Canadian politics should be or could be reoriented, from issues of territory, to some other basis of interests and identity, and, if so, whether we should restructure our institutions to reflect these alternative conceptions of political life. Over the long term, the axes around which politics is organized can change. Religion, once a fundamental organizing principle of Canadian political life, is so no longer. It has often been argued that the territorial divisions of Canada — and the structuring of our institutions around territory — are obsolete, and that we were about to move to a new set of dimensions. It has also been argued that the institutional framework has been a barrier to such reorientations. History shows, however, that all such predictions have been either wrong or wishful thinking. But it also shows that federal institutions have not been a barrier to the emergence of new groups, identities and issues. Indeed, federal institutions — by providing alternatives arenas for political action — may well have facilitated such developments. To displace more than 100 years of history in a fundamental reorganization of our political life is clearly impossible. Again, the real question to ask about Meech Lake is whether it erects major additional barriers in the way of the successful mobilization of the alternative groups.

The answers in the Meech Lake Accord are unclear. The revised amending formula does add an additional hurdle to eventual achievement of provincial status for the northern territories, though nothing prohibits much further movement towards *de facto* provincial status in dealings with the federal government. Native self-government in some form may be marginally more attainable now that Quebec will be a full participant in future constitutional reform efforts. In both these cases, however, it would appear that the primary barriers to achievement of the goals are not constitutional.

Recent debates have also given much more prominence to images of a multicultural Canada, as distinct from a dualist or provincial Canada. Some minimal symbolic recognition of this was given in 1982 and is preserved in the 1987 Accord. The long-run potential for a major reorientation of Canadian politics around ethnicity, especially in large urban areas such as Toronto and Montreal, is clearly great and has received far too little attention. But these changes will occur from the bottom up, and be much more manifest in some provinces and cities than others; hence they will probably be facilitated by federalism, and certainly will not be inhibited by Meech Lake.

By far the major perceived threat in Meech Lake to an alternative conception of community is the sense that non-Quebec women's groups have of a possible threat to equality rights in the distinct society provisions. Far better constitutional lawyers than I have argued both sides of this case elsewhere in this volume. Two observations are in order, however. First, to the extent that individual rights must be weighed against other considerations such as Quebec's distinct society, this is true already throughout the Constitution. Indeed, the recognition of the need to balance sometimes conflicting claims is built into the Charter itself — which is a blend of individual and collective rights — and into the very non-discrimination clause, s. 15, which simultaneously asserts the right of non-discrimination and the legitimacy of discrimination when used to overcome historic disadvantages. When a Constitution embodies a wide variety of values as ours did both before and after Meech Lake, then indeed, none can be absolute; weighing and balancing are inherent needs.

Second, the record of Canadian history is not that new movements displace older patterns; rather, it is that they blend and mix with them. The mobilization of new groups modifies the practices of federalism; federalism does much to shape the form and strategies of the new groups. Meech Lake ensures this dialectic will continue. Indeed, to the extent that Meech Lake marks the end of a period in which our politics was dominated by a preoccupation with ideological divisions about federalism, then the possibilities for new political coalitions are much increased. Thus, as long as Quebec politics was preoccupied with the politics of nationalism, then coalitions on other issues and across linguistic lines were hard to achieve. It is the waning of the polarization around nationalism — which Meech Lake both reflects and promotes — which, for example, makes it possible for the NDP to grow in the province by building on the social democratic tradition once tied to the Parti Québécois. Similarly, Meech Lake reflects the diminution of regional polarization within the rest of the country, and this makes more possible the emergence of a party system in which all parties have a base in all regions. If that is so, again, the possibilities for more "creative" politics along other than regional dimensions become much greater. Thus, it could be argued that Meech Lake, despite its focus on solving problems of federalism, does not lock us into a continuing politics of region and language, but rather, at least makes it more plausible to think about a politics less dominated by these themes, and thus more open to other themes. By helping resolve some conflicts within federalism, we may have liberated ourselves to turn attention to other issues and concerns.

Meech Lake, then, does not constitute a vision of the country, certainly not a single one. Rather it, along with 1982, captures multiple visions, without choosing among them. Exponents of any of the visions we have debated in recent years can find echoes of their model, but they will equally be reminded of the presence of others. Precisely because of its open-ended character, they will find that much is left to the political process. The spending power may mean that a federal government will be loathe to initiate new programs — but it provides much opportunity for an aggressive federal government, able to mobilize support. Federal-provincial collaboration on the appointment of judges may be co-operative and harmonious, but it may also be highly conflictual, and which level will win the conflict will depend, again, on the political support it can mobilize. Meech Lake, therefore, meets the criterion suggested above. It is not closed to any particular vision; it is permissive, rather than constraining. It leaves the outcomes — centralization on decentralization, harmony or conflict, the politics of region or of gender — undetermined.

In this, it is like all our constitutional documents. The British North America Act was full of contradictions; in it could be found elements both of Macdonald's quasi-unitary state and grounds for a much more decentralized Canada. We build these contradictions into our constitutional documents to be worked and reworked over time, because they are built into ourselves and into the fabric of the country.

CONCLUSIONS

If I am right in my argument that Meech Lake does not cast us into a rigid mould, and that its central characteristic is a rather cautious balancing act among several contending visions of Canada, I would also argue that is as it should be. While recognizing that Constitutions do have a symbolic, nation-building, legitimating and educating role, I think we should be very careful about that. Where there is little consensus on a single vision, then to try to embrace one is a recipe for conflict. It is a fallacy to think that if "the people" had been able to decide we would have been able to agree on some other vision. To try to set any vision in amber, by so writing the constitution as to forestall any deviation from it, is undesirable. In any case, as we have seen in the past, it would likely be futile; new forces and circumstances would eventually sweep it away. The capacity of Constitutions to shape national visions is limited; economic, social and political changes are far more important. In that sense, the Free Trade

Agreement is likely to be far more determinative of Canada's future than is Meech Lake.

The Canadian political nationality, as Donald Smiley[5] reminded us 20 years ago, cannot be based on any single nationalist vision; it must, instead, be based on a more pragmatic sense of wanting to do things together, and creating the machinery which will allow us to do that, in ways sensitive to the national and provincial dimensions of the country. I would add that it cannot be imposed from the top down. We make the country by living it, not in constitutional conferences and constitutional documents.

Is Meech Lake a reasonable balancing, a reasonable compromise among contending views? Is it a workable accommodation between the distinct society model central to all Quebec governments in our history, and a more dualist view of Canada? Is it a workable accommodation of federal and provincial responsibilities? Is it sufficiently flexible to accommodate future change, including responsiveness to new movements? Does it leave it open to future generations and movements, operating through political and legal processes, to shift the balance? The answer is broadly yes. I also ask whether one can imagine other outcomes which would achieve the goal of reconciling Quebec to the Constitution — the primary purpose of this round — while at the same time respecting the other constitutional values. It is very hard to do so.

---

5 Donald Smiley, "The Rowel-Sirois Report, Provincial Autonomy and Post-War Canadian Federalism" (1962), 28 Can. J. of Eco. and Pol. Sci. 54.

Appendix 1

CONSTITUTION ACT, 1867 (U.K.), c. 3
(SELECTED SECTIONS)

Powers of the Parliament

91. It shall be lawful for the Queen, by and with the Advice and Consent of the Senate and House of Commons, to make Laws for the Peace, Order, and good Government of Canada, in relation to all Matters not coming within the Classes of Subjects by this Act assigned exclusively to the Legislatures of the Provinces; and for greater Certainty, but not so as to restrict the Generality of the foregoing Terms of this Section, it is hereby declared that (notwithstanding anything in this Act) the exclusive Legislative Authority of the Parliament of Canada extends to all Matters coming within the Classes of Subjects next hereinafter enumerated; that is to say,—

. . .

1A. The Public Debt and Property.

. . .

3. The raising of Money by any Mode or System of Taxation.

. . .

24. Indians, and Lands reserved for the Indians.

. . .

93. In and for each Province the Legislature may exclusively make Laws in relation to Education, subject and according to the following Provisions:—

(1) Nothing in any such Law shall prejudicially affect any Right

or Privilege with respect to Denominational Schools which
'any Class of Persons have by Law in the Province at the Union:

(2) All the Powers, Privileges, and Duties at the Union by Law
conferred and imposed in Upper Canada on the Separate
Schools and School Trustees of the Queen's Roman Catholic
Subjects shall be and the same are hereby extended to the
Dissentient Schools of the Queen's Protestant and Roman
Catholic Subjects in Quebec:

(3) Where in any Province a System of Separate or Dissentient
Schools exists by Law at the Union or is thereafter established
by the Legislature of the Province, an Appeal shall lie to the
Governor General in Council from any Act or Decision of
any Provincial Authority affecting any Right or Privilege of
the Protestant or Roman Catholic Minority of the Queen's
Subjects in relation to Education:

(4) In case any such Provincial Law as from Time to Time seems
to the Governor General in Council requisite for the due
Execution of the Provisions of this Section is not made, or
in case any Decision of the Governor General in Council on
any Appeal under this Section is not duly executed by the
proper Provincial Authority in that Behalf, then and in every
such Case, and as far only as the Circumstances of each Case
require, the Parliament of Canada may make remedial Laws
for the due Execution of the Provisions of this Section and
of any Decision of the Governor General in Council under
this Section.

. . .

95. In each Province the Legislature may make Laws in relation
to Agriculture in the Province, and to Immigration into the Province;
and it is hereby declared that the Parliament of Canada may from
Time to Time make Laws in relation to Agriculture in all or any
of the Provinces, and to Immigration into all or any of the Provinces;
and any Law of the Legislature of a Province relative to Agriculture
or to Immigration shall have effect in and for the Province as long
and as far only as it is not repugnant to any Act of the Parliament
of Canada.

. . .

101. The Parliament of Canada may, notwithstanding anything in this Act, from Time to Time provide for the Constitution, Maintenance, and Organization of a General Court of Appeal for Canada, and for the Establishment of any additional Courts for the better Administration of the Laws of Canada.

. . .

106. Subject to the several Payments by this Act charged on the Consolidated Revenue Fund of Canada, the same shall be appropriated by the Parliament of Canada for the Public Service.

. . .

CONSTITUTION ACT, 1982 [BEING SCHEDULE B OF THE CANADA ACT 1982 (U.K.), C. 1] (SELECTED SECTIONS)

PART I

CANADIAN CHARTER OF RIGHTS AND FREEDOMS

1. The *Canadian Charter of Rights and Freedoms* guarantees the rights and freedoms set out in it subject only to such reasonable limits prescribed by law as can be demonstrably justified in a free and democratic society.

. . .

2. Everyone has the following fundamental freedoms:

(*a*) freedom of conscience and religion;

(*b*) freedom of thought, belief, opinion and expression, including freedom of the press and other media of communication;

(*c*) freedom of peaceful assembly; and

(*d*) freedom of association.

. . .

15. (1) Every individual is equal before and under the law and has the right to the equal protection and equal benefit of the law without discrimination and, in particular, without discrimination based on race, national or ethnic origin, colour, religion, sex, age or mental or physical disability.

(2) Subsection (1) does not preclude any law, program or activity that has as its object the amelioration of conditions of disadvantaged individuals or groups including those that are disadvantaged because

of race, national or ethnic origin, colour, religion, sex, age or mental or physical disability.

. . .

25. The guarantee in this Charter of certain rights and freedoms shall not be construed so as to abrogate or derogate from any aboriginal, treaty or other rights or freedoms that pertain to the aboriginal peoples of Canada including

> (*a*) any rights or freedoms that have been recognized by the Royal Proclamation of October 7, 1763; and

> (*b*) any rights or freedoms that now exist by way of land claims agreements or may be so acquired.

. . .

27. This Charter shall be interpreted in a manner consistent with the preservation and enhancement of the multicultural heritage of Canadians.

28. Notwithstanding anything in this Charter, the rights and freedoms referred to in it are guaranteed equally to male and female persons.

29. Nothing in this Charter abrogates or derogates from any rights or privileges guaranteed by or under the Constitution of Canada in respect of denominational, separate or dissentient schools.

. . .

PART II
RIGHTS OF THE ABORIGINAL PEOPLES OF
CANADA

35. (1) The existing aboriginal and treaty rights of the aboriginal peoples of Canada are hereby recognized and affirmed.

(2) In this Act, "aboriginal peoples of Canada" includes the Indian, Inuit and Métis peoples of Canada.

(3) For greater certainty, in subsection (1) "treaty rights" includes rights that now exist by way of land claims agreements or may be so acquired.

(4) Notwithstanding any other provision of this Act, the aboriginal and treaty rights referred to in subsection (1) are guaranteed equally to male and female persons.

PART III
EQUALIZATION AND REGIONAL DISPARITIES

36. (1) Without altering the legislative authority of Parliament or of the provincial legislatures, or the rights of any of them with respect to the exercise of their legislative authority, Parliament and the legislatures, together with the government of Canada and the provincial governments, are committed to

(*a*) promoting equal opportunities for the well-being of Canadians;

(*b*) furthering economic development to reduce disparity in opportunities; and

(*c*) providing essential public services of reasonable quality to all Canadians.

(2) Parliament and the government of Canada are committed to the principle of making equalization payments to ensure that provincial governments have sufficient revenues to provide reasonably comparable levels of public services at reasonable comparable levels of taxation.

. . .

PART V
PROCEDURE FOR AMENDING
CONSTITUTION OF CANADA

38. (1) An amendment to the Constitution of Canada may be made by proclamation issued by the Governor General under the Great Seal of Canada where so authorized by

(*a*) resolutions of the Senate and House of Commons; and

(*b*) resolutions of the legislative assemblies of at least two-thirds of the provinces that have, in the aggregate, according to the then latest general census, at least fifty per cent of the population of all the provinces.

(2) An amendment made under subsection (1) that derogates from the legislative powers, the proprietary rights or any other rights or privileges of the legislature or government of a province shall require a resolution supported by a majority of the members of each of the Senate, the House of Commons and the legislative assemblies required under subsection (1).

(3) An amendment referred to in subsection (2) shall not have effect in a province the legislative assembly of which has expressed its dissent thereto by resolution supported by a majority of its members prior to the issue of the proclamation to which the amendment relates unless that legislative assembly, subsequently, by resolution supported by a majority of its members, revokes its dissent and authorizes the amendment.

(4) A resolution of dissent made for the purposes of subsection (3) may be revoked at any time before or after the issue of the proclamation to which it relates.

39. (1) A proclamation shall not be issued under subsection 38(1) before the expiration of one year from the adoption of the resolution initiating the amendment procedure thereunder, unless the legislative assembly of each province has previously adopted a resolution of assent or dissent.

(2) A proclamation shall not be issued under subsection 38(1) after the expiration of three years from the adoption of the resolution initiating the amendment procedure thereunder.

40. Where an amendment is made under subsection 38(1) that transfers provincial legislative powers relating to education or other cultural matters from provincial legislatures to Parliament, Canada shall provide reasonable compensation to any province to which the amendment does not apply.

41. An amendment to the Constitution of Canada in relation to the following matters may be made by proclamation issued by the Governor General under the Great Seal of Canada only where authorized by resolutions of the Senate and House of Commons and of the legislative assembly of each province:

(*a*) the office of the Queen, the Governor General and the Lieutenant Governor of a province;

(*b*) the right of a province to a number of members in the House of Commons not less than the number of Senators by which the province is entitled to be represented at the time this Part comes into force;

(*c*) subject to section 43, the use of the English or the French language;

(*d*) the composition of the Supreme Court of Canada; and

(*e*) an amendment to this Part.

42. (1) An amendment to the Constitution of Canada in relation to the following matters may be made only in accordance with subsection 38(1):

(*a*) the principle of proportionate representation of the provinces in the House of Commons prescribed by the Constitution of Canada;

(*b*) the powers of the Senate and the method of selecting Senators;

(*c*) the number of members by which a province is entitled to be represented in the Senate and the residence qualifications of Senators;

(*d*) subject to paragraph 41(*d*), the Supreme Court of Canada;

(*e*) the extension of existing provinces into the territories; and

(*f*) notwithstanding any other law or practice, the establishment of new provinces.

(2) Subsections 38(2) to (4) do not apply in respect of amendments in relation to matters referred to in subsection (1).

43. An amendment to the Constitution of Canada in relation to any provision that applies to one or more, but not all, provinces, including

(*a*) any alteration to boundaries between provinces, and

(*b*) any amendment to any provision that relates to the use of the English or the French language within a province,

may be made by proclamation issued by the Governor General under the Great Seal of Canada only where so authorized by resolutions of the Senate and House of Commons and of the legislative assembly of each province to which the amendment applies.

44. Subject to sections 41 and 42, Parliament may exclusively make laws amending the Constitution of Canada in relation to the executive government of Canada or the Senate and House of Commons.

45. Subject to section 41, the legislature of each province may exclusively make laws amending the constitution of the province.

46. (1) The procedures for amendment under sections 38, 41, 42 and 43 may be initiated either by the Senate or the House of Commons or by the legislative assembly of a province.

(2) A resolution or assent made for the purposes of this Part may be revoked at any time before the issue of a proclamation authorized by it.

47. (1) An amendment to the Constitution of Canada made by proclamation under section 38, 41, 42 or 43 may be made without a resolution of the Senate authorizing the issue of the proclamation if, within one hundred and eighty days after the adoption by the House of Commons of a resolution authorizing its issue, the Senate has not adopted such a resolution and if, at any time after the expiration of that period, the House of Commons again adopts the resolution.

(2) Any period when Parliament is prorogued or dissolved shall not be counted in computing the one hundred and eighty day period referred to in subsection (1).

. . .

PART VII
GENERAL

52. (1) The Constitutiuon of Canada is the supreme law of Canada, and any law that is inconsistent with the provisions of the Constitution is, to the extent of the inconsistency, of no force or effect.

(2) The Constitution of Canada includes

(*a*) the *Canada Act 1982*, including this Act;

(*b*) the Acts and orders referred to in the schedule; and

(*c*) any amendment to any Act or order referred to in paragraph (*a*) and (*b*).

(3) Amendments to the Constitution of Canada shall be made only in accordance with the authority contained in the Constitution of Canada.

. . .

Appendix 2

1987 CONSTITUTIONAL ACCORD

WHEREAS first ministers, assembled in Ottawa, have arrived at a unanimous accord on constitutional amendments that would bring about the full and active participation of Quebec in Canada's constitutional evolution, would recognize the principle of equality of all the provinces, would provide new arrangements to foster greater harmony and cooperation between the Government of Canada and the governments of the provinces and would require that annual first ministers' conferences on the state of the Canadian economy and such other matters as may be appropriate be convened and that annual constitutional conferences composed of first ministers be convened commencing not later than December 31, 1988;

AND WHEREAS first ministers have also reached unanimous agreement on certain additional commitments in relation to some of those amendments;

NOW THEREFORE the Prime Minister of Canada and the first ministers of the provinces commit themselves and the governments they represent to the following:

1. The Prime Minister of Canada will lay or cause to be laid before the Senate and House of Commons, and the first ministers of the provinces will lay or cause to be laid before their legislative assemblies, as soon as possible, a resolution, in the form appended hereto, to authorize a proclamation to be issued by the Governor General under the Great Seal of Canada to amend the Constitution of Canada.

2. The Government of Canada will, as soon as possible, conclude an agreement with the Government of Quebec that would

(*a*) incorporate the principles of the Cullen-Couture agreement on the selection abroad and in Canada of independent immigrants, visitors for medical treatment, students, and temporary workers, and on the selection of refugees abroad and economic criteria for family reunification and assisted relatives.

(*b*) guarantee that Quebec will receive a number of immigrants, including refugees, within the annual total established by the federal government for all of Canada proportionate to its share of the population of Canada, with the right to exceed that figure by five per cent for demographic reasons, and

(*c*) provide an undertaking by Canada to withdraw services (except citizenship services) for the reception and integration (including linguistic and cultural) of all foreign nationals wishing to settle in Quebec where services are to be provided by Quebec, with such withdrawal to be accompanied by reasonable compensation,

and the Government of Canada and the Government of Quebec will take the necessary steps to give the agreement the force of law under the proposed amendment relating to such agreements.

3. Nothing in this Accord should be construed as preventing the negotiation of similar agreements with other provinces relating to immigration and the temporary admission of aliens.

4. Until the proposed amendment relating to appointments to the Senate comes into force, any person summoned to fill a vacancy in the Senate shall be chosen from among persons whose names have been submitted by the government of the province to which the vacancy relates and must be acceptable to the Queen's Privy Council for Canada.

MOTION FOR A RESOLUTION TO AUTHORIZE AN AMENDMENT TO THE CONSTITUTION OF CANADA

WHEREAS the *Constitution Act, 1982* came into force on April 17, 1982, following an agreement between Canada and all the provinces except Quebec;

AND WHEREAS the Government of Quebec has established a set of five proposals for constitutional change and has stated that amendments to give effect to those proposals would enable Quebec to resume a full role in the constitutional councils of Canada;

AND WHEREAS the amendment proposed in the schedule hereto sets out the basis on which Quebec's five constitutional proposals may be met;

AND WHEREAS the amendment proposed in the schedule hereto also recognizes the principle of the equality of all the provinces, provides new arrangements to foster greater harmony and cooperation between the Government of Canada and the governments of the provinces and requires that conferences be convened to consider important constitutional, economic and other issues;

AND WHEREAS certain portions of the amendment proposed in the schedule hereto relate to matters referred to in section 41 of the *Constitution Act, 1982*;

AND WHEREAS section 41 of the *Constitution Act, 1982* provides that an amendment to the Constitution of Canada may be made by proclamation issued by the Governor General under the Great Seal of Canada where so authorized by resolutions of the Senate and the

House of Commons and of the legislative assembly of each province;

NOW THEREFORE the (Senate) (House of Commons) (legislative assembly) resolves that an amendment to the Constitution of Canada be authorized to be made by proclamation issued by Her Excellency the Governor General under the Great Seal of Canada in accordance with the schedule hereto.

SCHEDULE

CONSTITUTION AMENDMENT, 1987

Constitution Act, 1867

1. The *Constitution Act, 1867* is amended by adding thereto, immediately after section 1 thereof, the following section:

Interpretation

2. (1) The Constitution of Canada shall be interpreted in a manner consistent with

(*a*) the recognition that the existence of French-speaking Canadians, centred in Quebec but also present elsewhere in Canada, and English-speaking Canadians, concentrated outside Quebec but also present in Quebec, constitutes a fundamental characteristic of Canada; and

(*b*) the recognition that Quebec constitutes within Canada a distinct society.

Role of Parliament and legislatures

(2) The role of the Parliament of Canada and the provincial legislatures to preserve the fundamental characteristics of Canada referred to in paragraph (1)(*a*) is affirmed.

Role of legislature and Government of Quebec

(3) The role of the legislature and Government of Quebec to preserve and promote the distinct

identity of Quebec referred to in paragraph (1)(*b*) is affirmed.

Rights of legislatures and governments preserved

(4) Nothing in this section derogates from the powers, rights or privileges of Parliament or the Government of Canada, or of the legislatures or governments of the provinces, including any powers, rights or privileges relating to language.

2. The said Act is further amended by adding thereto, immediately after section 24 thereof, the following section:

Names to be submitted

25. (1) Where a vacancy occurs in the Senate, the government of the province to which the vacancy relates may, in relation to that vacancy, submit to the Queen's Privy Council for Canada the names of persons who may be summoned to the Senate.

Choice of Senators from names submitted

(2) Until an amendment to the Constitution of Canada is made in relation to the Senate pursuant to section 41 of the *Constitution Act, 1982*, the person summoned to fill a vacancy in the Senate shall be chosen from among persons whose names have been submitted under subsection (1) by the government of the province to which the vacancy relates and must be acceptable to the Queen's Privy Council for Canada.

3. The said Act is further amended by adding thereto, immediately after section 95 thereof, the following heading and sections:

Agreements on Immigration and Aliens

Commitment to negotiate

95A. The Government of Canada shall, at the request of the government of any province, negotiate with the government of that province for the purpose of concluding an agreement relating to immigration or the temporary admission of aliens into that province that is appropriate to the needs and circumstances of that province.

Agreements

95B. (1) Any agreement concluded between Canada and a province in relation to immigration or the temporary admission of aliens into that province has the force of law from the time it is declared to do so in accordance with subsection 95C(1) and shall from that time have effect notwithstanding class 25 of section 91 or section 95.

Limitation

(2) An agreement that has the force of law under subsection (1) shall have effect only so long and so far as it is not repugnant to any provision of an Act of the Parliament of Canada that sets national standards and objectives relating to immigration or aliens, including any provision that establishes general classes of immigrants or relates to levels of immigration for Canada or that prescribes classes of individuals who are inadmissible into Canada.

Application of Charter

(3) The *Canadian Charter of Rights and Freedoms* applies in respect of any agreement that has the force of law under subsection (1) and in respect of anything done by the Parliament or Government of Canada, or the legislature or government of a province, pursuant to any such agreement.

Proclamation relating to agreements

95C. (1) A declaration that an agreement referred to in subsection 95B(1) has the force of law may be made by proclamation issued by the Governor General under the Great Seal of Canada only where so authorized by resolutions of the Senate and House of Commons and of the legislative assembly of the province that is a party to the agreement.

Amendment of agreements

(2) An amendment to an agreement referred to in subsection 95B(1) may be made by proclamation issued by the Governor General under the Great Seal of Canada only where so authorized

(*a*) by resolutions of the Senate and House of Commons and of the legislative assembly of the province that is a party to the agreement; or

(*b*) in such other manner as is set out in the agreement.

95D. Sections 46 to 48 of the *Constitution Act, 1982* apply, with such modifications as the circumstances require, in respect of any declaration made pursuant to subsection 95C(1), any amendment to an agreement made pursuant to subsection 95C(2) or any amendment made pursuant to section 95E.

95E. An amendment to sections 95A to 95D or this section may be made in accordance with the procedure set out in subsection 38(1) of the *Constitution Act, 1982*, but only if the amendment is authorized by resolutions of the legislative assemblies of all the provinces that are, at the time of the amendment, parties to an agreement that has the force of law under subsection 95B(1).

4. The said Act is further amended by adding thereto, immediately preceding section 96 thereof, the following heading:

General

5. The said Act is further amended by adding thereto, immediately preceding section 101 thereof, the following heading:

Courts Established by the Parliament of Canada

6. The said Act is further amended by adding thereto, immediately after section 101 thereof, the following heading and sections:

Supreme Court of Canada

101A. (1) The court existing under the name of the Supreme Court of Canada is hereby continued as the general court of appeal for Canada, and as an additional court for the better administration of the laws of Canada, and shall continue to be a superior court of record.

Constitution of court

(2) The Supreme Court of Canada shall consist of a chief justice to be called the Chief Justice of Canada and eight other judges, who shall be appointed by the Governor General in Council by letters patent under the Great Seal.

Who may be appointed judges

101B. (1) Any person may be appointed a judge of the Supreme Court of Canada who, after having been admitted to the bar of any province or territory, has, for a total of at least ten years, been a judge of any court in Canada or a member of the bar of any province or territory.

Three judges from Quebec

(2) At least three judges of the Supreme Court of Canada shall be appointed from among persons who, after having been admitted to the bar of Quebec, have, for a total of at least ten years, been judges of any court of Quebec or of any court established by the Parliament of Canada, or members of the bar of Quebec.

Names may be submitted

101C. (1) Where a vacancy occurs in the Supreme Court of Canada, the government of each province may, in relation to that vacancy, submit to the Minister of Justice of Canada the names of any of the persons who have been admitted to the bar of that province and are qualified under section 101B for appointment to that court.

Appointment from names submitted

(2) Where an appointment is made to the Supreme Court of Canada, the Governor General in Council shall, except where the Chief Justice is appointed from among members of the Court, appoint a person whose name has been submitted under subsection (1) and who is acceptable to the Queen's Privy Council for Canada.

Appointment from Quebec

(3) Where an appointment is made in accordance with subsection (2) of any of the three judges necessary to meet the requirement set out in

subsection 101B(2), the Governor General in Council shall appoint a person whose name has been submitted by the Government of Quebec.

Appointment from other provinces

(4) Where an appointment is made in accordance with subsection (2) otherwise than as required under subsection (3), the Governor General in Council shall appoint a person whose name has been submitted by the government of a province other than Quebec.

Tenure, salaries, etc., of judges

101D. Sections 99 and 100 apply in respect of the judges of the Supreme Court of Canada.

Relationship to section 101

101E. (1) Sections 101A to 101D shall not be construed as abrogating or derogating from the powers of the Parliament of Canada to make laws under section 101 except to the extent that such laws are inconsistent with those sections.

References to the Supreme Court of Canada

(2) For greater certainty, section 101A shall not be construed as abrogating or derogating from the powers of the Parliament of Canada to make laws relating to the reference of questions of law or fact, or any other matters, to the Supreme Court of Canada.

7. The said Act is further amended by adding thereto, immediately after section 106 thereof, the following section:

Shared-cost program

106A. (1) The Government of Canada shall provide reasonable compensation to the government of a province that chooses not to participate in a national shared-cost program that is established by the Government of Canada after the coming into force of this section in an area of exclusive provincial jurisdiction, if the province carries on a program or initiative that is compatible with the national objectives.

Legislative power not extended

(2) Nothing in this section extends the legislative powers of the Parliament of Canada or of the legislatures of the provinces.

8. The said Act is further amended by adding thereto the following heading and sections:

XII—CONFERENCES ON THE ECONOMY AND OTHER MATTERS

Conferences on the economy and other matters

148. A conference composed of the Prime Minister of Canada and the first ministers of the provinces shall be convened by the Prime Minister of Canada at least once each year to discuss the state of the Canadian economy and such other matters as may be appropriate.

XIII—REFERENCES

Reference includes amendments

149. A reference to this Act shall be deemed to include a reference to any amendments thereto.

Constitution Act, 1982

9. Sections 40 to 42 of the *Constitution Act, 1982* are repealed and the following substituted therefor:

Compensation

40. Where an amendment is made under subsection 38(1) that transfers legislative powers from provincial legislatures to Parliament, Canada shall provide reasonable compensation to any province to which the amendment does not apply.

Amendment by unanimous consent

41. An amendment to the Constitution of Canada in relation to the following matters may be made by proclamation issued by the Governor General under the Great Seal of Canada only where authorized by resolutions of the Senate and House of Commons and of the legislative assembly of each province:

(*a*) the office of the Queen, the Governor General and the Lieutenant Governor of a province;

(*b*) the powers of the Senate and the method of selecting Senators;

(*c*) the number of members by which a province is entitled to be represented in the Senate and the residence qualifications of Senators;

(*d*) the right of a province to a number of members in the House of Commons not less than the number of Senators by which the province was entitled to be represented on April 17, 1982;

(*e*) the principle of proportionate representation of the provinces in the House of Commons prescribed by the Constitution of Canada;

(*f*) subject to section 43, the use of the English or the French language;

(*g*) the Supreme Court of Canada;

(*h*) the extension of existing provinces into the territories;

(*i*) notwithstanding any other law or practice, the establishment of new provinces; and

(*j*) an amendment to this Part.

10. Section 44 of the said Act is repealed and the following substituted therefor:

Amendments by Parliament

44. Subject to section 41, Parliament may exclusively make laws amending the Constitution of Canada in relation to the executive government of Canada or the Senate and House of Commons.

11. Subsection 46(1) of the said Act is repealed and the following substituted therefor:

Initiation of amendment procedures

46. (1) The procedures for amendment under sections 38, 41 and 43 may be initiated either by the Senate or the House of Commons or by the legislative assembly of a province.

12. Subsection 47(1) of the said Act is repealed and the following substituted therefor:

Amendments without

Senate resolution

47. (1) An amendment to the Constitution of Canada made by proclamation under section 38, 41 or 43 may be made without a resolution of the Senate authorizing the issue of the proclamation if, within one hundred and eighty days after the adoption by the House of Commons of a resolution authorizing its issue, the Senate has not adopted such a resolution and if, at any time after the expiration of that period, the House of Commons again adopts the resolution.

13. Part VI of the said Act is repealed and the following substituted therefor:

PART VI

CONSTITUTIONAL CONFERENCES

Constitutional conference

50. (1) A constitutional conference composed of the Prime Minister of Canada and the first ministers of the provinces shall be convened by the Prime Minister of Canada at least once each year, commencing in 1988.

Agenda

(2) The conferences convened under subsection (1) shall have included on their agenda the following matters:

(*a*) Senate reform, including the role and functions of the Senate, its powers, the method of selecting Senators and representation in the Senate;

(*b*) roles and responsibilities in relation to fisheries; and

(*c*) such other matters as are agreed upon.

14. Subsection 52(2) of the said Act is amended by striking out the word "and" at the end of paragraph (*b*) thereof, by adding the word "and" at the end of paragraph (*c*) thereof and by adding thereto the following paragraph:

(*d*) any other amendment to the Constitution of Canada.

15. Section 61 of the said Act is repealed and the following substituted therefor:

References

61. A reference to the *Constitution Act, 1982,* or a reference to the *Constitution Acts 1867 to 1982,* shall be deemed to include a reference to any amendments thereto.

General

Multicultural heritage and aboriginal peoples

16. Nothing in section 2 of the *Constitution Act, 1867* affects section 25 or 27 of the *Canadian Charter of Rights and Freedoms*, section 35 of the *Constitution Act, 1982* or class 24 of section 91 of the *Constitution Act, 1867.*

CITATION

Citation

17. This amendment may be cited as the *Constitution Amendment, 1987.*